Law as Reproduction and Revolution

Law as Reproduction and Revolution

An Interconnected History

———

Yves Dezalay and Bryant G. Garth

UNIVERSITY OF CALIFORNIA PRESS

University of California Press
Oakland, California

© 2021 by Yves Dezalay and Bryant G. Garth

Suggested citation: Dezalay, Y. and Garth, B. G. *Law as Reproduction and Revolution: An Interconnected History*. Oakland: University of California Press, 2021. DOI: https://doi.org/10.1525/luminos.110

Library of Congress Cataloging-in-Publication Data

Names: Dezalay, Yves, 1945- author. | Garth, Bryant G., author.
Title: Law as reproduction and revolution : an interconnected history /
    Yves Dezalay and Bryant G. Garth.
Description: Oakland, California : University of California Press, [2021] |
    Includes bibliographical references and index.
Identifiers: LCCN 2021006465 (print) | LCCN 2021006466 (ebook) |
    ISBN 9780520382718 (paperback) | ISBN 9780520382725 (ebook)
Subjects: LCSH: Law—History. | Lawyers—History. |
    Sociological jurisprudence. | Law—East Asia—American influences.
Classification: LCC K150 .D49 2021 (print) | LCC K150 (ebook) |
    DDC 340.09—dc23
LC record available at https://lccn.loc.gov/2021006465
LC ebook record available at https://lccn.loc.gov/2021006466

29 28 27 26 25 24 23 22 21
10 9 8 7 6 5 4 3 2 1

Publication supported by a grant from
The Community Foundation for Greater New Haven
as part of the Urban Haven Project.

CONTENTS

Acknowledgments   ix

PART I. INTRODUCTION

1. Legal Revolutions, Cosmopolitan Legal Elites, and Interconnected
   Histories   3

PART II. LEARNED LAW AND SOCIAL CHANGE: THEORETICAL
ORIENTATION AND EUROPEAN GENESES

2. Sociological Perspectives on Social Change and the Role of Learned
   Law: Building on and Going beyond Berman and Bourdieu   19

3. Learned Law, Legal Education, Social Capital, and States:
   European Geneses of These Relationships and the Enduring Role
   of Family Capital   31

PART III. THE CONSTRUCTION OF THE UNITED STATES AS THE MAJOR
PROTAGONIST IN PROMOTING LEGAL REVOLUTION

4. US Legal Hybrids, Corporate Law Firms, the Langdellian Revolution
   in Legal Education, and the Construction of a US-Oriented
   International Justice through an Alliance of US Corporate Lawyers
   and European Professors   59

5. Social and Neoliberal Revolutions in the United States   75

PART IV. FROM LAW AND DEVELOPMENT TO THE NEOLIBERAL
REVOLUTION

6. India: Colonial Path Dependencies Revisited: An Embattled Senior
    Bar, the Marginalization of Legal Knowledge, and Internationalized
    Challenges   101

7. Hong Kong as a Paradigm Case: An Open Market for Corporate
    Law Firms and the Technologies of Legal Education Reform—as
    Chinese Hegemony Grows   121

8. South Korea and Japan: Contrasting Attacks through Legal
    Education Reform on the Traditional Conservative and Insular Bar   137

9. Legal Education, International Strategies, and Rebuilding the Value
    of Legal Capital in China   164
    Coauthored with Zhizhou Wang

10. Conclusion: Combining Social Capital with Learned Capital:
    Competing on Different Imperial Paths   193

Notes   203
Bibliography   207
Index   223

ACKNOWLEDGMENTS

We are very grateful for the support of the American Bar Foundation and its Executive Director, Ajay Mehrotra, which, combined with support from the University of California, Irvine, and its Deans Erwin Chemerinsky and Song Richardson, allowed us to complete our research for this book. Bryant Garth's sabbatical from Southwestern Law School also facilitated the initiation of this project in 2012. We are grateful to the more than 60 individuals we interviewed specifically for this book and for the more than 150 interviews we drew upon from our previous book, *Asian Legal Revivals* (2010). This kind of comparative work also requires collaboration with local expertise to gain scholarly insights, to connect to individuals and research sites, and to help avoid mistakes. We would like to single out those who have been especially helpful. For India, we thank Upendra Baxi, Mona Bhide, Jayanth Krishnan, Nick Robinson, and especially Swethaa Ballakrishnen, who served as a key point of entry into the world of the National Law School graduates. Professors Ballakrishnen, Krishnan, and Robinson made very helpful comments on a draft of Chapter 6. We also thank Raj Kumar for hosting a full day visit to the Jindal Global Law School. For Hong Kong, we owe a continuing debt to Carol Jones and thank David Law for his perspective from the University of Hong Kong. Both made helpful comments on Chapter 7. For South Korea we drew especially on JaeWon Kim, Seong-Hyun Kim, K.S. Park, and Jae-Hyup Lee, and the latter two made helpful comments on Chapter 8. We thank Professor Park also for inviting us to visit and present work to the University of Korea Law School and Professor Lee for inviting us to visit and present work at Seoul National University Law School. We appreciate the careful reading of our Japanese section by Kay-Wah Chan and the opportunity to engage with leading Japanese scholars, including Atsushi Bushimata, Daniel Foote, and Dan Rosen, at the Asian

Law and Society Conference in Taiwan in 2017. Finally, for China the two primary authors of the book are grateful for the collaboration of Zhizhou (Leo) Wang, our co-author for the China chapter, who has made an invaluable contribution. We thank Philip McConnaughay for hosting us and inviting us to present our work at the Peking School of Transnational Law, in Shenzhen. For China, in addition, we also are very grateful for comments and guidance from Sida Liu and Benjamin von Rooij. Finally, we are grateful for Robert Gordon for his reading and criticisms of Chapter 5, on transformations within the United States.

PART ONE

Introduction

1

Legal Revolutions, Cosmopolitan Legal Elites, and Interconnected Histories

The global rise of financial capitalism and neoliberal economics over the past thirty to forty years has helped produce a "legal revolution" (Berman 1983) in much of the world. Tangible results of this process include the proliferation of large corporate law firms—a US invention—in the major capitals of the world and, more recently, a trend toward legal education reform geared toward those corporate law firms and US approaches to legal education. The current legal revolution, like the earlier one in the United States, is associated with a modernist commitment to meritocracy, which can be deployed against entrenched legal elites—even oligarchies—held together by family or quasi-familial capital. The strong impact of this revolution is apparent in the major countries of Asia, including the subjects of this study—China, Hong Kong, India, Japan, and South Korea.

Our book is about this revolution and the very different ways it is playing out in those countries. But it is also about how such revolutions both attack legal hierarchies and are central to their reproduction. Richard Abel's well-known work on the legal profession emphasized professional control of markets and "the production of producers" (e.g., Abel and Lewis 1989–90) as keys to the success of the profession. In contrast, we argue that control of the production (and reproduction) of producers is applied mainly to protect those at the top of the legal hierarchies. In other words, the key strategy is not so much to restrict internal and external competition through monopoly and limited entry into the profession; rather, it is to enforce an internal hierarchy that reserves access to the top positions to a cosmopolitan elite blessed, most typically, with inherited legal capital and degrees from highly selective schools. Such elites include descendants of the French "noblesse de robe," notable "jurists" in Brazil, high court advocates and judges in India, and, in places like China, Japan, and South Korea, families with sufficient resources that their children will excel on national examinations and rise to the most respected positions.

3

Those who occupy positions at the top are typically presented as having risen through meritocratic processes, when actually they have depended heavily on family, social, and economic capital, which includes access to exclusive universities and law schools. The mix of meritocratic and social capital varies from place to place and over time, but the dynamics of elite reproduction are general.

Even where the ideology of meritocracy seems dominant, as in the United States, partnerships in elite corporate law firms are open mainly to graduates from a relatively small number of law schools—that is, to those who have been schooled since birth to compete for such positions (Markovits 2015; Dinovitzer and Garth 2020). This reproduction of the "one percent" requires, as Markovits has noted, "massive, sustained, planned, and practiced investment, from birth or even in the womb"—"equivalent, economically, to a traditional inheritance of between 5 and 10 million dollars per child" (Markovitz 2015: 9). The most elite positions reproduce the advantages of social class in other ways as well. Even if someone from outside a society's privileged families "wins the economic lottery against all odds, there is a social glass ceiling. The positions of cultural, economic and political leadership—the trappings of the upper class—are much less open to them than to those who from birth and privileged education accumulate the less obvious forms of [social and cultural] capital" (Jodhka, Rehbein, and Souza 2018: 85).

This process goes back to the creation of the legal profession in medieval Italy around the University of Bologna. The top rewards of law practice have always gone primarily to a handful of individuals with strong family connections, access to substantial resources to support long years of study away from home, and expertise in cosmopolitan legal knowledge—beginning with the Roman Corpus Juris rediscovered in Italy in the eleventh century. An enduring feature of the legal profession is the survival of the inheritors of this role and of the habitus (Bourdieu 2012) that has sustained it over the centuries. Yet this system is neither linear nor unidirectional. Indeed, it is unstable and full of contradictions and detours, in part because those at the top erect barriers to preserve their places and those of their children. Challengers promoting meritocracy or a stronger emphasis on scholarly capital confront complacent legal establishments at the top of the national hierarchy. Bourdieu's sociological insights about the tensions between and complementarity of family and meritocratic capital help explain how these challenges play out (2012; 2015).

The dynamics of these challenges and the changes they generate can be understood through the concept of "legal revolution" developed by Berman (1983). Berman focused on major revolutions such as the Gregorian and Protestant revolutions, but his approach can be applied to smaller ones as well. Legal revolutions typically are characterized by the presence of relative newcomers challenging complacent legal elites who are too close to power and disinvested in legal scholarship. The newcomers combine their meritocratic and scholarly achievements to attack the legal establishment; at times, their legal theories gain salience as these "rebels" forge links with emerging political groups that are also rising against the status quo. The scholarly investment and orientation of political groups may also relate to shifts in imperial power that provide opportunities to challenge local legal and political power. Domestic legal shifts in the nineteenth century, for example, took place in relation to a shift in imperial policies away from economic exploitation toward a more moral and missionary approach offering a larger role for the legitimacy provided by law and lawyers. Changes in imperial centers provided local opportunities to build on law. The legal challengers ultimately refurbished and revitalized the traditional hierarchies by reaching the top of the profession and connecting with the new political elite. But as Bourdieu suggested (2012), the upstarts may themselves become complacent, conservative, and too eager to elevate family capital over scholarly capital.

Examples of the complexity of these processes abound. In the 1970s, law and development missionaries in many countries used the prestige of US legal education to challenge traditional legal oligarchies that had long resisted scholarship, meritocracy, and reforms in legal education—oligarchies such as the prominent Indian grand advocates who opposed Nehru's social reforms, and Brazilian jurists (professors, politicians, and public intellectuals with prominent legal names). The initial "failure" of reforms gave birth to a later generation who used their expertise and foreign connections to recreate the challenge by importing from the global North not only corporate law firms but also new schools to serve them. But here, as elsewhere, there were further twists and turns. The aspirational Harvard of India, the National Law School of Bangalore, founded in 1986, was a legacy of the idealistic law and development movement and of internal politics challenging the complacency of the elite bar. But it changed quickly, from a school committed to training public interest advocates to serve NGOs to the first of many National Law Schools focused on producing corporate lawyers. The US-oriented teaching produced lawyers who easily slotted into the new corporate law firms that had established themselves following India's economic liberalization. Yet many of these same graduates are now themselves challenging the traditional bench and bar.

Benton and Ford (2016) describe how Britain in the nineteenth century legalized colonial administration as well as interaction with trading partners, thus connecting the power of local elites to cosmopolitan legal expertise and imperial governance. The same process of co-optation into law and imperial power was evident even in countries that under pressure from Western empires emulated the practices of the Western colonial powers. The long and interconnected history of these practices is evident to this day, for example, in the leading law faculties in Beijing, which are distinguished by their cosmopolitanism—in particular, their expertise in Western legal theories. This is striking—China, never a Western colony, has reproduced the habitus of the cosmopolitan legal elites.

The processes that Benton and Ford describe suggest that the position of these cosmopolitan legal elites investing in formal law cannot be taken for granted. Law always exists in relation to underlying social structures and a multitude of methods of dispute resolution. In the nineteenth century, for example, locally embedded justices of the peace in the colonies competed against the formal law controlled by British Queen's Counsel (Benton and Ford 2016). The lesson of legal pluralism is that the place of mafias, tribes, religions, political parties, and customary law may ebb and flow depending on the power and embeddedness of formal law and its lawyers relative to those who seek to challenge them in the name of other authorities. Sida Liu (2020: 699), for example, discusses the changing role of Chinese lawyers in relation not only to state bureaucrats, market brokers, and political activists but also to "barefoot lawyers" or "basic level legal workers." Those who challenge formal law and its practitioners may replace it with other legitimating ideologies.

We cannot depict all of the twists and turns of the descendants of the small group of cosmopolitan elites that built the legal profession in medieval Italy, but we want to note that our narrative does not preclude shifts in direction that affect the role of law and lawyers. Our focus here, however, is on the relationship of legal oligarchies in Asian countries to the relatively powerful legal revolution emanating initially from the United States and identified with neoliberalism and financialization.

Some of the institutional changes associated with this neoliberal legal revolution, especially the boom in corporate law in the United States, which began in the 1980s and continues, with some hiccups, into the present, are already the subject of an established scholarly literature (e.g., Galanter and Palay 1991; Gordon 2008). The story that leading legal scholars tell is mainly one of growth in the market for corporate legal services resulting from the economic changes associated with liberalization and deregulation (see Boussebaa and Faulconbridge 2019). Law firm expansion and growing wealth are seen mainly as consequences of more general economic trends that have produced a much greater demand for corporate legal services.

The same phenomenon is now evident in much of the world. Comparative studies of the legal profession emphasize the importance of corporate law firms in many countries besides the United States. In particular, the work being done at Harvard University by David Trubek, David Wilkins, and their colleagues emphasizes that there has been a boom in corporate law in places where its practitioners are a relatively new phenomenon—most notably, Brazil, China, and India among the emerging economies (Wilkins, Khanna, and Trubek 2017; Gross Cunha, Monteiro Gabbay, Garcez Ghirardi, Trubek, and Wilkins 2018). Other scholars see the same trend in Latin America (Gomez and Pérez-Perdomo 2018). Europe, we should note, developed corporate law firms earlier, although well after the United States (Dezalay 1992). Again, the expansion and economic success of corporate law firms emulating those in the United States is attributed largely to changes in the local and global economies—liberalization and globalization. These scholars also point to the rise in prestige and wealth of those in the corporate sector as evidence of some convergence with the US model (albeit with local variations).

These literatures tend to accept the rise of corporate law firms in the United States and abroad as natural and inevitable—as the modernizing result of growth in demand among corporations for the services of well-trained lawyers in large organizational settings (Wilkins, Trubek, and Fong 2020; Abel and Lewis 1988–89). Other characteristics—high prestige; very high salaries, especially for partners; and hiring on the basis of merit (i.e., high grades from top law schools)—are typically seen as features that go along with corporate law firms' growth and expansion.

Neither the demand for the specific services of corporate lawyers nor the prestige of this sector can be taken for granted, however. It was not inevitable that corporate law firms would succeed when exported to settings outside the United States, and of course such "success" takes a form that depends on what was already established in the importing nation's legal field (Dezalay and Garth 2002; 2010). Success in transforming a legal field, which includes carving out a credible role for corporate law firms, requires actors and processes best depicted as legal revolutions challenging the existing legal oligarchies.

The arrival of the corporate law firm disrupted relatively stable structures. There was a two-stage process that varied by local context. Corporate law firms initially were outside the mainstream and ostracized by local legal elites, who did not initially embrace the potential demand pushed by US-style globalization. Corporate law firm entrepreneurs eventually found ways to draw elites in and gain acceptance. Stage two then involved entrepreneurs seeking to reshape legal education so as to align it with corporate practice.

The entrepreneurs of the "globalization of legal education" embrace the need to "modernize"—that is, Americanize—other countries' methods. Initiatives include promoting the JD or equivalent to replace the much more prevalent undergraduate legal education; placing greater emphasis on clinics and experiential learning; recruiting full-time professors instead of relying on part-timers; and using devices such as Harvard's Socratic method rather than passive lectures in order to encourage student engagement. The entrepreneurs, many of whom did graduate studies in the United States and then went home to "reinvest" them, also promote scholarship produced to a "global standard," derived largely from US interdisciplinary approaches.

The globalization of legal education is the theme of a rapidly growing literature celebrating and promoting these entrepreneurial initiatives (e.g., Steele and Taylor 2010; Gane and Huang, 2016; Jamin and van Caenegem 2016; Harding, Hu, and de Visser 2017). Our goal, however, is not to hail an emerging organizational convergence or an agreement on "best practices." Our focus is sociological—specifically, on the contests over legal education as part of the process of making legal revolutions that provide a central place for corporate law firms at or near the top of the hierarchy. The US model often challenges familial and quasi-familial establishments, which find themselves battling against change.

This existing literature tends to adopt the perspective of the US-influenced side in the contested legal revolution—that of corporate law firms, legal educational reform, and meritocratic versus familial criteria for advancement. Our approach aims to place this literature in the context of the long history of cosmopolitan legal elites and legal revolutions more generally, including the neoliberal revolution in major Asian countries. For example, instead of looking for evidence of an emerging trend consistent with US interests and practices, we focus on the actors in the local battles and on the stakes they face.

We recognize that studies of lawyers and the legal profession do not usually take the form of long histories going back to the origins of the legal profession. Giovanni Arrighi, in a new preface to *The Long Twentieth Century: Money, Power, and the Origins of Our Times* ([1994]2010), takes an approach similar to ours and helps explain what we hope to accomplish. Arrighi noted that his work, inspired in part by Braudel, pushed him into "recasting his investigation into a much longer time frame." Our research has similarly drawn us more into "excursions into the past" to make sense of present developments. Arrighi writes that he sought to avoid the trap of "the treacherous terrain of world historical analysis" (xii) identified with Immanuel Wallerstein (e.g., 2004) by following Charles Tilly's recommendation, which was to "deal with more manageable units of analysis than entire world systems" (p. xiii)—in his case, financial systems. Through our specific focus on the role of cosmopolitan legal elites, which in recent decades have variously resisted and participated in a legal revolution involving corporate law and complementary legal education, we can perhaps make a similar and related contribution, by showing new developments in Asia as "reflections on structures and processes that had been in place since the sixteenth century" (p. xv) or earlier.

ORGANIZATION OF THE BOOK

Our book has four parts. After this introductory chapter, the next three parts address three moments central to understanding the colonial legacies in our Asian case studies. The first part also sets the stage for the later chapters with a chapter on our theoretical approach. Chapter 2 explores the idea of legal revolution, the tension *and* complementarity between social and familial capital and scholarly and meritocratic capital, and the centrality of colonialism and imperialism to the interconnected histories we develop in the case studies. The chapter goes "beyond Berman and Bourdieu," whose theoretical perspectives on law and social change are central to the approach we take in this book. The chapter also draws on Lauren Benton and Lisa Ford's (2016) recent work on British colonialism and law.

We begin in Chapter 3 with the founding of the medieval law faculty at Bologna, which represents the starting point of the long history studied in this book. In the aftermath of Bologna, we focus especially on two diverging paths: cosmopolitan elites in Britain veered toward an approach that de-emphasized scholarly capital in favor of apprenticeships and familial capital; while on the European Continent faculties of law kept up the role of scholarly capital that had characterized medieval Bologna and the study of civil and canon law. In the countries we study, the British and German models of state and law were imposed or adopted in the nineteenth century, with China and Japan adopting the German model under imperial pressure, Korea following Japan, and Hong Kong and India shaped by British colonialism. The cosmopolitan legal elites in those countries have never been simple replicas of the West; rather, the process of local embedding has rendered them as distorted mirror images of Western institutions.

The second period explores the development of the hybrid that became the basis for US "anti-imperial imperialism." The current legal revolution stems from the rise of US power in imperial competition. As the United States grew stronger and became more active in foreign policy, its models for education and corporate law became ripe for export, including by means of the well-documented "law and development movement" in the 1960s and 70s. The new legal revolution, unlike the earlier law and development movement, is not mainly a product of affirmative legal export policies. While it builds on that history, today it is much more about *import*—that is, importers are taking advantage of the huge new global market in the post–Cold War period. They are drawing on the legitimacy of law and legal approaches in the United States in order to take on and challenge their local legal oligarchies in the name of modern corporate legal practice and legal education.

Chapter 4 shows how the US approach to legal education and corporate law originated in the context of meritocratic reforms at Harvard Law School under Langdell and associated famously with the case method. The reforms at Harvard and that university's growing production of Wall Street lawyers were essential to legitimating the corporate law firm—an institution that mixed social with meritocratic capital and thus was well-positioned to serve and prosper during the Gilded Age (Coquillette and Kimball 2016). The hybrid represented a revolutionary break within the United States. It transformed the structures of the field by legitimating corporate law firms at the top of the hierarchy, supplying considerably more legal talent for representing corporations, and facilitating a concomitant huge expansion of demand for the legal services of the kind that corporate law firms provided. The legitimating of the new supply was necessary for the new demand to take root, contrary to the assumptions made by demand side theorists (Abel and Lewis 1988–89). Through this process, corporate partners came to occupy the top of the US legal hierarchy, and they have not ceded that position despite a number of challenges. The law professors who emerged in the United States drew on the Continental European legacy that valued law professors highly. And even though the elite law schools were open mainly to the well-to-do, they maintained a real selection process and provided rigorous training (Coquillote and Kimball 2016).

As Chapter 5 shows, the relative openness of the legal profession in the United States has made it possible for corporate law firms to survive and adapt to significant state transformations, including the New Deal, the welfare state, and the rise and worldwide spread of conservatism and neoliberalism. The diffusion of neoliberalism abroad, beginning especially in the 1990s, was led by economics, but it came with and gained strength from the diffusion of corporate law firms—often in tandem with investment banks. Legal entrepreneurs found a propitious climate for promoting the formation of such law firms in many different settings outside the United States.

The US hierarchy that placed corporate partners at the top was historically unique. Who sits at the top of the legal field—whether corporate lawyers or others—depends very much on the local context. Historically, for example, in Latin America the "jurist"—professor, public intellectual, litigator, politician—has been at the top. In India, the top of the profession has been the domain of leading senior barristers, termed "grand advocates" by Galanter and Robinson (2018), and of the judges of the most prominent courts, while in Japan and South Korea, the top has been exemplified by judges and prosecutors. The historical differences are profound and continue to shape the hierarchies even as they are disrupted by the institutionalization of corporate law firms outside the United States.

The third period, discussed in Part IV, presents Asian case studies of the ascendance, especially in recent decades, of US models associated with the neoliberal legal revolution. The international legitimacy of the US model provides opportunities for local scholars and legal entrepreneurs to challenge the entrenched legal oligarchies that control access to elite legal positions. But here, too, we find a local, distorted variation of the US model.

The case studies reveal continuities in the monopolistic strategies of those at the top of the local legal hierarchies produced by imperial processes. Those strategies link together domestic political power, hegemonic and imperial relationships, and social and family capital. Also, a small core of elite law schools plays a central role in both the reproduction of legal elites and the "modernist" challenges associated with legal revolutions. Each case study examines the impact of the legal revolution within a particular national legal field. Local impacts differ substantially because of complex variations in local structures of power.

We begin with India (Chapter 6), where we see much evidence of the legal revolution, such as new US-oriented law schools and a proliferation of corporate law firms, but where we also see resistance by a strongly entrenched legal oligarchy comprised of the grand advocates and high judiciary. Hong Kong (Chapter 7), another former British colony, provides a dramatic contrast: it quickly adapted to the global balance of power, including the neoliberal revolution, but also to the growing power of China in the world and in Hong Kong.

Chapter 8 contrasts South Korea and Japan. Japan's colonial relationship with Korea from 1905 until the end of the Second World War strongly marked South

Korea's legal system and legal profession. The faculties of law and the legal profession were Japanese-led replicas of what had been established in Japan after the Meiji Revolution. The similarities make especially stark the differences in how each country has enacted and accommodated the recent legal revolution emanating from the United States. Both countries, to be sure, have absorbed much of that revolution, including the presence of a magic circle of corporate law firms and a prominent reform in legal education toward the JD as opposed to the LL.B. But South Korea, in contrast to Japan, overcame the resistance of the core of the legal establishment (in the Judicial Research and Training Institutes) through an almost classic legal revolution according to the Berman formula.

Chapter 9 on China provides a counterpoint to the other case studies. China's long-established internationalized legal elite played a major role during the Republican Period and also helped constitute both the Kuomintang and the Communist challenge to it. This group, purged during the Anti-Rightist Campaign and the Cultural Revolution, came back after the Cultural Revolution to rebuild legal education and again imprint it with international expertise and scholarship centered on highly selective and elite schools in China. Graduates today go abroad in very large numbers, especially to the United States, and they dominate the top legal positions, including in the expanding corporate and in-house law sectors. This internationalized sector of the legal profession has adapted to changes in the field of state power. The most recent shift in Chinese power has been away from the "liberalism" and "rule of law" of the 1990s more toward a Chinese version of "rule by law." The domestic power of the internationalized group has grown as the role of law increases in the state and the economy.

The particulars of the diffusion of corporate law firms and related legal education reforms depend on evolving contests between familial and scholarly capital, as well as between lineage and meritocracy. The case studies show that in these Asian countries, the confrontation between the US-style corporate law firms and law as historically practiced (or not) can be quite dramatic, with China notable because it almost eradicated the legal profession during the Anti-Rightist Campaign and the Cultural Revolution. The other countries also illustrate what legal entrepreneurs encounter when promoting corporate law firms and related changes in legal education. Entrepreneurs, to be sure, can bypass existing legal hierarchies by ignoring them, as the Big Four accounting firms appear to be doing (Wilkins and Ferrer 2018). But the resistance that slows or stops the entrepreneurs (and that held up the Big Four in the past) mobilizes from inside the core of the legal fields. This entrepreneurship/resistance process is well-illustrated in our case studies. Despite the very different backgrounds and colonial histories, in every case we see a strong effort by groups allied with corporate law firms to reform and globalize education, including through new law schools and the US-copied JD degree. The conclusion in Part IV examines some of the themes emerging from the case studies and revisits the theoretical perspective.

SOME OBSERVATIONS ON METHOD
AND TERMINOLOGY

This book builds on our previous books, especially *Asian Legal Revivals: Lawyers in the Shadow of Empire* (2010) but also the Hong Kong chapter of *Dealing in Virtue: International Commercial Arbitration and the Construction of a Transnational Legal Order* (1996). The research for those books involved more than fifty interviews in each country studied, including Hong Kong, South Korea, and India. We have expanded our work here to include China and Japan. For China, we were fortunate to collaborate with Zhizhou (Leo) Wang. For Japan, which we study in conjunction with South Korea, we did not conduct interviews *in* Japan but were able to draw on leading authorities, especially at a conference in 2017. In 2017, we conducted twelve interviews in China (one by Wang), fifteen new interviews in Hong Kong, twenty-three in India, and thirteen in South Korea. Our method, as in previous works, has been to combine historical accounts, scholarship on law and the legal profession, and even newspaper and other Web sources to extend our knowledge. Interviewees included legal scholars and academic leaders, corporate and other lawyers, NGO lawyers, and social scientists. The interviews focused on career trajectories, including investments in politics and the state, links to foreign contacts and expertise, and strategies that interviewees individually and collectively use to build professional credibility.

The book also builds on our previous work theoretically. Our earlier work examined especially the divide between US and European approaches to law and governance, with the US approaches ascending (*Dealing in Virtue* 1996; *The Internationalization of Palace Wars: Lawyers, Economists, and the Contest to Transform Latin American States* [2002]), and we expanded that approach to examine the role of empire and imperial competition in *Asian Legal Revivals* (2010). We believe that our focus here on the genesis of the legal profession allows us to deepen the theoretical framework to explore not only the differences and similarities in interconnected histories but also the relationship between law and social change involving cosmopolitan elites, stemming initially from medieval Bologna, and legal revolutions seeking to shake them up.

Finally, we wish to clarify some terminology. We use terms such as lawyers, pure law, elites, neoliberalism, and the state to simplify the narrative, but we recognize they are terms that hide the fluidity and complexity of what is deemed to be represented by those names. That is why Bourdieu's concept of the field—especially the legal field and the field of state power—is so useful. It can be clumsy, however, to always use that term in the text. With respect to elite, it is not meant to depict some fixed group. The divide between the few and the rest is an evolving one, and any reification of the categories of elite versus non-elite is misleading. The Bourdieusian framework we employ is concerned with the evolving structure of legal fields that produce particular hierarchical relationships. The habitus and institutions embedded in the field are more important than categories of elite and non-elite. The key point is that the impacts of the legal revolutions we explore in this book, including the neoliberal revolution, are shaped by those occupying the centers of professional power and influence in the field, who may resist and/or seek to turn them to their advantage.

PART TWO

Learned Law and Social Change

Theoretical Orientation and European Geneses

THE TWO CHAPTERS IN THIS PART EXAMINE the role of learned law or scholarly legal capital in social change and stability from two vantage points. The first chapter is more theoretical. It draws first on two notable scholars, Harold Berman and Pierre Bourdieu, to develop a theoretical orientation for the relationship between learned law and social change. Berman is famously associated with his historical concept of "legal revolution," which he applied to major transformations such as the Gregorian and Protestant revolutions. Central to the legal revolutions were alliances between new producers of scholarly work and emerging new political movements.

We next discuss the evolution of Bourdieu's sociological approach to the legal field, which we have drawn on in our prior work (e.g., Dezalay and Garth 1996; 2002; 2010), exploring in particular Bourdieu's account of structural contradictions inherent in the reproduction of legal capital, since legal capital—that which is valued in the legal field—comes both from inheritance and from scholarly achievement. The play of this structural contradiction, which is at times a false contradiction, is one of the elements we see in the processes of legal revolution. It helps account also for alternating periods of "boom and bust" in particular legal fields. The chapter shows the ways in which we seek to go beyond these two scholars, and it concludes on the need to add the importance of the imperial and related North–South dimensions (drawing on Benton and Ford 2016).

The second chapter in this part (Chapter 3), is more historical. It explores the invention of learned law, schools of law, and law professors, examining the relationship between education and the position of law and lawyers in Europe as it developed in the medieval period and beyond. It depicts the European structures that evolved out of that period, but it also highlights a central theoretical point that comes out of Chapter 2. The positions of holders of legal capital are quite mobile, operating among many different spaces. These people can modify their strategies and the positions they take in relation to the historical and political context that valorizes one or another of these spaces. The histories illustrate the theoretical perspective of the legal field as fluid and shifting while maintaining a kind of crossroads position—between religion, state, community, and so on. This focus—hinted at by Bourdieu's lectures on the state discussed in Chapter 2 (2012: 556)—facilitates an analysis of the role of lawyers as courtiers and diplomats between different fields of power, but also and more importantly, it facilitates analyses of the relationship between learned, familial, and political strategies in periods of transition between political regimes. This same paradigm also takes into account the diversity of connections between law and state in different national spaces and in different contexts. The chapter argues that there is a process of relative decline in the value of scholarly capital.

Finally, the chapter shows that the role of lawyers as brokers and converters of capital is evident also in colonial settings and in countries, such as Japan and China, that adapted under pressure to westernized legal systems. They therefore show the same patterns of boom and bust that we see in Europe and elsewhere. These chapters set the stage for Part III, which examines the variations on the same processes in the United States. which have led to the spread of corporate law firms as part of what can be seen as the current global legal revolution.

2

Sociological Perspectives on Social Change and the Role of Learned Law

Building on and Going beyond Berman and Bourdieu

The sociological perspective in this book builds on the work of the sociologist Pierre Bourdieu and the legal historian Harold Berman, both of whom examined the question of the role of law and lawyers in social change and social continuity. Each also examined the role of learned law and legal education in these processes and sought to connect law professors and learned law with changes in economic and political power. A general theme that can be found in various ways in both scholars is stated bluntly by Van Caenegem: "law professors serve the powers that be" (1987). That truism masks the very complex processes that allow that relationship to continue through eras of political and economic change.

Bourdieu emphasizes the links between law professors and the field of state power, highlighting the role of lawyers generally as brokers between different forms of capital. He also makes explicit the tension within legal fields between family capital and meritocratic and scholarly capital. Berman offers a historical model of law and revolution that focuses on the alliances between relatively marginal academics and emerging political, religious and social groups. Both insights are important for us to understand the relationship between law professors, legal scholarship, family capital, and the growth, spread, and rise in prestige of corporate law firms in the United States and in many other countries. This chapter introduces the perspectives of these scholars while suggesting that to acquire a deeper understanding, we need to include the imperial dimension missing in their approaches and destabilize the categories and theories these scholars offer—including Berman's category of revolution in "law and revolution."

BOURDIEU: FROM THE LEGAL FIELD TO THE FIELD
OF STATE POWER

Bourdieu began his work specifically on law and the legal profession with his well-known lecture on "the force of the law" (1986). The focus of that lecture was especially on the role of formal law, law professors modeled on the German *Professorenrecht*, and lawyers serving the state. Much can be learned, to be sure, by examining the relationship of pure law and law professors to the field of state power. This early lecture on law, however, draws too much on the German model. Anglo-American lawyers, in particular, who developed through the autonomization of legal fields at the margins of the state, do not fit the German model.

Bourdieu wrote relatively little about law after "The Force of Law" (1986). After that effort, he did not return to this theme outside of a few short texts: "Les robins et l'invention de l'Etat" (in Bourdieu 1989: 539–48); "Les juristes, gardiens de l'hypocrisie collective" (1991); and "Esprits d'etat: genese et structure du champ bureaucratique" (1993). But he made a number of references to the history of law and lawyers on the occasion of his last series of courses on the state offered at the College de France in 1991 and recently published as *Sur l'Etat* (2012; in English as *On the State* in 2015).

These recently published documents illustrate how Bourdieu had deepened his analysis beyond the theoretical hypotheses developed in "The Force of Law." Bourdieu moved in this later work to treat the legal market more generally, in the process underscoring a central point of our study—how the demand for legal services is in large part constructed by what the producers offer. His course of lectures also examined the genesis and reproduction of the position of holders and producers of legal capital in relation to changing state power structures. He proposed an analysis "in terms of the field, that is to say a differentiated space" (2012: 516). He then examined different groups of lawyers ("jurists" in the English translation of his *juristes*) differentiated by their social origins, their education, and their proximity to royal power.

The first group is the lawyers of the state, who contribute to the creation and legitimation of states and state power. They represent what can be termed the bureaucratic pole of the legal field, and thus are distinguished from the second category, which is the "noblesse de robe," the "officiers de justice," who control the high courts. The ideology and objectives of the latter group were inspired in part by the British model of courts as restraints on royal power. In France this group relied in particular on one key institution, the Parisian Parlement, to which the king had delegated the power of applying the law, in this way establishing legal autonomy as a limit on royal power. The third category Bourdieu specifies is that of the "lower legal clergy . . . speaking and being spokespersons for the collective will, popular will, etc., according to the transhistoric alliance between 'the intelligentsia proletaroïde' as Max Weber pointed out and the popular classes" (2012: 515).

These categories move beyond the earlier work on law and the legal profession, but the categories that Bourdieu uses, while helpful, limit his analysis. First, the categories mask the relative ease with which lawyers can switch roles as the state and social contexts change. Even at the individual level, lawyers may shift from, for example, gaining notoriety by representing a social movement to becoming lawyers for the state or members of high courts. Lawyers serving the state may evolve into spokespersons for a political group. Second, the categories themselves are misleading, because the roles that lawyers play are fluid and constantly evolving at the individual and group level. Bourdieu noted but did not develop the insight that the legal field was a "space of many dimensions [where] things shift in relation to each other" (2012: 518). The holders of legal capital are quite mobile, operating among many different spaces. They can modify their strategies and the positions they take in relation to the historical and political context that valorizes one or another of these spaces. This fluidity challenges the idea that the legal fields of France, Germany, or Great Britain, as prominent examples, are best understood only through the analyses of particular dominant types. The situation is much more nuanced. The histories of legal fields shift and evolve in relation to exchanges of all kinds of capital.

A familial and quasi-familial dimension is one of the keys to these exchanges. Bourdieu highlights the tension between inherited family capital and meritocratic or scholarly capital in legal education and in the legal field (2012). There is a structural contradiction inherent in the reproduction of legal capital, since legal capital comes both from inheritance and from scholarly achievement. On the one hand, legal capital is defined in opposition to aristocratic capital or nobility, assigning value to individual merit and scholarly competence rather than inherited title or family lineage—the earned diploma as against the inherited title of nobility. On the other hand, as Bourdieu observes, those at the top of the legal field seek to be recognized as akin to nobility—"noblesse de robe" in France and its equivalents elsewhere. For example, in the top judicial hierarchy of France prior to the French Revolution, the holders of "legal offices" purchased from the king defended the principle of dynastic reproduction against meritocratic promotion (2012: 510). This claim to the status of nobility was also sustained in many places by barriers to entry—as much cultural as financial—that reserved places in schools of law solely for the most privileged of the "cadets" of aristocratic lineage, who were sustained in their studies by their families or as beneficiaries of the support of powerful religious or civil protectors (Brundage 2008: 121).

There was conflict between fractions of lawyers who sought to valorize different forms of capital in the field. For example, the inheritors of the "noblesse de robe," characterized by their family and social capital, occupied the top of the hierarchy in part because of their lineage. They opposed new arrivals seeking to forge a career out of their learned competence, their personal merits, their managerial skills, or their eloquence on behalf of the disadvantaged. This structural contradiction helps explain how learned capital came to be devalued—and how the most intellectual fraction of the legal field was correspondingly marginalized and thus fell into obsolescence, even decline.

The most flagrant example of this decline in the value of learned capital is the evolution of the Inns of Court in Great Britain, which lost all intellectual function following the triumph of barristers around 1750; the latter then imposed recruitment by co-optation and apprenticeship, in conformance with their social origins and political strategy (Prest 1986). One can see this same propensity elsewhere in the histories of faculties of law: they become places where "scholarship" involves little more than reproducing doctrinal exegesis dominated by "guardians of the temple and the texts," who seek to minimize jurisprudential evolution and refuse to take new social realities into account. As Bourdieu remarked in the conclusion of "The Force of Law," in such circumstances, any reinvestment comes from new entrants, typically the "underdogs," who struggle to renew jurisprudential science. They may, for example, attempt to import ideas from the social sciences with the aim of gaining recognition within the law for new social interests, for which they seek to be the legal spokespersons.

These internal battles quite often are very beneficial to the legal field generally in terms of innovations; even so, the process can be quite dramatic and conflict-laden. As Bourdieu noted, "At the core of the field, one kills oneself for things that are imperceptible . . . little changes which, often, are not intelligible except to people who operate within the particular universe." Opposing sides may be completely taken by the logic of symbolic confrontation. They may even fail to see that "they may be in the process of sawing off the branch on which they are sitting. Very often, the dominant group can contribute to weaken the fundamentals of their domination because, taken by the logic of the game . . . they forget that they go a little too far" (2012: 502). The "passion of internal fights" may therefore become suicidal.

Bourdieu adds later on that "legal capital is not only a capital of theories . . . [but also] a species of permanent exchange between practical innovations . . . and theoretical innovations destined to legitimate small conquests in practice" (533). However, he did not develop this insight on the role of legal capital as a site of exchange. As this comment suggests, it is not just about major or sustained confrontations; it is also about a constant process of adjustment through exchanges of symbolic and other capital. Political alliances, elite schools, imperial connections, corporate power, and family dynamics can all be absorbed within the symbolic bank of legal capital.

Bourdieu hinted at the structural tendency to disqualify scholarly production in relation to social and family capital, leading to imbalances in the legal field. But he did not develop this point. As we have noted, the imbalances lead to periods of boom and bust regarding the credibility of lawyers and learned law. To be sure, in societies with long legal histories, the process of decline that comes in part from resistance to any innovation—or more precisely, the loss of credibility in law that results from that resistance—typically occurs relatively slowly, especially given the weight of the capital accumulated over a period of centuries and inscribed in institutional, symbolic, and linguistic structures endowed with a certain permanence. But the booms and busts are nevertheless evident.

Bourdieu's neglect of this boom-and-bust process relates to the relatively little attention he paid to the role played by family capital in the habitus of actors seeking to enhance their positions in the legal field. Passionate confrontations within the field are not inconsistent with family alliances in the interests of the field and its hierarchies. Family capital can be and often is turned into legal capital. Successful investments in meritocratic legal capital lead also to the production of families and quasi-families at the center of the legal field. This process goes back to medieval times. Martines (1968), for example, shows that individuals with family capital could gain doctorates from the University of Bologna, use a combination of family capital and learning to obtain diplomatic assignments and courtier positions, and then perhaps found or join a school. At that point, the students around him could support themselves through consulting and teaching, becoming quasi-familial or familial when bright pupils ended up marrying the professor's daughters. These mixtures of family and scholarly capital explain how, in a real sense, the process began and ended with family capital playing a central role in the legal field.

There are many modern examples of this enduring process. Indian advocates and judges provide a vivid illustration of the importance of family capital; indeed, we see that in India, family capital plays a key role within the bar, among the elite law firms that challenge some of the bar's privileges, and even in challenges to the bar from social scientists close to law (Chapter 6). Another Asian example can be taken from Eric Feldman's study of law professors in Japan (1993). The bright and relatively meritocratic students selected for the path to legal academe, he noted, often married into the family of the professor mentor (Feldman 1993). Mexican "camarillas" involving professors, politicians, students, and others are another paradigmatic example of the blending of scholarly and familial capital (Dezalay and Garth 2002).

Sacriste's analysis of the rise of a new generation of scholars in France in the late nineteenth century is an earlier European example (2011). These young scholars built up their power in alliance with new political groups and in opposition to conservative and complacent law professors. The history of this scholarly and meritocratic move includes a number of examples of the new generation of challengers marrying into the older legal families associated with the status quo, thus blending family capital with legal scholarly capital (Sacriste 2011). These marital alliances between newcomers and families with established social capital are indeed legion in the world of law schools and faculties of law. These largely neglected processes are central to the booms and busts—and adaptations—that we see in legal fields. The tension between inherited family capital and meritocratic scholarly capital that Bourdieu noted is in fact central to the processes of change and continuity in legal fields.

Another key to Bourdieu's account of change and continuity relates to his focus on how lawyers serve as go-betweens among different fields of power and successive variations in the field of state power. Drawing on Skinner (1978), he particularly stressed "the role of the great religious ruptures in the construction of the state" (Bourdieu 2012: 528). Consistent with Berman's basic hypothesis, elaborated on below, Bourdieu found that internal conflicts are crucial to the history of legal fields, including their genesis, their crises, and their reformations. Pursuant to this, Bourdieu explored the central hypothesis of a parallel genesis for law and state, a theme he took up again in his 1993 article. Bourdieu contended that legal capital accumulated through competitive struggles between religious and royal power: "The jurists, at bottom, served the Church and used resources furnished largely by the Church to construct the State against the Church. . . . The State was constructed on the model of the Church, but against it" (526).

These contributions by Bourdieu pointed to the existence of double agency: lawyers built their strength in the field of state power by working back and forth between church and state. The concept of double agency helps account for the role of lawyers and how they acquired it. Yet the category of double agent may be somewhat misleading. Brundage (2008) showed that, during the medieval period, familial processes blurred the categories on each side of the double agency. Ambitious individuals seeking to advance within the state could hit a glass ceiling because they were outside the circle of the royal or noble families. They might then move closer to the church, and indeed bishops were often the key sponsors of study at the University of Bologna. The complex ways in which church and state blended at the familial level challenge double agency as such.

In sum, the familial processes hinted at by Bourdieu are central to understanding the processes of change and continuity in legal fields. They also undermine many of the categories that define the study of law and the legal profession, such as practitioners versus professors, apprenticeship versus academy. The categories mask who occupies those positions, and what their characteristics are, as well as their elite roles within the positions. In general, to use Bourdieu's term, the habitus of actors within legal fields draws on and seeks the accumulation of family capital.

BERMAN'S LEGAL REVOLUTIONS

In the introduction to his first book, *Law and Revolution*, Harold Berman wrote that "the Western legal tradition has been transformed . . . by six great revolutions" (1983: 18). Berman's own research covered three of these revolutions: first, the Gregorian reforms (1983); next the Lutheran reforms; and finally the English revolution (2003). The Gregorian revolution, named after Pope Gregory (1073–1085), who played a key role in it, was both a social movement and the very first mobilization of "legal" authority. The reforms gave the Catholic Church and the

Pope authority over emperors and kings through a new division of society into separate ecclesiastical and secular spheres. The social movement was led by the clergy, which in the process "became the first translocal, transtribal, transfeudal, transnational class in Europe to achieve political and legal unity. It became so by demonstrating that it was able to stand up against, and defeat, the one preexisting universal authority, the emperor" (108). Key to its success was the mobilization, for the first time, of collections of canon law and a return to earlier Church writings consistent with the Gregorian program. This canon law became central to the teachings at the University of Bologna and elsewhere, along with the Justinian compilation of Roman civil law rediscovered—probably not coincidentally—at the same time. Yet as Berman also shows, the victory came with compromises that enhanced the legitimacy of secular power as well.

The *problématique* that Berman developed for these dramatic revolutions can be expanded to help explain other, less dramatic transformations, both legal and political. The principal heuristic merit of Berman's *problématique* is that it facilitates an analysis of the processes of both rupture and recomposition that occur simultaneously in the field of state power and in the field of legal representation and practice. The processes play out through alliances and converging strategies that shake up and realign the boundaries between the two universes. Modernist leaders and reformers construct new modes of government by relying on a small group of relatively meritocratic producers of learned law, whom they can then make their influential advisers. The scholars furnish them not only with legitimate legal arms for battles to gain power but also with collaborators predisposed to participate in the new governance regime. As stated in the introduction, Berman's model inspired the second sociological insight we use in this study—the competition and complementarity between lawyers (interpreted broadly as actors in the legal field) and the state.

Berman limited his research to revolutions that were both political and religious. But the same *problématique* can be extended to regime transformations such as from a monarchy to a republic, or from colony to independent state. We use it here to clarify major political reorientations, such as the New Deal and the welfare state in the United States, as well as the retreat over the past several decades from the welfare state to neoliberalism. In each of these moments, whatever the intensity and violence of the political-ideological breaks, transformations within the legal order are part of the recomposition of scholarly learning, legal practice, and state governance. Hierarchies may change, but they are also relatively stable, as is seen in the enduring role of the partners of elite corporate law firms in the United States. The *problématique* developed by Berman retains its heuristic strength in these situations and may usefully be expanded to cover them. It also works well for the legal revolution we trace in Asia in Chapters 6 to 9, which made a place for relatively prestigious corporate law firms and their practices in legal fields where they had not previously been welcome.

The approach provides analytical tools to explain how, through an internal dynamic, these successful readjustments operate, as well as how they are able to preserve the relative autonomy of the legal field with respect to the holders of political power. That autonomy, as shown famously by Kantorowicz (1997) and others (e.g., Thompson 1975), is the basis of the social credibility of legal institutions and the reason why the law may serve political leaders and further legitimate their power. For these transformations to happen, the law must at the same time shift to the new power alignment—professors (and others) serving the powers that be—and, principally through developments in learned law, reaffirm its autonomy.

According to Berman, change involves converging political and legal strategies successfully working through a kind of osmosis between the two spaces, leading to the emergence of new legal hierarchies conforming to the interests of the new holders of power. One question about this process is how the two sides – law and state power – diverge so as to allow new strategic alliances to come into play. Reformers and political opponents of the status quo must get together with legal "young Turks" who are ready to risk their capital of legal authority by questioning established legal hierarchies consolidated out of prior configurations of the field of state power.

From our vantage point, Berman misses some of the dynamics of this process, which leads producers of learned law to risk their careers (and more) by forming alliances with potential modernist leaders seeking to gain power and legitimacy in the field of state power. No doubt there is the pull of potential new leaders and movements, but there is also a push from within the legal field. New entrants into the field seek to advance by investing in learned law to show their ability to excel in the scholarly world. But what they often confront is a status quo that has devalued legal scholarship and learned law relative to the familial and social capital that is comfortable with the current political arrangement. The newcomers feel therefore that scholarly capital itself is devalued.

The new producers, while placing their doctrinal expertise at the service of these new regimes, also deploy political resources to invest in the reproduction of legal learning. This investment is not inconsistent with initial opposition to the hierarchies of the legal field and its *doxa* of independence with respect to the holders of political power. The vehemence of the challenge goes with efforts to reshape legal scholarly representations to conform to the new dominant ideologies, and the overinvestment in legal science serves to legitimize the innovations as part of the existing tradition of legal science—now skillfully reinterpreted. Despite being quite politically marked, therefore, the new legal discourse is assimilated into the discourse and tradition of law—with its universal and almost timeless pretensions.

There is a constant process of change and adjustment in the legal field. As noted earlier, Bourdieu stated at one point in the lectures that "legal capital is not only a capital of theories . . . but it is a species of permanent exchange between practical innovations . . . and theoretical innovations destined to legitimate small conquests in practice" (2012: 533); but he did not develop this insight in terms of the role of legal capital as a site of exchange. This constant process of exchange is part of the explanation as to why the revolutions are not that revolutionary in terms of the hierarchies of the legal field.

At the same time, as we have noted, there is also a continuing familial dimension that is part of the assimilation of the new into the old. Change takes place, as we have noted, but the enduring hierarchies in the legal field, and their relationship to societal power, make the term revolution questionable in important respects. Even in Berman's archetypical examples of law and revolution—the Gregorian and Protestant revolutions—the conversions and reforms that took place kept social and legal hierarchies largely in place.

The meritocratic element of the revolution on which we focus here, which includes the more rigorous selection of students as well as better training within law schools, is quite obvious. But the new corporate law firms and law schools in the periphery, including in South and East Asia, take a more elitist and perhaps even plutocratic approach. What is in part a conservative counter-revolution exported abroad is also a huge departure from the idealist law-and-development projects that were the basis earlier of importing and exporting of US legal technologies and approaches.

The current developments also raise interesting questions about Berman's equating of the Lutheran and Anglican revolutions. The Lutheran story perfectly fits his hypothesis that reformist policies were coupled with the meritocratic reproduction of legal knowledge. Yet the Anglican emergence of the common law, instead of being scientific and meritocratic, happened at the opposite end of the spectrum. It can be seen as an elitist counter-offensive to impose the political recognition of the gentry and merchants at the expense of the scholarly reproduction of legal knowledge. The more recent episodes in legal palace wars that we explore in this book—especially in Chapter 5 and Part IV—thus suggest new factions of the financial elites gaining entry and claiming a larger share of the fields of law and state power (for similarities with the French legal field and field of state power today, see Vauchez and France 2017).

EMPIRES, BLOWN-UP MIRRORS, BOOMS AND BUSTS

The European powers used law in somewhat different ways in support of their colonial adventures. The approach depended in part on the role of the existing population and the amount of colonial settlement that took place, shifts in domestic politics in relation to colonialism, and the related importance of groups seeking to conquer, exploit, or civilize the subjects of colonial governance. Nevertheless, there were key similarities generating similar impacts. The Western colonizers, especially the British, built up law in part by finding or creating counterparts to the kings, barons, and advocates at home. They elevated or co-opted individuals, naming them as quasi-judges, quasi-lawyers, and quasi-nobles, as part of a process of legalizing and legitimating empire. As noted by Benton and Ford (2016), some form of law and legal order emerged through these improvisations. The Dutch acted similarly when they co-opted and empowered the Javanese elite so that they could negotiate a "legal" arrangement with them. The United States in the Philippines in the late nineteenth century followed the Spanish practice of appointing the most prominent local *ilustrados* in each town and province to positions of governance. They had been named *gobernadorcillos* and tax collectors under Spanish rule, and the same group became politicians and "lawyer-statesmen" under US rule. Stanley Karnow's history of the Philippines under US rule is appropriately titled "In Our Image" (1989).

In many respects, these co-optations and quasi-conversions created *faux*-counterparts to what was found in the governing country. Building on Bourdieu, we see colonial legal fields as images produced by mirrors that inflate and exaggerate what is seen in the core of the empire. Bourdieu saw legal fields as symbolic fields constructed around the opposition and complementarity between the much smaller field of production—pure jurists at the core of the legal field—and the much larger field of those who use legal capital in various ways (cf. merchant, soldier, and sage in Priestland [2012]). But the mirror effect is both to exaggerate the larger part around the law and the impact of the sporadic investment from the core.

In the colonial legal field, the second and larger circle around the law was much broader and more extended than in the centers of the empire. It was more diversified in space and time, and it was fluid and evolving as a consequence of professional and colonial competition. As suggested by Benton and Ford (2016), it included colonial administrators, including those who controlled the exploitation and circulation of gold in Latin America; merchants and justices of the peace, who often were the first to apply some version of colonial law; and agents who interacted on the borders of the legal field, including soldiers, as Steinmetz (2007) showed, and missionaries in many places, including India. These interactions led to hybrid statuses between north and south, including, for example, the *ilustrados/* lawyer-statesmen in the Philippines and the legal gentlemen-barristers in India (Dezalay and Garth 2010).

The inner circle of the legal field—most identified with pure law—was important but distant from the colonial territories. Its relative lack of presence in the colonies meant that its role was *ad hoc* and episodic, as described by Benton and Ford (2016). Nevertheless, the center in London played a central role in colonial governance, for it controlled the "despotic dominions"—for example, the abuses of power by those given positions as justices of the peace. That control came from a combination of legal capital (often the barristers and judges) and political capital (through relationships with the government and Parliament). The resources of the legal core thus played a prominent role in colonial governance. Because of the size and fluidity of those around the law or pretending to use the law on the peripheries, in particular, there were many opportunities to intervene with resources from the core of the legal field in London. The logic is similar to what we see with Berman, but here there were many *ad hoc* mini-revolutions. The two-tier structure exacerbated the mini-revolutions that broke out between agents with shifting and frequently divergent interests and resources in the colonies.

In certain favorable circumstances, in addition, there were successful movements for independence, nourished in part by legal investments that played out on the periphery but that were built from the scholarly and symbolic legal capital produced by and bestowed in the metropolitan center. Well-known examples are the Indian barristers of the Congress Party and the graduates of the Academy of Chiquisaca who led independence in Argentina (Bohmer 2013).

In sum, there were, in effect, overextended imperial legal fields, with internal and external conflicts breaking out around the colonial peripheries but also in the imperial legal cores. There were also boomerang effects and "symbolic telescopes," as evident in notions such as the Indian Raj as a British laboratory, and the similar idea of the Comaroffs that colonial experiments served as "petri-dishes for imperial reformers" (2011) (cf. Oguamanam and Pue on "fighting brigades" [2007]).

The exaggerated mirrors that structured the colonial legal fields were more fragile than those in the European colonial powers. Over time, local social capital became much more embedded in the imported colonial legal capital (Dezalay and Garth 2010). The resulting social structures led to relatively rapid conversions, such as those just mentioned, from nabobs of the law to leaders of independence, or from officers of Spanish kings to Latin American revolutionaries. But even then, the conversions masked the centrality of family capital.

To return to our elaboration of Bourdieu's discussion of the relationship between family capital and scholarly legal capital, we can see an exacerbated boom-and-bust phenomenon in the peripheral ex-colonies and in countries that adopted legal reforms under threat of colonization. Legal capital, once converted into and embedded in family capital, becomes central to the habitus of actors in the legal field, which makes it that much easier to discredit the role of lawyers and law. It also makes it relatively easy at times to convert, however shallowly, and bring in a new revival or boom period in the law, such as the one tied to US hegemony, which operates in the same way as in colonial empires in the past. But the resulting conflict between family capital and legal capital generates resistance, even a bunker mentality opposed to "modernization."

CONCLUSION: BEYOND GRAND NARRATIVES OF LAW AND THE LEGAL PROFESSION

Our goal is not to produce a grand narrative that starts with Roman law or medieval Bologna and then proceeds up to the present day, showing the emergence of fixed categories such as civil law, common law, and more generally the idea of "legal families." Bourdieu did indeed move beyond the dichotomy of professors and state lawyers to see different models of law and the state, but his categories still mask the fluid and shifting nature of the relationships. Similarly, Berman's depiction of the relationship between law and revolution neglects the way that the same processes of change he uncovers are ongoing as the legal field absorbs and converts new and competing forms of capital into the bank of legal capital. There are story lines, to be sure, and we pursue certain of them in this book, but the processes are fluid and constantly shifting as they produce adaptations within the various legal fields.

Berman and Bourdieu saw the need to explain the interaction of meritocratic scholarly movements and legal and social change. Berman highlighted the revolutionary change that comes when new legal scholarly investment connects to emerging social movements, a process that tends to have the conservative effect of rebuilding and relegitimating the prevailing legal hierarchies. Bourdieu suggested that it was important to grasp the relationship between meritocratic scholarly capital and familial capital in order to understand the structure of the legal field. In this book, we stress the constant boom and bust that takes place in law and the legal field as actors continue to invest achievements in the legal field into familial accumulation, which paves the way for delegitimation and devaluation—a bust that then paves the way for new investment and potential new booms such as the one associated with corporate law firms and related reforms in legal education (discussed in Part IV).

The study of the role of law in change and continuity requires us to look beyond the comparative national contexts taken up by Berman and Bourdieu. So we turn to the more complex *interconnected* national and transnational stories that are vital to understanding legal change. These stories must include colonial and imperial activities, which play key roles in processes of constructing legal capital and determining what goes into it. Imperial competition helps shape and define the values of local capital in many different settings through links to dominant colonial or imperial powers. At the same time, the imperial processes create mirrors, in such a way that the actors who occupy such posts as lawyer, judge, or professor exaggerate and to some extent distort what exists in the colonial power. The family power also becomes more entrenched, and the resistance to meritocratic and scholarly capital more pronounced. In this way, in many of these contexts, a bunker mentality develops in opposition to legal change.

Finally, we emphasize again that our goal is not to create a new grand narrative. Our theoretical approach is built around capital conversion, fluidity, and constant processes of change that are generally also stories of continuity in the hierarchies of the legal field. The challenges are absorbed so as to rebuild—at least for a time— the legitimacy of the legal field. Our emphasis on processes, therefore, means that we focus not on a unified history but rather on explaining the genesis of the processes and approaches that emerged early in the history of the legal profession, became part of colonial competitions, and are still quite evident today.

3

Learned Law, Legal Education, Social Capital, and States

European Geneses of These Relationships and the Enduring Role of Family Capital

The strong linkage between legal and social capital is a by-product of the competition between empires in Western Europe (Burbank and Cooper 2010). There was a Roman model for constructing and administering vast and fragmented empires, one that continued for many centuries in Constantinople, though it was structured very differently there by the Moslem caliphate and later the Ottoman Empire. The Roman model went in a different direction in Western Europe. There, the Roman institutional framework of governance was appropriated quite rapidly by new ruling elites—in particular, by a mix of the Roman Catholic elite and the landed aristocracy (cf. Schmidhauser 1997). The rapid demise of Rome as a centralized site of power contributed to lasting competition and fighting among peripheral regional elites, with only a few limited attempts (such as that of Charlemagne) to recreate a more coherent set of institutions and rules over a vast territory. All of this meant that the more ambitious rulers could only expand their territory through alliances with powerful aristocratic families and their complex systems of feudal clientelism among the lesser nobility.

The development of the legal profession in Europe took place in this specific context, which required compromising with feudal institutions of power. That meant accommodating family ties and capital as well as a system of seigneurial justice, the latter a hybrid of customs and some remnants of Roman law. Thus, the embeddedness of law in social hierarchies and capital is at the core of the historical construction of political power in Western Europe (in contrast to the completely different approach to managing imperial power in the Ottoman Empire, which carefully avoided any compromise with local elite families) and the related history of the legal profession. The specific broker or double agent role of elite lawyers (and those who have followed the same model) is a product of this history. The classic volumes on the origins of the legal profession by Lauro Martines (1968) and more recently James Brundage (2008) demonstrate the complicated processes whereby family capital was converted into legal and diplomatic capital.

LEARNED LAW AND THE TRANSFORMATIONS IN MEDIEVAL AND RENAISSANCE ITALY

Learned law, associated especially with the University of Bologna, wherefrom it expanded to other universities, was an important tool for mediating the interplay of jurisdictions in the service of emerging power relations. The circumstances that led to this are explained in Brundage's (2008) work on the formative period, 1140–1230. He details the close relationship between the rise of canon law, closely linked to the Gregorian Revolution and the Catholic Church's efforts to free itself from lay control, and the revival of Roman law especially through the rediscovery of Justinian's Digest late in the eleventh century (Berman 1983). These parallel yet related developments led to the two degrees offered by the University of Bologna: the doctorate in civil law based on the newly recovered Corpus Juris Civilis, and the doctorate in canon law after the latter part of the twelfth century.

Ambitious scholars recognized the prestige associated with Roman law and the Corpus Juris, and canon law scholars drew increasingly on Roman law as well. According to Brundage, they began "to align themselves intellectually more with Roman law than with theology. They borrowed ideas, insights, tools, and techniques from their civilian counterparts with increasing frequency and enthusiasm, yet at the same time they sought to preserve their autonomy from civil law as well as from theology" (2008: 125). Already by 1200, according to Brundage, there were two distinctive sets of "operating rules, a specialized literature, and a distinctive way of approaching problems" (155). The power of this learned law became apparent. The practitioners of Roman and canon law gradually became "aware of their collective identity as an advantaged social group during the latter part of the twelfth century" (155). They used their tools to "attach themselves to the elite classes that ruled Western society" (155).

On the civil side, "the recovery of the juristic learning embodied in Justinian's Digest came as a powerful, almost intoxicating revelation to western European scholars. . . . Medieval jurists learned from the Digest how to frame sophisticated legal arguments, how to manipulate legal categories, how to analyze problems, and how to find solutions to them" (Brundage 2008: 77). This prestigious and sophisticated set of universals corresponded to a growing number of opportunities to put those universals to work. Economic developments, especially in northern Europe, provided one type of opportunity: "The Corpus iuris civilis offered a system of commercial and municipal law that could be adapted to meet those needs. Its attractiveness was enhanced, not diminished, by its antiquity and its association with Roman imperial power" (95).

Meanwhile, the emerging canon law provided the Church with tools for strengthening its reform movement. As Brundage notes, "each of these claims carried legal implications, as reform leaders were acutely aware" (2008: 79). The learned law could be deployed to support the reforms. The reform movement attracted people "gifted with brains, energy, and ambition," who "discovered that those with specialized knowledge of the law fared distinctly better than those without it" (80). Learned law, once mastered, provided them with a key weapon.

Within the Church and outside it, "between the 1140s and the 1230s, the lawyers went from strength to strength" (Brundage 2008: 166). The successes of individuals armed with the new learned law meant that wealthy families found it "advantageous to send one or more of their sons to study law at a university in order to improve their chances of beating out competitors in the contest for prestigious appointments in church or state" (220). The rigorous education meant that graduates were well-suited to "the highest courts, providing sound legal advice to clients, both public and private, for serving as judges, and for administrative careers in either church or civil government" (269). Accordingly, "by the mid-twelfth century clever and enterprising men could already make a living, often quite a comfortable one, from the teaching and practice of civil or canon law" (203).

The leaders of the city-states in medieval and Renaissance Italy took advantage of the intellectual infrastructure in place to mediate among emerging jurisdictions and social and political groups. Roman law was available to serve these emerging groups. As Berman noted, "Roman law was called 'a handmaiden of canon law': it could equally have been called a handmaiden of imperial law and a handmaiden of the positive law of the emerging secular kingdoms and city-states. It was, however, always a handmaiden" (1983: 205). Law-trained individuals possessed the tools to offer legitimate solutions to disputes and social problems in the language of the highly respected learned law. Law graduates could shift and circulate among jurisdictions and powers, including the church and the state. Upward mobility was achieved through that circulation, based on legal knowledge that could be used as a weapon by either side.

There is evidence that these developments were fluid. It is noteworthy in this regard that the students who paid the professors at Bologna held back their payments to ensure that the professors would not leave to take advantage of other opportunities to market their expertise. The rapidly changing religious and political world had opened up opportunities to apply familial, legal, and diplomatic capital to new problems and conflicts. Lawyer brokers and double agents thrived within a fragile and constantly shifting social and political environment (Brundage 2008).

The founding of the powerful city-states late in the medieval period amounted to an affirmation of their legal and political autonomy at the expense of older feudal, imperial, and religious regimes. But those older jurisdictions continued to exist and to confront one another and the city-states, at all levels—commercial, military, territorial. The management of those confrontations added a powerful international dimension to the construction of state law. The multitude of turf battles among overlapping and competing state institutions provided one of the principal markets for legal experts. They could interpret texts so as to justify the claims of one or another side; they could act as arbitrators or consultants in proceedings before powerful groups or authorities (including, for example, the Council of the Seigneurie of Florence or the Papal Courts). Martines thus noted that "overlapping jurisdictions [were the] source of many conflicts [and] legal knowledge [represented] a useful weapon on both sides" (1968: 251).

The law patricians produced at Bologna and comparable schools drew on their cosmopolitan capital to achieve their positions at the top of a new "noblesse d'etat," which drew on more than individual states. Elite jurists positioned themselves very early as courtiers of the international in the name of the universal principles of learned law, which were deemed valid for civil law as well as for canon law. In fact, if we look deeper into the process, we see that the success of the learned capital was inseparable from investments in cosmopolitan capital. These jurists had acquired their cosmopolitan capital through journeys they took at a very young age as well as the long years spent at prominent universities such as Bologna, where they met their counterparts from other cities. They took advantage of numerous opportunities to grow their international capital, be it in legal practice or in the service of the state.

A practice that assisted them was that certain judicial activities were reserved for "foreign" judges. This tradition, which goes back to the model of the Roman Empire, was justified in the name of impartiality. Judges from city-states not involved in a dispute were considered more neutral than their local counterparts for the purpose of deciding disputes. In this way, adversary parties were prevented from mobilizing extended family and clientelist networks.

This imperial holdover helped build cosmopolitan connections and experience, but in fact it represented but a small part of the international market for legal expertise among the new states. The mix of relational and learned capital acquired by the offspring of old patrician families furnished useful instruments that allowed the new holders of power in the city-states to manage confrontations between rival cities, be it commercial or political. This resort to "legal diplomacy" meant there was less call to resort to military action, which would have risked disrupting the merchant economies.

As Martines showed (1968), these international legal courtiers served many functions: negotiating and drafting treaties, drafting legal opinions where there were potential differences of interpretation, and providing arbitration in order to avoid the use of force between rival cities. Finally, for the ambassadors to Rome, these jurists also fulfilled a double function: to advise and negotiate the numerous fiscal and jurisdictional relationships between the religious and state authorities; and to handle judicial proceedings involving important individuals before the Papacy. The market involved legal expertise with legitimacy across borders, access to which was reserved for the descendants of the great patrician families—those able to take full advantage of a learned capital claiming to be universal through combination with cosmopolitan relational capital.

This trans-frontier dimension in early European legal history helps clarify the analysis developed by Kantorowicz (1997). Kantorowicz developed the truism that lawyers serve power by providing a legitimacy that protects the interests of the powerful; at the same time, those who hold power accept some limits on that power in exchange for legitimacy. But Kantorowicz was focusing on one site—the state. The availability of multiple sites to construct cosmopolitan capital offered legal elites the additional advantage of being able to play on two or more scales. They could construct their professional autonomy and credibility in part through cosmopolitan circles and then put their expertise in the service of the new holders of state power; this allowed the further acquisition of the capital of political influence vital to continuing professional success. The descendants of aristocratic and patrician families therefore played a powerful role in the construction of the modern state in part because they could rely on family resources that permitted them to connect themselves to trans-frontier power through networks situated above—but also within—the city-states.

This history is consistent with the theoretical perspective of the legal field as fluid and shifting while maintaining a kind of crossroads position—between religion, state, community, and so on. This focus—hinted at by Bourdieu's lectures (2012: 556)—facilitates an analysis of the role of jurists as courtiers and diplomats between different fields of power; but more importantly for our purposes here, it facilitates analyses of the relationship between learned, familial, and political strategies in periods of transition between political regimes. This same paradigm also takes into account the diversity of connections between law and state in different national spaces and in different contexts. More generally, as noted above, this approach helps explain and demonstrate the paradox formulated by Kantorowicz: the clerks of the law affirmed their autonomy with respect to power even while putting their expertise in the service of power. As shown by numerous works of history (Martines 1968, Brundage 2008, Whaley 2001) consistent with this theoretical approach, the relative mobility of jurists—for example, between different royal courts or principalities and the hierarchies of the church—was the best guarantee of their autonomy in the sense that it permitted them to break from those holders of power who were too heavy-handed or who undertook activities that threatened the clerks' credibility.

The embedding of legal fields within national fields of power thus was combined with a relative mobility of legal professionals. They could circulate among different national spaces on the basis of their expertise and claims to universality, undertake strategic reconversions during political transitions, and provide continuity between successive regimes.

As discussed in the previous chapter, revolutionary (or lesser) changes, be they religious or political, are opportunities for factions of legal elites to update legal doctrine in sync with the political objectives of new ruling groups seeking allies and privileged collaborators. Part of this process involves investment in meritocratic scholarly capital to challenge and ultimately relegitimate the legal order and its hierarchies.

What emerged from the relatively fragile creation of a new profession and new site of knowledge production continued to shift and absorb new movements and sources of power. The law school at Bologna, as scholars have noted about the earliest European universities generally, was born between states and the church.[1] Developments in Germany built on and continued this central role of the universities and their professors despite transformations in state power.

PROFESSORENRECHT AS AN ONGOING ELITE STRATEGY AROUND STATES: FROM NOTABLES AND MEDIATORS WITHIN THE FRAGMENTED HOLY ROMAN EMPIRE TO A LEARNED ELITE MOBILIZED IN A "CATCH-UP" STATE STRATEGY PROMOTED BY BISMARCKIAN PRUSSIA (AND EXPORTED ALSO TO MEIJI JAPAN)

Germany represents both a break from and a continuity with what Brundage and Martines depicted. The continuity relates to the structure of the Holy Roman Empire, which lasted from about 800 to 1806. The Holy Roman Empire, centered on part of what today is Germany, was divided into countless individual entities governed by kings, dukes, bishops, and other rulers, who governed their lands independently of the Roman Catholic emperor. The emperor's power was limited strongly by local leaders. The half dozen universities in Germany that began to open late in the fourteenth century played precisely the same role as Bologna in the medieval and later periods. Doctoral degrees from these universities helped legitimate professors and law graduates, who offered their knowledge to broker disputes between and among state and church entities. As described by Whaley (2012: 47), the professors and law graduates drew on the Roman Law heritage— "interpreted by legally trained officials through the conceptual language of Roman law"—as well as other sources, to maintain a strong tradition consistent with the role of lawyers with doctorates from Bologna.[2] The lawyers thus inhabited a context very similar to that of Bologna in the twelfth century. It is no surprise, then, that there was strong continuity in the mix of family capital, law schools, and shifting broker roles across different jurisdictions: the conditions were perfect for it.

As Berman shows, the Lutheran revolution early in the sixteenth century challenged the conservative mix of religious authority and royal power (2003). That revolution developed and was consolidated on the basis of an alliance between emerging scholars—theologians or jurists—and new leaders—princes, bishops, and merchants (Berman 2003: 66). After this revolution, however, professors and lawyers continued to occupy the privileged position that flowed from their proximity to the various holders of power they advised and served on the basis of their doctrinal authority. The high prestige of professors in particular meant they were consulted by high courts in cases involving important questions of law—a practice termed *Achtenversendung*.[3] These practices reaffirmed the collective stature of the professoriate within the legal field, as well as more generally regarding the interpretation and definition of legal norms.

The Holy Roman Empire provided a perfect space for continuing the mix of practices that had evolved in Bologna. However, the situation changed substantially with the transformation in Prussia associated with the revolution-from-above launched by the Prussian monarchy. There was a break in the legacy of the Holy Roman Empire when Prussia emerged as the most powerful state in the weak empire. There was a rather large legal profession in Prussia—some 1,200 attorneys—around the year 1700, and their reputation was poor: "Though not very often aristocrats themselves, many attorneys were associated with aristocratic interests—as legal advisers, agents, or administrators. . . . Their qualifications were extremely uneven" (Rueschmeyer 1997: 208). They were blamed for a legal system geared toward the aristocracy: "Dominated by aristocratic interests, the administration of justice was cumbersome, slow, and incomprehensible to intelligent outsiders. . . . Attorneys were blamed for the ills and contradictions of this system of justice, a system they did not control" (208). So the Prussian state in the eighteenth century "sought to reform and regiment not only the system of justice dominated by the aristocracy but also the size, composition, and competence of the Bar" (208). In 1713, accordingly, the bar was purged of more than half its members. The idea was not just to reduce the size of the bar but "to change its character" as well (208).

This offensive conducted by the Prussian bureaucracy enabled it to consolidate royal power at the expense of the feudal aristocracy, implement its "catch-up" economic strategy, and at the same time restore the authority of judicial institutions while rationalizing and imposing on them more meritocratic and rigorous recruitment practices. In this way, "the new order represented an authoritarian rule by professional, highly educated administrators which was based on compromises with the nobility and concessions to the aspiring bourgeoisie, especially the educated bourgeoisie. . . . While traditional privileges were de facto retained, education became 'now the official mainspring of privilege'" (151). The professors produced a kind of pure law while at the same time acting under the control of the state government.

Yet this break did not fundamentally challenge the relationship between the legal and political fields as posited by Berman. On the contrary, this bureaucratic relaunch of law was supported by an alliance with the professors and thus entailed a reinvestment in legal learning as well as more meritocratic lines of recruitment. The proximity between the hierarchies of law and the seats of power led to a logic of connivance. As Rueschmeyer noted, in serving the interests of the landed aristocracy and the merchant class, legal and judicial expertise tended to mix with the ensemble of government, including the aristocratic and merchant elites. This risked weakening the credibility of institutions of government, which appeared to be mere instruments of political power.

The rise of Prussia thus led to continuity *and* rupture in the German legal field. The continuity was evident in the continuing strong role of professors and their pure law; the break, in a weakening in the *noblesse de robe*, who found themselves replaced by the high civil service. With the rise of codification, there was also more control by the state over the professors. The Prussian Code of 1794 was based largely on customary and Roman law, and in that sense it was conservative; yet as the embodiment of state law, that code circumscribed the professors, who had long used the combination of scholarly and family capital to take the lead in combining Roman and customary law. This elite of the professors reasserted a somewhat different role as the authoritative spokespersons for the codes.

Within the Weberian model of "*Professorenrecht*," there is a division even to this day between two kinds of faculty members. The dominant producers—those with the authority "to speak the law"—are characterized by their ability to combine academic competence with an important mix of political and social capital. This divide continues in the present. A German grand professor states that it is a matter of the difference between "true professors" and those who, lacking the power to mobilize multiple forms of social and political capital, are mere "teachers" (*lehrers*), contenting themselves with their contributions to legal knowledge but without the social authority to "speak the law" (interview with Dezalay). That authority flows from networks and alliances within the world of law—from the judicial hierarchy and the elite of the bar—but also from within the field of state power and parliamentary politics, as well as from the world of business and activism—labor unions, NGOs, and even the media.

The story of Prussia and the decline of the *noblesse de robe*—in relation especially to the high civil service—was made still more complex by the plurality of approaches within the Holy Roman Empire and Germany. With respect to the development of the high civil service, these approaches evolved directly from the model of the Roman Empire. Parts of the territory within the Holy Roman Empire—and, later, Germany—resembled the British, with lawyers serving other holders of power, including bishops and landowners, creating a mix of feudal justice; other parts had quasi-lawyers brokering customary law through justices of the peace instead of relying on codification.

The coexistence of these different relationships suggests that the standard opposition between the civil code and the common law makes much of a very late development in the legal field. It appears, in fact, that the development of national codes related less to different "legal cultures" and more to efforts to strengthen the role of state power as a component of state-led industrialization as states attempted to compete with the British. The export of codes from France and Germany coincided with efforts to buttress state power (e.g., in Japan and in Argentina) in addition to legal legitimacy. The chapters on South Korea, Japan, and China in Part IV fit this general model.

THE REINVENTION OF FRENCH ADVOCACY AS CIVIC AND PARLIAMENTARY RHETORIC: FROM TRIBUNES OF THE NEW ENLIGHTENED BOURGEOISIE TO LEADERS IN PARLIAMENTARY POLITICS

The decline in the value of learned capital was far sharper in France than in Germany. Variations from the paradigm established in medieval and Renaissance Italy stemmed in large part from the eighteenth-century transformation of the high judicial positions in France into ones that could be bought and sold and passed on through inheritance. This push in favor of family capital shifted the hierarchies of the French legal field.

This weakened the law faculties' control over the reproduction of professionals. Bell (1994: 70) points out that the French bar was a "nursery of dignitaries" and the means of access to positions of power in and around the state. But the restrictions created by the venality of the legal system created incentives for the less wealthy members of the bar to find other means of gaining power and asserting their expertise, be it professional, scholarly, or civic. They found new openings in revolutionary politics, as tribunes and leaders. This was the beginning of a professional valorization that made defending the public and the citizen a new source of prestige, which developed in conjunction with flourishing printing presses and public scandals (Bell 1994: 83).

There were attempts to improve legal education, such as under Louis XIV in the late seventeenth century, but they did not succeed. Carbonneau notes that prior to the French Revolution, "despite the integration of national French law into the law school curriculum and the revival of the system generally, the reforms . . . had failed to offset the decline of legal education. The Facultes de droit were content to see their task as the preparation of practitioners who, paradoxically, were trained in classical oratory, and the precepts of Roman civil law and canon law" (1980: 452).

The new opportunities linked to the tribune role helped change how members of the French bar were recruited. This led to a change in lawyers' professional profile (Bell 1994: 84). The earlier generation had sought to be "high priests of the law" and to validate their technical skill, their legal science, and their political wisdom; the new arrivals valued rhetorical and theatrical skills that allowed them to speak effectively for various causes. They valued "genius, a good voice and the art of touching hearts" (Bell 1994: 94). Nevertheless, even if this new approach to practice was dressed up in the language of civic virtue and lack of concern about money, the profits were not insignificant: "barristers' careers reached new peaks as a result of the public's endless taste for sensational causes célèbres" (94).

This shift in the legal profession's "mindset"—from that of dignitaries serving the constitutional monarchy to that of tribunes for the public—happened in tandem with an expansion in recruitment to the bar. Reforms prior to the French Revolution had already abolished the monopoly of the organized bar and opened the profession to all law graduates. The bar's monopoly control of the market for political pamphlets free of royal censorship gave lawyers a central role in constructing and feeding public opinion. "Factums" describing particular arguments were disseminated by the thousands: "Factums take the place of judicial rulings and direct those of the judge" (Voltaire); "your judges will be, even without realizing the fact, compelled or restrained by the Public, by the most widely spread opinion. It is thus the Public we must instruct, convince and win over" (Linguet) (Bell 1994: 85). The strategy whereby lawyers were converted into tribunes for the public and political causes permitted this group to dominate the emerging market for political representation even if it meant sacrificing the organization of the bar. This explains the paradox of revolutionary assemblies dominated by advocates acting to abolish the bar.

After the revolutionary turmoil passed, Napoleon restored the professional structures, albeit while restraining their autonomy. The French Civil Code was part of this strategy to circumscribe the bar and the judiciary. But the role of advocate-politician and champion of public opinion was sufficiently profitable that it reappeared when political circumstances allowed. Young advocates from the urban middle classes gained fame in the courts and in the press by denouncing the government's abuses of power. Indeed, even today in France, access to elite legal positions is determined by performance at the Conférence du stage, which is nothing but a competition in public speaking.

The need to maintain credibility by mobilizing legal resources in the political field did impose restrictions in terms of investments in business law, which meant that business lawyers occupied only the margins of the legal field. But political profits, as noted above, were not trivial, even if they had to await the arrival of the "république des avocats" in the late nineteenth century for the consecration of this strategy of the advocate as a notable professional in the political field.

The strong connection between law and politics helped continue to marginalize the production of legal learning that characterized the eighteenth century. In a recent book calling for the modernization of the teaching of law, Christophe Jamin, the founding director of the law faculty at Sciences Po, wrote: "We know that the old faculties of the Ancien Régime were nearly abandoned at the time the

Revolutionaries suppressed them in 1793: the professors barely gave their lessons and the students no longer attended in mass. Better to learn the law at the office of a practitioner than to go and follow, in Latin, the vague teachings of Roman law and canon law, with lessons on French law being almost negligible" (2012: 34).

After the faculties of law were re-established by the Napoleonic reforms, professors were limited to the function, in Jamin's terms, of "repeaters of the imperial catechism about the codes" (36), and they were quite reticent with respect to new disciplines, such as history and political economy. To illustrate the intellectual poverty of this manner of teaching, Jamin quotes Flaubert, who referred to his years of studying the law as evoking "huge amounts of boredom" (39).

The mandate for legal education after the Napoleonic revolution was summarized by Carbonneau as follows: "education in the law schools would be restricted to the texts of the codes and the principles of private French law. The professors would teach private law by dictating their comments on the codal provisions to their students" (1980: 455). Courses that went beyond the codes, such as philosophy of law, legal history, and natural law, were not taught. The codes then also dominated French scholarship: they were seen as "definitive and immutable works; this attitude gave rise to a casuistic tendency to give the codal texts primacy over legal principles and fostered a belief in mechanical jurisprudence" (455).

To better situate the professional context and clarify its internal criticisms, we can rely on the historical research by Sacriste in *La république des constitutionalistes* (2011), which covers the years 1870 to 1914. He describes the faculties of law as essentially professional schools. This characterization especially applied to provincial faculties, which responded to the demands of local practitioners, who sought to ensure the reproduction of highly segmented regional legal worlds in which the professors were themselves highly involved. The professors were thus much closer to the pole of legal practice than to the intellectual pole: "The production of written works—articles, notes on jurisprudence, treatises or manuals—did not constitute a valued criterion of professional excellence" (2011: 48). And the professors spent much of their time and resources in their legal offices, "pleading most often themselves or providing written opinions for the benefit of the local bourgeoisie" (48).

The dominance of civil law professors in faculties of law was directly linked to their integration into these parochial legal worlds, which reproduced while educating the inheritors of the local notables of the bench and bar in the rules established by the Civil Code. With teaching activity dominated by the exegesis of texts, all innovation was, if not excluded, at least marginalized—*a fortiori* any reference to new ideological currents or new disciplines such as sociology and other social sciences that emerged in new intellectual circles close to the reformist milieu, such as the School of "sciences morales et politiques."

All of this makes it easier to understand why the young upstarts of the faculties of law, whose learned expertise was going unrecognized—by the hierarchy of professors of civil law as well as by the notables of the bar—were inclined to form alliances with emerging political leaders. Such alliances offered positions and careers that could valorize their capital of legal authority. The success of these promotional strategies came from the ability to put forward a new scientific legitimacy that conformed to the university's new model of academic excellence encouraged by the new political leaders. In this manner the partisans of these reforms in legal education were also able to bring scholarly value where the actual production of that value had been lacking (121). They offered continuity and legitimacy to those who brokered the change.

The role of the legal academy and the professoriate underscores that there is a more limited role in France for the legal profession in the governance of the state than there is in Germany (or Great Britain or the United States). As in Germany, however, there are professors who combine family and learned capital with a series of connections to the field of power. They can draw on the learned investments of those less endowed with social capital to support their own careers and paths as power brokers and agents of legal change. They may also be advocates or judges or have other links to the kinds of elite lawyers who connect, absorb, and broker emerging forms of capital into institutional and legal investments (Kawar 2015). The interconnected elite, including prestigious professors of law, is central to both continuity and change in the law, the profession, and the relationship between lawyers and the state. The meritocratic investment in the narrative of change and continuity is not inconsistent with the continued relative depreciation of investment in learned law in France and in the many countries whose legal education systems have followed the post-Napoleon French pattern (e.g., Bohmer 2013 for Argentina).

This French variation departed in different ways than Germany from the medieval model of lawyer-brokers using their command of Roman civil law or canon law to serve and mediate between different jurisdictions and sources of power, including customary law. But the continuity in the history, as in southern Germany, was not consistent. There were patterns within the French empire—in the coastal trading areas of Africa, for example—of negotiated justice that involved in effect legally trained courtiers operating between French and indigenous power (for Tunisia see Gobe 2013).

ITALY: BUILDING THE STATE
AND BROKERING POWER

Italy at the time of unification in 1860 had professions that "preserved the original features of arrangements in the country's previous regions" (Mazzacane 1995: 80). The universities by this time had "largely fallen into decay and dispute" (80). Professors "simultaneously practiced as lawyers or magistrates" (84), and attendance at universities for students and professors was poor: "Professors and students were largely indifferent to the university," and indeed many classes were taught in professors' homes (84). In addition, "teaching in the university was trapped in the mechanical transmission of an ancient 'culture of cloisters' which was entirely irrelevant to professional problems and needs" (87).

The key to the legal profession was that "legal professionals were the members of the bourgeoisie imbued with a rhetorical and humanistic culture who possessed the greatest expertise in politics and institutions" (81). This was especially true in Naples, where "the dominant role occupied for centuries by the judiciary and the Bar in the city explains the poor regard in which the university was held" (81).

Naples and its lawyers in the nineteenth century "played a decisive role in . . . the building of the Italian state" (81). Working from all parts of Italy after a diaspora of exiled southern lawyers, they provided the architecture of a "national jurisprudence" (82). Part of the story is that the bar—*avvocatura*—in Naples during the decade of rule by Joseph Bonaparte had to learn the French codes and more generally the French legal system (83), and this knowledge and experience helped them provide later leadership. The center of know-how, however, was not the universities. The center of the legal field was private practice. Naples was "truly the city of lawyers," noted Savigny after visiting Naples in the mid-1820s (83). For Savigny and other German observers, this dominance of private practice and the weakness of public universities meant "backwardness" (86).

Mazzacane, however, notes the importance of "private colleges, academies, and institutions" (86), where the judiciary and the bar transmitted learned law. Because Savigny focused on the role of professors in public universities, as in Germany, he left these entities out. Yet they played a crucial role in a transition to the new legal code (89). The universities insisted on staying focused on Roman law, whereas the private schools tied together the older traditions and the new approaches identified with French law (90). The vicissitudes of governance brought some repression with respect to the private schools, including exile for leading members of the legal profession; however, the ascent to the throne of Fernando II in 1830 introduced an openness that "reinvigorated the private schools. Now directed by leading lawyers, they were able not only to provide training of immediate practical usefulness but also to adopt new approaches and to broach new fields of study" (93). The offices of "certain lawyers" evolved into "power-houses of legal culture and southern liberalism" as well as "civil education" (94). The leading lawyers brought ambition and learning to a program that saw law as "the perennial link among the human generations" (95).

Political activities again led to many being exiled, and the diaspora "spread among jurists the most typical paradigm of the Neapolitan legal professional: the lawyer-professor-politician adept at switching from one role to another and often combining all three of them in one person" (99). They drew on ties to major institutions, "cultural and political reform" activities, "the close study of foreign developments in order to keep abreast of them, [and] finally liberalism and *laissez-faire* economics" (99). After unification they were key "artificers of the 'national legal science"' (99). They invested heavily in the state as the "engine of modernization" (100), and since a major task of the state was to handle regional and local issues and conflicts, the lawyers' market expanded further through opportunities to serve the "mediatory function that they had always performed" (103).

Musella (1995) illuminates this classical brokering role of Italian lawyers before and after unification. He notes that after unification, the key to success was through "legal work that enabled these lawyers to establish the connections and relationships that they required to build their political careers" (315). Also, "a political career became the final and indispensable accomplishment for the successful lawyer, because it enabled him to forge close connections with the inner circles of state administration" (316). That career typically began with family connections: families were "the first network" (317), and indeed professional training was typically in the office of family or family friends (317). For example, the sons of the wealthy urban bourgeoisie as well as rural landowners found places through family connections in the offices of prominent lawyers. Marriage was also important in extending family ties: "In many cases, a member of the professions already belonging to a family of professionals would resort to marriage to establish new relations, and to buttress his social position further" (318). In some places, professionals typically married "women from the propertied class" (319), while in others, "the son of the property-owner . . . married the daughter of the professional" (319).

The web of connections with the state and the social world enabled lawyers to "operate in two different spheres" (320) that worked together. Wealthy clients helped political careers, and politicians in turn helped wealthy clients. The lawyers operated in the national government but also at local levels. In sum, "political and professional activities thus fused and reinforced each other. Many leaders of those years [after unification and into the twentieth century] were at the centre of manifold and disparate interests which gravitated around the local administrations, and in many cases they became the legal and political representatives of those economic groups which built their fortunes on public resources" (328). Lawyers were "the brokers *par excellence* within civil and political society" (333). This role, which went with a relative downgrading of universities and scholarly capital, had much in common with what we see in Great Britain in the next section.

FROM THE EARLY CONSTRUCTION OF THE COMMON LAW TO THE IDEOLOGY OF THE RULE OF LAW: THE POLITICAL RISE OF A SOCIAL ELITE OF BARRISTERS AND THE DEMISE OF DOCTORS OF LAW AS KING'S OFFICERS

Great Britain provides a similar example of a variation of the classic medieval model in terms of highlighting the importance of private practice over academic learning. In Britain, private barristers ascended while Bologna-inspired doctors of the civil law were eclipsed.

As Berman documented, the rise of the common law, beginning especially in the latter half of the twelfth century, was built on a delegation of power by English kings to feudal lords while the king spent time outside of England (Berman 1983: 440). The hybridization of British feudal status with expertise borrowed from canon law and Norman practices helped create a process that the Crown could later borrow from and compete with. Henry II began to increase the royal investment in courts with the creation of the King's Bench and the expansion of the writ system, among other activities. These became the basis of the common law as it emerged, taking that name a few centuries later.

Prior to the emergence of the common law, a group of learned judges in England sought to use the prestige of Roman and canon law to influence and legitimate emerging British law (McSweeney 2019). Bracton's Treatise, published in the mid-thirteenth century, provides evidence of the influence and prestige of Roman and canon law in Britain. As shown by McSweeney,

> the authors of Bracton were people who, for reasons specific to the way English judicial careers were developing in the early and middle decades of the thirteenth century, saw canon law and, more particularly, Roman law as attractive models for the work they were doing in the royal courts. They used Roman law to make the case that the common law was a body of knowledge that should only be applied by justices who had mastered it through a long period of study and practice. . . . In this time before the common law was yet the common law, when its nature was contestable, the justices and clerks wanted to show that it was a constituent part of the universal law of the Latin West.

They sought to identify emerging British law and judges with the prestige of the law coming from Bologna. But the effort to build the credibility of the emerging common law on Roman law did not succeed:

> From 1290 . . . the king regularly appointed practicing lawyers to the Common Bench and the court coram rege. By the middle of the fourteenth century, the crown was turning primarily to lawyers to fill vacancies on the judicial bench. The community of justices and clerks focused on a particular set of textual practices envisioned by the Bracton authors could not have survived long, if it ever really came into being.

The rise of the common law led to the development of barristers, who, from the fifteenth century, were trained at the Inns of Court through a process that could last ten years and could be compared to education at a "finishing school" (Prest 1986). Those who accumulated sufficient social and learned capital were ideally suited to serve as agents and intermediaries for the monarchy or the landed aristocracy—defending independence against royal or religious power. They provided advice and resolved disputes, serving also as justices of the peace. The autonomy of the bar was thus constructed on the basis of capital and activities attuned not only to legitimation but also to maintaining equilibrium within the field of political power. Since they were recruited from within the elite of the landed gentry—and to some degree from the new merchant bourgeoisie—the barristers trained and socialized at the Inns of Court were predisposed to become the representatives of the two social groups to which they were already well introduced (Lemmings 1990). These learned gentlemen became both the champions and the guardians of an equilibrium among various powers against the absolutist claims of the monarchy supported by the bureaucrats and jurists of the state.

While retaining their privileged relationships with the new ruling classes whose interests were now represented in Parliament, these legal practitioners succeeded in legitimating their jurisdictional monopoly and affirming their autonomy with respect to the holders of power. This strategy of autonomization was facilitated by the fragmentation and decentralization of the field of power in the context of the civil war and religious battles favoring the emancipation of cities and the growth in power of an alliance between the gentry and the merchant bourgeoisie. The strategy also drew on a mode of familial reproduction through co-optation and apprenticeship under the aegis of the Inns of Court, which reinforced the sociological homogeneity of this professional guild, which was dominated by a hierarchy of barristers controlling the judicial power and the learned authority of the law.

This double control of the production of law and the reproduction of lawyers allowed the barristers to thrive in the litigation market. Their monopoly gained credibility because it rested on the affirmation of the need for the law to be independent with respect to the holders of state power, be it central or local. At the same time, however, the guild structure kept the bar very closed and small in number and promoted the decline of the role of the Inns of Court. Intellectual activities diminished at the inns, which lost their role in educating the descendants of the elite.[4]

The universities, including Oxford and Cambridge, did not pick up the slack. Since medieval times, Oxford and Cambridge had been teaching Roman and (until the Reformation) canon law, but law professors were unable to compete with the bar with respect to the common law. The history of law faculties is one of low prestige, and until recently, those who joined the legal profession either as solicitors or barristers were unlikely even to bother with an undergraduate law degree before going through the practical programs of the legal profession. Law professors had little prestige and were thought of as merely teachers; they were respected by neither the rest of the academy nor the legal profession (Twining 1994).

Berman noted that unlike the Gregorian and Protestant revolutions, the revolution associated with the English transformation in the seventeenth century was facilitated by a cohort of barristers and judges (coming from the bar), who made the effort to revamp learned law: "the authors of the first treatises on English law were not professors but judges and practicing lawyers, and their treatises in fact strongly affected the fundamental structural and institutional changes in the English legal system that took place in the late seventeenth and early to mid-eighteenth centuries" (Berman 1983: 184). Berman noted that earlier legal theory was primarily professorial whereas the new English legal theory was "primarily judicial in its origin and nature" (184). The legal profession became "guardian not only of the positive law but also of legal science" (184). The bar therefore upgraded the role of learned law and the role of law and lawyers in governance. According to David Lemmings, even after the settlement of 1689, "politics in general and parliamentary business in particular was expressed in the language and lore of the courtroom" (1990: 184).

Lemmings documents the role of the bar and the judiciary—led by relative outsiders—at a time when industry and global trade were being transformed. Consistent with the "revolutionary" scenario depicted by Berman, Lemmings shows the role that outsiders played in remaking commercial law with the rise of trade and commerce: "Barristers who were able to adapt to the changes in English society tended to be men who were not closely identified with its ancient institutions" (177). Lemmings includes the key figure of Lord Mansfield among the outsiders. Lord Mansfield, who was educated in Scotland, became the leading figure later in the century in remaking and systematizing the emerging English commercial law. This relatively outsider group was also linked to politics: a "sizeable number of barristers were also MPs during these years and they played an important part in the activities of the legislature" (178).

The connection of this expertise to the strong personal relations central to the elite of the bar is evident in Kostal's book about the relationship between law and the railroad industry in England in the nineteenth century (Kostal 1994). Lawyers played a key role with that industry, not just as lawyers but also as brokers and even investors. They created the necessary legal and financial instruments to facilitate that industry's growth and guaranteed its value to potential investors (many of them their clients). They also coached the new entrepreneurs (many of them amateurs or engineers) in this sophisticated new technology, negotiated with the landed aristocracy (also their clients) for the sale of land at huge prices, and when necessary lobbied in Parliament to get a private bill authorizing these railroads to operate. Many lawyers were also investors, and profited enormously during the railroad financial boom—which ended with a huge crash and an enormous wave of litigation (again to their huge profit). Despite growing resentment at their enormous legal fees (estimated at more than 30 million pounds), particularly after the crash when small investors lost their investments and the entire industry was financially strangled, most of these lawyers managed to survive the crisis untouched.

Even more interesting is the hierarchical diversity of treatment. After twenty years, Parliament imposed a fee limitation on solicitors, but the dozen elite Queen's

Counsel who had built a cartel to act in front of the parliamentary committees managed to continue for decades until the railroad industry was consolidated. Their peers tried timidly to discipline them, but their recommendations were easily bypassed. The only revenge was to exclude them from the prestigious ladder toward judgeships and political appointments on the pretext that their practice was too specialized and not intellectually challenging enough to qualify them for judicial appointment. Nevertheless, the elite lawyers serving the railroads enjoyed a tremendous period of success.

Kostal's explanation for this central and highly profitable role is based on the barristers' strategic position between the landed aristocracy (whose trust they enjoyed since they were frequently second sons or poor cousins), the railroads, and Parliament (where that aristocracy was well represented). The legal construction of this new industry thus served to build a compromise between the new entrepreneurs and the landowners, who relinquished some of their property rights for a huge price (corollary of the huge legal fees)—either directly through the brokering of their family solicitors or after an enormously costly legal battle in the parliamentary committees granted the power of expropriation. The high legal costs also served as a barrier to entry, thus excluding less wealthy players from the competition. Elite barristers in particular played a key role mediating among business interests, the state, and the landowning class that dominated the state. Those same barristers continue to hold this leading position despite efforts to build up the position of legal education and the role of solicitors in multinational business and finance.

Returning to the railroads, the experience of Great Britain provides a telling confirmation of the role of elite barristers as leaders of the legal field—and also above and around it, through their close connections to family capital, the state, and economic power. We cannot provide detailed comparisons here, but it is highly suggestive to contrast the English experience with the German one, where elite lawyers within the state bureaucracy played the most prominent role in constructing the railroads, and France, where state engineers and private entrepreneurs were at the forefront (e.g., Mitchell 2000). For Italy, we do not have details on railroad construction, but the depiction of elite lawyers in Italy as being closely linked to local, regional, and national governments, urban wealth, and private property, suggests a general role very similar to what Kostal found in Great Britain.

The institutional location of the key actors, the relevance of lawyers, and the place of lawyers who "count" thus varies according to the different national experiences. The US experience with railroads, to add one more example, involved alliances between an emerging group of corporate lawyers, the so-called robber barons, and state power (e.g., Martin 1992). This comparison shows how these very different professional and political paths produce different institutional and regulatory landscapes—as well as different profiles for those who lead in shaping those landscapes. At the same time, the classic lawyer strategy of brokering, converting, and absorbing what is emerging outside the legal field can be seen in each of the contexts.

Finally, we can recap the low investment in learned law by the British barristers and a complementary lack of respect for law professors in the universities. The bar had very little respect for the academic work of professors, and professors often even considered themselves failed members of the bar. The legal scholarly tradition at Oxford, for a notable example, was extremely poor until very recently. Taking up a chair in philosophy of law at Oxford in the 1950s, H.L.A. Hart noted that the form of typical scholarship was a very mild and formal critique of judicial decisions (Lacey 2006: 157). Hart wrote, "What is odd about the whole faculty (there are 4–5 exceptions) is that they regard themselves as a pack of failed barristers and a weak version of the Real Thing in London" (2006: 157).

As noted above, a law degree until very recently was not even the preferred undergraduate degree for admission to the bar or the solicitors' branch. Family capital, secondary school at Eton and Harrow, and graduation from Oxford and Cambridge were the key credentials for gaining access to elite careers. As David Sugarman wrote about the mid-1960s, "Relative to their Continental European or United States counterparts, English law faculties were small, poorly resourced and failed to attract a fair share of the best talent among university students and from within the legal profession. . . . Most lawyers, and virtually all superior court judges, had not read law at university but had learnt what they thought of as 'law' in legal practice. Judges usually expected sycophantic praise, and legal academics normally obliged" (2009: 8). In William Twining's words, "One of the recurring themes that runs through debates and histories of legal education in most common law countries is the low prestige of law schools and the low status of academic lawyers, both within the universities and in the eyes of the profession" (1994: 25).

THE RELATIVE DECLINE OF SCHOLARLY CAPITAL IN FAVOR OF FAMILY CAPITAL

The European stories, including those of France and especially Great Britain, point to a relative decline in the value of scholarly capital in favor of scholarship dominated by the exegesis of civil codes, by conservative and relatively static approaches to scholarship, and by the elevation of the role of dinners at the Inns of Court over any pretensions to learned activity; all of this was consistent with the relatively higher value of family capital as opposed to learned legal capital. In such settings, despite important exceptions such as the rise of the constitutional law scholars in France, the continuing strong role of German professors of law, and the role of the learned British judiciary in building British trade and commerce, there were few ongoing mechanisms to keep law and legal discourse abreast of new political interests, new disciplinary approaches, and new political regimes. There were cycles of more or less investment in scholarly and meritocratic capital versus family capital, but family capital over time maintained a very strong role. These European histories reflect a relative devaluation of scholarly capital over time.

This decline was especially noteworthy during the post–Second World War years. In none of the European countries discussed above were lawyers central to the field of state power. The welfare state developed through various expertises, among which law was not of primary importance. Neither the bar, the solicitors, the French legal academy, nor the German legal academies retooled after the Allied victory in a way that placed lawyers and the law at the top of the hierarchy of governing expertise. Lawyers as brokers and capital converters were not open enough to the new social movements and social science expertise. Lawyers primarily provided legitimacy for the state in a manner that had not changed substantially since the Prussian era and the Napoleonic regime. The British welfare state similarly went around the deeply conservative English bar (e.g., Abel-Smith and Stevens 1968). Family capital continued to play the major role in the reproduction of the legal professions—leaving relatively little place for more open and meritocratic scholarly investment.

IMPERIAL SOCIETIES, IMPERIAL RULE, AND INDEPENDENCE: RELATIVE MARGINALIZATION OF LAW AS STATE GOVERNING EXPERTISE

The European examples illustrate interrelated histories built on the legacy of the Roman Empire and the medieval construction of the legal profession—shaped subsequently by the rise of the city-states. The German experience linked to Prussia has particularly privileged the "true professors" at the top of the professional hierarchy but also above and around the legal field. The related French experience has professors in a similar role, but the elite brokers are a group of notable *avocats* connected to the courts as well as to the faculties of law. The top of the English bench and bar assumes a comparable position in Great Britain (and offers a much more minor role for legal academics), and leading Italian advocates/brokers are central to the Italian legal field. Who the key actors are in the legal field in a specific country during a specific period—professors investing in political alliances, *avocats-tribunes* or QCs embedded in oligarchic elites—is the product of strategic battles involving competing factions of legal elites (either well-established reformist hierarchies building on their mix of social and professional capital or ambitious and successful newcomers). And even if there are fairly stable hierarchies in different countries, lawyers still may adopt the full range of strategies—including learned and familial strategies and speaking for marginal groups—seen in classic medieval practices. It is, then, a dynamic and highly contested process where the values of different forms of capital constantly change. Detailed comparative study, is, therefore, essential if we are to understand the construction and operations—and constant change—of these elites.

There is also continuing mutual influence, which comes in part from the fact that lawyers in a great number of settings come in contact with their counterparts among elites and within law, interact with them, learn from them, and borrow from them both to maintain their position and credibility and to manage processes of change. They build hybridizations seen as institutional innovations. Each national variation involves newcomers whose promotional strategies, in alliance with modernist rulers or entrepreneurs, are built on borrowed institutional transplants.

The export of these models—and of approaches to colonies—tended to occur with different patterns associated with competition among European imperial powers. In each case, what was exported was at best a truncated version of what existed at home. Also, the interest in investing in law and lawyers varied over time and in different places. Imperial powers sought conquest, natural resources, trade, and the religious conversion of indigenous peoples, among other things, and the investment in law accordingly varied substantially.

The British had the longest and most varied experience with law. The export of law typically began with local justices of the peace, as in India, and these men often came initially from the merchant class. There was also typically a double aspect to the justice system that the British promoted abroad. The top tier of justice was for the British in the colonial setting; a second-class system sufficed for indigenous people. There was a long evolution in places like India, however, that included the incorporation of locals initially educated at the Inns of Court or evolving from local *vakils* into advocates. The most successful of the local advocates became known as the "nabobs of the law" in India because of the great wealth they acquired through litigation, especially of land disputes (Dezalay and Garth 2010).

Later in the imperial relationship, law became a central component of the legitimation of the British Empire. As detailed by Benton and Ford (2016), early in the nineteenth century the British Empire built a structure of international law through officials of all ranks in the empire constantly promoting legal discourses and solutions to augment and lock in what the British imagined as a structure of imperial governance well beyond the places of formal colonies. The structure of core and periphery in the law, as a part of this process, was put in place and survived the end of colonialism. Late in the nineteenth century, the Dutch in at least Indonesia invested in some of the same processes of co-option through law and through education abroad, but the British had a longer and deeper commitment to this.

In contrast, the Germans were late to colonize, and law played a minor role in their colonies. As Steinmetz showed, different sectors of German society dominated different colonial relationships (2007). In East Africa, for example, the army ran the show. In Asia, merchants were the dominant players in shaping colonial governance, while in the various island colonies most of the investment was by more meritocratic scientists. In none of these cases, however, did law play a major role. France, like Germany, also did not invest much in law in their governance of the French empire (S. Dezalay 2017; Burgis-Kasthala 2018). Legal education in French Africa, for example, was essentially nonexistent prior to independence (S. Dezalay 2017). In some places, law and lawyers became important, most notably in Tunisia (Gobe 2013), but the overall story was one of very little investment in the export of the French legal profession and law.

We do not focus here on the former Spanish colonies, but we can note that the Spanish empire in South and Central America was somewhat different. Legal education came relatively late in the race for gold. Ultimately, however, it became a key credential for the elite of mainly Europeans, who assumed the major places in governance, and it helped integrate local criollos and Europeans; but law itself was not very important (Pérez-Perdomo 2006). Accordingly, the law degree became embedded in the fabric of the elite families that dominated Latin America after independence, exemplified especially by Chile and Brazil. Legal education was a way to select those who served as cosmopolitan politicians and brokers with the colonial state. But again, a key feature of that domination was that the law-trained oligarchs were above the law, occupying a variety of roles in and around the state and economic power. Law practice had very little to do with what was taught in law school, and elite law graduates only incidentally practiced law.

In the South and East Asian countries that we study in this book, the legal revolution we focus on is in large part a product of the United States as it evolved through and after the colonial legacy of the British. The British relationship has been especially important in shaping the role of law and lawyers in India and Hong Kong. The role of Germany in particular is also evident in East Asia, but that influence came mainly through Meiji Japan's self-conscious effort to mimic the role of law in Prussia—both to demonstrate to the West that Japan was sufficiently "civilized" to justify the benefits of international law and to justify the strong Japanese state (Flaherty 2013; Yukihiko 1997). Japan imposed that model of governance on Korea (and Taiwan) during the period of colonial domination from the turn of the twentieth century until the end of the Second World War, and the Chinese borrowed from Japan for the same reasons Japan borrowed from Germany. Leading Japanese and German law professors long maintained their influence in Korea and China in a kind of legal core-and-periphery relationship. As we shall see in later chapters, the legal revolution we describe challenges both the Japanese/German legacy and the legacy of the British Empire.

One feature we see in the legal transformation we depict in this book is the role of the codes in shaping legal education. Thus the French and French-inspired civil codes were especially attractive to elites in South America, who used them to strengthen their power in the newly independent states (Bohmer 2013). The later Prussian and German codes, in contrast, were more attractive to reformers in Japan and China, consistent with the influence of the Prussian model of the state. In both cases, the emphasis on codes helped reshape legal education and produce the mix of learned and family capital that the most recent legal revolution coming from the United States has challenged. According to Baade, "virtually all late-twentieth century civil lawyers have received their legal education from professors of law at university faculties . . . with emphasis on a codified body of private law" (2001: 232). It is the product, in his words, of "forces set free by the French Revolution" (233). The educational innovation followed on the system introduced in 1806 in France: "That new method was, in essence, the teaching of the texts of the new law [—the 'Cinque Codes'—] by rote pursuant to a detailed uniform curriculum prepared by the Ministry of Education" (227). This rote method and model of legal education more generally represents part of the structure attacked in recent decades in Korea, Japan, and China by the US-led legal revolution, which, as noted above, began after the Second World War and gained momentum especially after the end of the Cold War.

The role of lawyers as brokers and converters of capital is evident in colonial settings and in the countries that adapted under pressure to Westernized legal systems. They therefore show the same patterns of boom and bust that we see in Europe and elsewhere. We turn now to the United States, where the same processes led to the emergence of the key components of today's legal revolution.

The Construction of the United States as the Major Protagonist in Promoting Legal Revolution

AS NOTED IN PART II, the study of the role of law in change and continuity requires us to look beyond comparative national contexts and examine the more complex *interconnected* national and transnational stories that are vital to understanding legal revolutions. These stories must include colonial and imperial activities, which play key roles in processes of constructing legal capital and determining what goes into it. Imperial competition helps shape and define the values of local capital in many different settings through its links to dominant colonial or imperial powers. The dominant imperial power or powers help define what makes law legitimate and seemingly "universal."

Our theoretical approach is built around capital conversion, fluidity, and ongoing change—with changes also reflecting stories of continuity in the hierarchies of the legal field. Challenges are posed, and then absorbed so as to rebuild—at least for a time—the legitimacy of the legal field. We focus especially on challenges related to familial capital versus scholarly and meritocratic capital, and on the relationships between law and lawyers and the state. In this regard, the previous chapter was intended not to provide a unified history but rather to show the beginnings of the processes and approaches that emerged early in the history of the legal profession and became part of colonial competition. We now turn to the United States, not because any grand narrative leads us there, but rather because that nation has emerged out of these fluid and shifting processes as the main protagonist in the legal revolution that is the subject of this book.

The structure of the legal field in the United States has shifted over time. We can say, though, that the current structure has its roots in internal and international developments in the late nineteenth and early twentieth centuries. These are discussed in Chapter 4. Central to the US transformation was a group of meritocratic newcomers associated with legal education reform at Harvard University, who formed alliances with gentlemen lawyers, corporate law firms, robber barons, and anti-corruption reformers. Elite US lawyers and academics late in the nineteenth century also borrowed from German universities, drawing on the credibility of European-based international law to create a hybrid form of legal education and a kind of US exceptionalism as an anti-colonial imperial power exporting its own universals around the world.

The second chapter in this part (Chapter 5) traces the booms and busts that have replenished and maintained the legal capital associated with the alliance of elite legal education and large corporate law firms. An enduring feature of the legal field in the United States is that its history of few barriers to entry makes it more open to legal revolution than is the case in countries with more homogeneous and closed legal professions. Legal scholarship moves more quickly to adapt to changing political and social movements. But there are still booms and busts, and we trace three major periods in US history—the New Deal, the civil rights era, and the present age of local and global neoliberalism. The rise in the importance of law professors and legal scholarship is part of that account. The ability of corporate law firms to maintain their position at the top of the legal hierarchy despite strong political change has become an enduring feature of the US legal field.

US Legal Hybrids, Corporate Law Firms, the Langdellian Revolution in Legal Education, and the Construction of a US-Oriented International Justice through an Alliance of US Corporate Lawyers and European Professors

The United States is the most important protagonist in the legal revolution that is the subject of this book. The shifts in the US legal field over time, especially since the domestic and international developments of the late nineteenth and early twentieth centuries, are the subject of this chapter. We describe the processes that led to the rise of the corporate law firm to the top of the US legal hierarchy and the relationship between those firms and the reforms to legal education led by Harvard Law School. The process involved the same patterns of boom and bust we have seen elsewhere as lawyers broker political, social, and economic changes over time. The more specific historical transformations were from a colonial legal profession oriented toward British governance, to cosmopolitan elite lawyers as leaders of the American Revolution, to the Jacksonian period of challenge to that elite, and then, after the Civil War, to the rise of corporate law firms and partners to the top of the profession. The corporate firms, which emerged first on Wall Street, blended gentleman-lawyers with a group of meritocratic newcomers—a variation of the story of the relationship between family capital and meritocratic and scholarly capital. The corporate lawyers gained relative autonomy through public service; they represented robber barons but were also anti-corruption reformers. Then late in the nineteenth century, they borrowed the credibility of continentally based scholars and the international law they promoted to recast the United States as an "anti-colonial" imperial power that was beginning to export its own universals around the world.

The early colonial period was characterized by strong hostility to lawyers (e.g., Henretta 2008). The colonial lawyers gradually gathered strength, however, partly as a result of their service to the British administration. Around 1700, according to Henretta, "a new legal regime staffed by lawyers was coming into existence in British North America. An important cause was the program of imperial administrative and legal reform undertaken by legal officials in the 1680s" (564–65). By 1720, there was a "nascent system of common law courts" (569) and a more English style of procedure and advocacy. As elsewhere, lawyers who settled in the colonies prospered through their service to the colonial administration.

It is unclear how many lawyers there were in the colonies prior to independence (Konefsky 2008: 71), but it can be said that "the social power and influence of colonial lawyers far exceeded their numbers" (71). Legal arguments were central to the American Revolution and to the crafting of the Constitution. Clearly, then, the position of lawyers was relatively strong at the time of independence. Not surprisingly, after the war lawyers sought to be the "American aristocracy" that Alexis de Toqueville would identify in the 1830s (74). But the prominent role of elite lawyers linked to the former colonizer did not go uncontested.

There persisted an enduring populist antipathy to legal elites. North America, as Nancy Isenberg (2016) notes, was largely populated not by industrious strivers for upward mobility celebrated in US mythology, but rather by what the English in particular saw as a population surplus of vagrants and others unable to survive in England. Many of these settlers became squatters as part of the movement west. Isenberg vividly depicts these "white trash" and shows how uneasily they coexisted with the elite leaders of the American Revolution, many of whom were lawyers. Descendants of these settlers have kept alive the anti-elitist stance of this group, with implications for the role of lawyers.

The Jacksonian revolution in the 1820s and 30s attacked legally educated leaders in the name of the more rural and uneducated group identified with the descendants of the squatters and vagrants (124). When Andrew Jackson ran against John Quincy Adams in 1824, for a notable example, Jackson's supporters praised their candidate as "self-taught" and noted his lack of diplomatic experience as meaning he was "less contaminated than the former diplomat Adams by foreign ideas or courtly pomp" (125). As Isenberg states, "the class comparison could not have been ignored. Adams had been a professor of rhetoric at Harvard," whereas Jackson sprang from a common family (125). The elite law of the period was waning in influence, anti-elite populism was on the ascendant.

This popular movement around Andrew Jackson "created a difficult environment for 'the natural aristocrat in America' with attacks on lawyers peaking in the 1830s" (Katcher 2006: 345; Stevens 1983: 5). Local bar associations declined in importance during this period, to the point of collapse (5), as did standards for admission to the bar (Friedman 2005: 237). Oral bar examinations became relatively "casual" (Stevens 1983: 25), enough so to lead to a decline in institutionalized legal education. The requirement of study in a lawyer's office for admission to the bar became less strict. Proprietary schools that had "been absorbed by or affiliated with a college" shrank in number (Katcher 2006: 345): "Towards the middle of the nineteenth century, fewer than ten university-affiliated schools existed, with altogether only 345 students" (345). Bar associations that had existed since colonial times waned and essentially "collapsed after 1800" (345).

The rise of Jacksonian democracy, anchored in the west among a lower class of migrant squatters, meant more generally that there was little respect for law and lawyers and for lawyers as natural aristocrats. But all of this led to backlash against the Jacksonian era that opened up opportunities to relegitimate what Toqueville had celebrated, and relatively elite education began to return before the Civil War and in its aftermath. Yet even though the bar had begun to grow as restrictions on membership were lifted, by 1860 there were still "only a few cracks in its façade of social class" (Konefsky 2008: 86). Stratification within the legal profession continued to exist but began to be identified much more with clients as corporate wealth began to build. Railroad attorneys emerged as part of what Konefsky describes as "a segmented and stratified profession . . . reinforced by social kinship and family networks" (89). The profession was much larger than in England or on the Continent, but it retained an elite core traceable to before the American Revolution. As we shall see, the leading corporate lawyers in the United States naturally looked to build connections with the long-established and respected European legal elites.

The United States also began to develop a hybrid system of legal education broader than the British system of apprenticeship, which was based largely on family capital. It drew inspiration in educational matters mainly from England at the time of independence. This meant that the first law schools were largely modeled not on the universities in England, which had little to do with preparing people for admission to legal practice, but instead on the practical apprenticeship that was then the practice of the English bar. The Litchfield School in Connecticut, which operated from 1784 until 1833 (Coquilette and Kimball 2015: 33), is one famous example of this kind of education. Harvard Law School, founded in 1817, also drew inspiration from that model of apprenticeship. But the elite members of the bench and bar in the United States were also inspired through their own readings of the Corpus Juris Civilis, scholarly works on Roman and Continental law (40–41), and Blackstone's lectures at Oxford beginning in the mid-eighteenth century on the laws of England (62–63). Though immersed in the common law, they shared a scholarly interest in formal legal theory linked to Roman and canon law. They imbibed legal formalism less from schooling and more from individual study linked to European legal history. The colonial version of legal training and learned law was thus a hybrid model that very early did not fit the categories of law school versus apprenticeship or civil law versus common law.

Harvard Law School became the most important US law school soon after its founding, and a small group of aspiring elites from the North and the aristocratic slave-owning South enrolled there to build on and legitimate their family capital for careers as lawyers and politicians. The professors who taught at Harvard Law School, especially under Joseph Story in the years prior to the Civil War, focused their learned output on legal treatises: "The treatise drove the curriculum, the faculty's scholarship, and the pedagogy" (166). The treatises were the basis for teaching as well as guides to future legal practice; they simplified teaching to groups and built also on professors who were notables more generally in the legal profession (173). Treatises took advantage of established names in the profession and bolstered reputations largely made outside of the legal academy.

From its inception, various other features of US education helped distinguish US law schools from their European counterparts. The success and autonomy of the medieval university, as noted, was based to a great degree on "its ability to operate in the space between church and state" (Labaree 2017: 18). In the United States, the relationship between church and state was different. US education generally arose, as Labaree noted, "in a setting where the market was strong, the state was weak, and the church was divided" (18). Accordingly, "neither church nor state could establish dominion over this emerging institution, and the market gave it the ability to operate on its own" (18). While "European universities lost much of their autonomy in the early modern and modern period, as the authority of the church declined and they became increasingly subordinate to a state whose rational-legal authority grew beyond challenge" (18), US universities have been able to thrive in the very competitive marketplace outside the state. Private universities—or public ones that behave just like private ones—are at the top of the hierarchy in the United States, while public universities hold sway in Europe.

Competition in the United States led to a proliferation of universities and, later, law schools. There was no US national church, and as one consequence, different religious groups competed to build religion-based colleges. Furthermore, the abundant land in the United States led to the construction of schools, including many colleges, for the purpose of attracting settlers and enhancing land values. Thus, as Labaree notes, the United States had 50 colleges and universities in 1850 but 811 by 1880, compared to 10 in the United Kingdom in 1880, 22 in France, and 160 in all of Europe (27). The large number of schools and the relatively open market became a characteristic of legal education as well in the United States.

MERITOCRACY AND CORPORATE LAW AT HARVARD

The naming of Christopher Columbus Langdell as the new Dean of the Harvard Law School in 1870 was a key moment in the transformation of the legal profession and legal education in the United States. His appointment was part of Continental-inspired academic upgrading of Harvard University promoted by Charles Eliot, the new president, inspired by two years of studying education in Europe. Langdell, a graduate of Harvard Law School, came from relatively modest means, and that background made him a passionate believer in academic merit as opposed to family capital. He would invest that belief, with mixed success, in his vision of legal education. He also brought to his deanship a particular practical experience that strongly shaped his agenda.

After graduating from Harvard Law School in 1855, he had begun to practice law on Wall Street. By 1860 his practice was thriving. Indeed, according to Coquillette and Kimball (2015), he helped establish a potential "new role in litigation," characterized by "the extensive written brief that was beginning to displace the weight of oral argument in complicated cases arising from large and intricate commercial transactions in the burgeoning economy of the growing nation" (308). These complex documents took advantage of the resources of the emerging corporate law firms, whose clients were able to pay huge legal bills. Yet Langdell grew disaffected with the New York City bench and bar, which he linked to corruption and Tammany Hall politics (Kimball and Brown 2004). His learned briefs made a stark contrast, no doubt, to the style of practice that prevailed in the New York courts.

Langdell's goal at Harvard was to "elevate and legitimate legal practice and the legal profession . . . through demanding legal education" (Coquillette and Kimball 2015: 319). That meant avoiding any talk of "fairness and policy." Such arguments played into the hands of Tammany Hall and undermined "the idea of legal science, the purpose of a university law school, and fundamentally the principle that cases are decided by law, not the whims of judges" (319). The "merchant class," whom he had represented, "demanded that cases be conducted 'by trained judges . . . and governed by known precedents rather than desire to do justice" (326), which could be used as an excuse to rule against corporations. Property and contract rights would be enforced by properly trained lawyers and judges schooled in the formal law (334). Langdell lamented that successful practice in New York did not "necessarily depend on legal expertise and that absent such dependence, the legal system and entire polity were at risk." His commitment was to "legal science," which he identified with "formal consistency" (334).

His belief in legal science was also consistent with his focus on academic merit. It is noteworthy that he refused to dine with the academic overseers as part of an interview for the deanship at Harvard. Also, he sought to hire not the notables of the law—judges and famous lawyers—who had dominated Harvard's law faculty, but rather recent graduates whose only claim was that they had excelled academically. The teaching of law was to be a career, consistent with the forefront of the "movement to professionalize faculty that emerged at universities in the United States" in the decades between the Civil War and the First World War (385). Langdell battled with faculty over hiring decisions and faced resistance from those more invested in a professional hierarchy that favored the notables. Several times, in fact, "professional reputation trumped Langdell's principle [of merit] in hiring" (393). Nevertheless, according to Coquilette and Kimball, the principle of hiring on the basis of "academic merit" had triumphed by 1900 (401).

Also controversial was Langdell's rigor in grading. He did not want to make it easy for those with family capital to gain a law degree; they had to commit themselves to the task. It is telling that his critics complained that faculty conflict could have been avoided "if Mr. Langdell had been a gentleman" (402). In fact, Langdell fought against the system controlled by gentlemen. In addition, the casebooks that Langdell and his followers created formalized and systematized the law. The education that Harvard provided with the new case method and academic rigor was just what Wall Street wanted and, as noted earlier, what Langdell had sought to bring to New York City and elsewhere.

Langdell joined with the emerging corporate law firms to battle against the existing legal establishment, which at the time was composed of a combination of legal notables, inheritors of family names and capital, and urban power brokers. His fight on behalf of merit and neutral legal science was not entirely successful, but it still had a powerful impact on the legal profession. The corporate law firms made a place for the new and more meritocratic law graduates, building on the formula of Sullivan and Cromwell, which combined family capital, represented by Cromwell, with the more meritocratic credentials of Sullivan.

The "marketplace of legal education" (415) was transformed: "The job market began to favor the strongest students at the most demanding school. Already in the mid-1880s, the Law School was 'unable to fill all the places in lawyers' offices which have been offered" (415). Most importantly, corporate law jobs became the goal of those attending the top law schools, and "students seeking to enter leading firms began to flock to the Law School ... in the 1890s . . . bolstered by the emergence of law practices serving large industrial corporations during the economic expansion." Harvard and then schools such as Columbia and Yale participated in this boom as "the corporate law firm rose to the apex of the legal profession in the late nineteenth century" (471). For elite firms, litigation skills began to take second place in their practices to skill with complicated commercial transactions.

In short, "the success of case method teaching at [Harvard] Law School was therefore associated with the shift in the nature of the legal expertise and with the hiring criteria of elite law firms" (471). Langdell had largely succeeded in his efforts to transform legal practice. The legitimacy of the law school/corporate law firm alliance was furthered by the commitment of Harvard Law School to meritocratic admission and the close attention paid by the firms to law school grades.[1] It was not that social class was irrelevant in the law firms or in the law schools. For example, there were important social clubs and activities at Harvard to which elites had privileged access (585). And the criteria for admission to Harvard Law School depended on the "quality of the college degree" (474), which actually made it very difficult for graduates of Catholic schools, for example, since very few were on the acceptable list. There were none in 1893, and only later was Notre Dame added. Women were not admitted, minorities were very few, and the entry of Jews had a spotted history despite prominent graduates such as Louis Brandeis and Felix Frankfurter.

Langdell and allies in the corporate law firms and legal academia helped bring meritocratic scholarship and academic excellence to the elite of the legal profession, and this, combined with the rising status of corporate law firms, brought new credibility to the profession generally. In addition, as noted below, the corporate law firms that gained prominence did not neglect the importance of social capital. To be sure, they hired the meritocratic Harvard graduates, but they coupled those hires with recruits from the upper crust of New York bourgeois society (for the situation in the 1960s, see Smigel 1964).

The success of these well-trained corporate lawyers was impressive. At one level the success was in gaining credibility for a retooled elite of the legal profession. The Wall Street law firm had initially faced resistance within the bar for adopting the role of hired gun for the so-called robber barons, who included J.P. Morgan, Andrew Carnegie, and John D. Rockefeller (see, e.g., Powell 1988 on the rise of the city bar). Even so, those corporate firms were soon at the top in terms of professional prestige. They reshaped the professional elite through a combination of public service, family capital, meritocracy, and cosmopolitanism (Gordon 1984). This hybrid institution combined elements of the European-developed roles of power broker between state and private power, tribune for social causes, and upholder of state power.

By the early twentieth century, the public service activities of the Wall Street lawyers-statespersons included working with their clients to build philanthropic foundations to support moderate social reforms (thereby containing pressures for more fundamental social change). They continued to serve and profit from their corporate clients, but they also built autonomy by helping enact rules that tamed some of the excesses of competition and corporate power. The law firms prospered, and their clients in turn benefited from rules of the game that allowed them to operate more legitimately and still thrive. In the Progressive Era, these lawyers and their allies in the high courts and the government effectively absorbed, contained, and channeled external challenges to their clients and their position by steering those challenges toward moderate and relatively unthreatening legal reforms (Kolko 1965, detailing the roles of, in particular, Philander Knox and Elihu Root, two major corporate lawyer-statespersons).

The law schools modeled on Harvard late in the nineteenth century also increased the importance of academic lawyers as such in the United States. Teaching was increasingly being conducted by full-time professors charged with producing legal scholarship. The Langdellian revolution was the key to the emergence of what Thomas Grey (1983) called "classical legal orthodoxy" as well as to the beginning of "legal thought" in the United States. As Tomlins (2000) has shown, the development of the case method, legal science, and full-time legal academics was in part a competitive response to the rise of the social sciences in the universities modeled after those of Germany. These developments helped shift the US legal field in the direction of more prestige for legal academics than was the case in the British system (which the United States had inherited). And that shift was only just starting.

US law professors with academic legal theories were not at that time highly respected members of the legal hierarchy. The corporate bar, as Langdell had hoped, took advantage of the "legal science" developed through full-time professors and the case method at Harvard to bolster their own credibility. They in effect outsourced training and sorting for selection into corporate practice to the leading law schools, beginning with Harvard. But Langdell's successful exclusion of "professional reputation" as a basis for hiring meant that professors were not the type of people the elite of the bar most respected. Also, the corresponding commitment to hiring top graduates a few years after they had finished law school and committing them to full-time teaching and scholarship limited those graduates' opportunities to build stature by combining practice with teaching.

There was therefore an unequal division of labor: a key role of law professors was, in addition to training law students in legal science, systematizing and cataloging the law as pronounced by high court judges responding to the arguments of leading practitioners (Shamir 1995). The American Law Institute, founded in 1923 with funding from the Carnegie Foundation, and spearheaded by Elihu Root, reflected this balance of power (Legemann 1989). Academics were to be "reporters" providing a systematization of an area of law; notable judges and practitioners would then examine the "restatement" and shape it to fit their perspectives. Felix Frankfurter in 1915 stated this understanding at an American Bar Association annual meeting: "What we need are doctrinal writers—men who labor steadily upon law as an organic whole, who produce tentative working hypotheses to be tested, revised and modified as the actualities of the controversy require. For the work of the law schools must meet the tests and suffer the modifications of practical experience. Bench and bar will apply such tests and make such modifications" (in Boyd 1993: 18).

The legal academic profession was at the early stage of building autonomy from and parity with practice. Academics adopted a position that was more reformist and that began to be more open to social science than that of the practitioners or the pure Langdellian formalists (Auerbach 1976: loc. 943). Auerbach observes that "law teachers were distinguished by their sensitivity to the sociolegal implications of [social problems coming with urbanization and industrialization]" (loc. 943). Roscoe Pound noted the "need . . . for teachers trained in economics, sociology, and politics, who were thereby equipped 'for new generations of lawyers to lead the people'" (loc. 996.).

Prior to the Great Depression, put more strongly, law professors "were marginal" both to the academy generally and to legal practitioners (loc. 952). Legal theory produced by academics was of relatively little importance in academic or public policy debates. The rise of legal education in the United States did not therefore mean a replication of the German model of learned professors speaking the law. The leaders of the legal field were the elite corporate practitioners and the most prominent judges, and they looked to Europe when they sought law professors with prestige. When they needed academic credibility both within and outside the United States, they used cosmopolitan connections with European law professors (see below).

After the wave of activity in the Progressive Era, these leaders of the corporate bar had become relatively complacent. By the time the Great Depression hit, they were closed off from new social movements and the increasingly important social science disciplines. They were generally quite content with legal education that emphasized only the formal law and that produced lawyers using that education to fight for corporate interests and property rights in the courts and in the legislatures. Their own reform efforts in legal education, led by Elihu Root and continuing into the 1920s, were strategies mainly to attack the proliferating night law schools that served immigrants and others who lacked the credentials to attend the elite schools (Boyd 1993; Auerbach 1976). Graduates from those schools, to return to Langdell's concerns, were more likely to be closer to urban machine politics than to the pure law taught at Harvard. The boom period had come to an end—the elite of the bar had adopted a defensive posture and begun to lose credibility.

As discussed below, the leaders of the corporate bar strongly opposed the New Deal and the reforms associated with it, and this provided an opportunity for a new and expanded academic/political alliance to reshape but also preserve the hierarchies of the legal field and the power embedded in them. Before discussing the Depression and the New Deal in Chapter 5, however, it is important to examine the interconnected rise of international law and an international legal field built out of elite cosmopolitan connections.

As noted in Chapter 3, a trans-frontier dimension played an important role in early European legal history. Lawyers constructed their autonomy and credibility in part by operating in multiple sites above but also within the city-states. They acquired a cosmopolitan capital that allowed legal elites to play in national as well as transnational fields. In particular, the descendants of aristocratic and patrician families played a key role in the construction of the modern state because they could rely on family resources that permitted them to connect themselves to trans-frontier power through networks inside and outside the city-states. We see the same mechanism operating with legal elites involved in the emergence of the field of international law late in the nineteenth century.

REMAKING CORPORATE HIRED GUNS INTO
"MERCHANTS OF PEACE": NATIONAL ORIGINS
OF AN INTERNATIONAL FIELD

The story of the development of an international legal field is indeed part of the interconnected histories of competing European empires and the growing power of the United States. We see the complementary forms of academic, political, and philanthropic capital, providing what we shall call "International Justice" with its initial accumulation of expertise, mixing diplomatic skills with the professional legitimacy of the key national legal fields.

The alliance that produced what became International Justice had on one side Europe, with Continental professors seeking to promote new learned disciplines marginalized within the doctrinal hierarchies that dominated their milieu (cf. Sacriste and Vauchez 2007; Sacriste 2011); and on the other side of the Atlantic, a small elite of Wall Street lawyers seeking to enhance their legitimacy as lawyers-statespersons (Dezalay and Garth 2010; 2016). The latter invested the resources of their long-standing patrons, the "robber barons," whom they had converted into philanthropists/statespersons, into learned European law idealized as an instrument of universal peace.

The individuals who engaged in the creation, institutionalization, and routinization of new legal practices and institutions had in common the accumulation of multiple expertises and resources—national and cosmopolitan; they were jurists/diplomats and lawyer/entrepreneurs (Koskenniemi 2001). This alliance emerged in part because of the multiple roles occupied by each side—professors on the European side who served also as diplomats, and US corporate practitioners with learned and cosmopolitan resources as well as close ties to economic and political power.

They also had in common—even if in varying degrees—the ability to mix their learned expertise with practice in politics, diplomacy, or business affairs. These combinations made them well-suited to take part in conflicts, negotiations, or mediations that involved an overlap between different systems of national or trans-national rules—a legal complexity of which they often were the principle architects (cf. Gordon 1984; generally, Kantorowicz 1997). They played multiple roles in the service of the increased competition between imperial societies, but they also sought to limit the risks of competition by building legal channels toward the peaceful resolution of conflicts. These masters of legal rhetoric, before and after the First World War, were at ease with a discourse characterized by oppositions. This increased the value of their skills as mediators and negotiators—between, for example, ideals such as international peacemaking and realist claims for national sovereignty or even imperialism (cf. Mazover 2012: 73 on the dubious support brought by the founding fathers of international law for the "civilizing" mission of King Leopold in the Congo).

GENESIS OF A "LEGALIST" EMPIRE

The research of Benjamin Coates into the saga of the New York & Bermudez (NY&B) Company, part of the giant US Asphalt Trust, and its contracts with the Venezuelan government to exploit and market asphalt (2015), helps illuminate the elements of the early history. The Venezuelan government seized the implicated Venezuelan property in 1904, and the company failed in its legal efforts to gain redress in Venezuela. So the NY&B turned to Washington for assistance, seeking to mobilize US power on behalf of corporate power. The company's hands were not particularly clean, however. It had engaged in some shady activities, including bankrolling an effort to overthrow the Venezuelan president, who it felt was giving it trouble. Instead of calling for gunboats, the State Department under Elihu Root requested information on the legal merits of the claim. The company then hired as its counsel America's pre-eminent international lawyer, John Bassett Moore of Columbia Law School. Moore was to make the case to James Brown Scott, the State Department solicitor, and to Root, the Secretary of State and former Secretary of War. Moore framed the issue as seeking to secure the power of the United States to, at the very least, compel the Venezuelan president, Cipriano Castro, to submit to binding arbitration.

For Root and Scott, this matter was not cut and dried. They wanted to avoid the much criticized specter of the State Department intervening—including with threats or uses of force—on behalf of US companies that did not merit that support. Consistent with the elevation of legal argument promoted by Harvard and the Wall Street law firms, these lawyers had faith in the law, and they had sought to professionalize the State Department consistent with that vision. They wanted to make an assessment on the basis of legal arguments. They valued neutral arbitration and sought to replicate it within the State Department.

Moore made his case by citing his own treatises and the European authorities, who at the time were the most prestigious internationally. He argued in a subtle way that the Venezuelan legal system was not up to "civilized standards" and therefore not to be respected, and he reminded Scott that there were occasions justified by European authorities in international law when intervention to protect private interests was permitted. Scott, who was at the same time recruiting Moore to join the newly formed American Society of International Law, considered the arguments carefully, and found for the company.

President Theodore Roosevelt then supported a convenient and timely coup in Venezuela. The new president, seeing that he would have to submit to arbitration, settled the dispute. Moore's fees for his representation amounted to $27,500. His work promoted his own interests, and those of his corporate client, as well as the interests of a cosmopolitan international law tilted toward the West. Root in fact saw this as vindicating an approach favoring law, courts, and arbitration as central to international relations. Coates (2015) writes that "Root shared his exuberance with [Andrew] Carnegie. . . . Carnegie was also a strong critic of imperialism and an advocate for international law and peace and liked this approach. In 1910 he would donate $10 million to establish the Carnegie Endowment for International Peace. Root became the new organization's president, while James Brown Scott, the State Department solicitor, became its secretary" (405). Drawing on his own credibility and Carnegie's wealth, Root helped build international law more generally in the United States and abroad. Indeed, he received the Nobel Peace Prize in 1912 for his work on the Permanent Court of Arbitration.

Through all these activities, the US "anti-imperial" (Dezalay and Garth 2010; Coates 2016) empire expanded, enhancing corporate power abroad and legitimating corporate expansion and empire as according to the rule of law. Furthermore, and not incidentally, the elite of the US legal profession gained both prosperity and respect. The story can be seen as a relatively early episode setting the stage for the judicialization, legalization, and globalization that are now viewed as characterizing recent decades. Root and Scott worked to build international law and ultimately courts as well to bring order to fraught issues in international relations, in this case by ascertaining the legal merits of both the investing company and the host country to avoid gunboat diplomacy while protecting property and contract rights. The incident was one of many steps at the time toward the rule of law; it also precipitated greater investments in international law through philanthropy.

The corporate lawyers' international strategy was consistent with their domestic strategy, in that they helped produce rules such as antitrust that in part reined in their clients—better both to legitimate and to serve them (Dezalay and Garth 2010). The clients gained credibility at the price of submitting to rules. In the asphalt case the credibility came from submitting to international law as determined by Root and Scott. The lawyers also gained power as the experts in international law, which was deemed central to the emerging rules of the game for international relations, attested to, for example, by their positions in the American Society of International Law and their connections to European allies, who at the time possessed more authority in international law. As with respect to US domestic politics, Root understandably felt that an international regime of relatively legalistic courts and arbitration would favor the interests of his clients just as the domestic courts did at home. The same legalism taught at Harvard Law School could serve nationally and internationally (for the Latin American story of "empire and networks," see Scarfi 2017).

A legalist empire, in contrast to competition with "old Europe" empires, was consistent with an open door for US global investment and influence (Rosenberg 2003). The legalist empire was and remains part of an elite strategy in the United States. Because of the central role played in the past by law and lawyers, it seems inevitable in retrospect that law would play such a prominent role in US foreign relations, but the international field could have been ceded to the military and to diplomacy. The late nineteenth century, however, was a propitious time for legal discourse and legitimacy in the United States and in Western Europe because, as Mazower shows, the empires of Old Europe were subject to considerable criticism, which provided an opening for lawyers to offer rules, more legitimacy, and related claims to promote a more legalized and legitimate empire as part of a "civilizing mission" (Mazower 2012).

One reason why Root and others had so much faith in international courts (and in courts generally) relates to the concept of core and periphery. Those with the most credibility in interpreting the law were those closest to the core of the legal profession, who included European and linked US law professors, such as Moore. In the United States, these were the lawyers closest to the corporate law firms. Furthermore, the law originated in and embodied the interests of Europe and the West in protecting private property. Thus, the Venezuelans had to depend on legal arguments to show that their country was "civilized," and they also were forced to rely on peripheral authorities such as scholars from Argentina to support a position closer to that of the southern states and more distant from corporate property rights.

This does not mean that the Western (or northern) position was inevitably the winning one, but it does mean that the law tilted in favor of Western interests. The law had evolved in such a way as to favor prevailing power and property while offering rules that provided legitimacy (Kantorowicz 1997). Those characteristics are embedded in the law's core. The civilized versus uncivilized distinction also merits elaboration. Again, as Mazower shows, uncivilized countries did not enjoy the protections of international law. Thus, to gain access to the group of civilized nations, they had to show that they respected the rule of law (see Flaherty 2013 on Meiji Japan as a prime example). Yet even after they had done that, they found themselves within a field that favored the interests of the West and the authorities recognized as credible in the West. Law is a field with hierarchies of authority, and a price of playing within the field is submitting to that hierarchy. As Coates specifically notes, Root and his allies could be utterly certain that an independent international court would be consistent with US imperial interests and US hegemony (Coates 2016).

Furthermore, these leaders on both sides were also directly engaged in legal learning as an instrument for progressive reform, be it as professors (cf. Sacriste and Vauchez 2007; Coates 2016) or as lawyers-statespersons mobilizing the resources of financiers-philanthropists (exemplified again by Root as a lawyer and Andrew Carnegie and John D. Rockefeller as sources of philanthropy). The new international legal practices appeared first as spaces of learned investment and academic debates that constructed an idealized representation of quasi-virtual institutions in order to indicate what they could or should produce in the future. Far from being born fully formed, however, this slow and uncertain emergence of the field of International Justice was a complex process that today can be understood by analyzing the internal battles these new legal elites fought within national legal fields—as well as, by ricochet, the competition between national legal models as it played out in the new transnational spaces.

This analysis requires that we take into account hierarchical structures and related political alliances that are the product of very different national histories. In this regard, the differentiation between the legal models is not limited to the classic divide between common law and civil law, or the Weberian differentiation between *Professorenrecht* and practioners' law. The international competition between different national models of legal hierarchies and different divisions of labor relates also to the potentially antagonistic strategies of "clerks" of law in fields of state power. As noted in Chapter 3, there are two classic bases of political authority: royal officers and professors who place their competencies in the service of religious or royal bureaucracies (Berman 1983; 2003; see also Martines 1968; Brundage 2008); and learned gentlemen who mobilize their legal expertise in order to control royal power on behalf of the gentry and the rising merchant class.

This divide is blurred, however. The emerging hegemonic society, the United States, reinvented itself through a *de facto* hybrid of two different modes. In the United States, law professors and law schools play a large role today; in Great Britain, by contrast, the rise of the barristers led to the dismantling of law faculties for more than three centuries. The difference between the legal fields of the Continental professors and that of US practitioners was therefore somewhat more ambiguous than a simple Weberian opposition between practitioners' law and *Professorenrecht*.

In sum, the general competition—which does not preclude convergence—between the two models, differentiated by the hierarchy of professional positions and by the alliance strategies of the notables of law within national fields of power, provides the context in which transnational spaces emerged in the nineteenth century, over whose course European imperial powers battled not only for military control of overseas territories but also for control of the definition of international legal practice.

THE EXACERBATION OF IMPERIAL COMPETITION IN THE EARLY TWENTIETH CENTURY

The confrontation between hegemonic attempts to control international law in Europe was complicated by the growing role of US lawyers. Indeed, US corporate lawyers controlled considerable resources—philanthropic, political, and commercial—and they could deploy those resources to promote alternative conceptions of law and International Justice. Those conceptions conformed to their own interests as well as to those of the large corporations that were their clients and patrons. The professional and state strategy of these US practitioners led also to a position close to the Continental model—and more concretely to their investing in the production of learned law in the service of reformist or modernizing politics. Langdell's strategy at Harvard became a pillar of this upgrading of the law. As noted earlier, in addition, the strategy was helpful as a means to disqualify and to some extent absorb—through some meritocratic opening up of law firms and elite law schools—the rising tide of lawyers from émigré backgrounds, who were moving into populist and clientelist politics after low-prestige training in night law schools.

To be sure, as with respect to all symbolic transfers (Bourdieu 2002), this importation remained very partial. Even as they invested in learned scholarship, the Wall Street practitioners made sure they maintained control over the production of law in the United States, in part through the private status of most leading law schools and their links to the corporate law firms. Indeed, it took a long time for these US professors to acquire close to the authority on stating the law that characterizes the German *Professorenrecht*. At the same time, while investing in reformist state politics, the elite corporate lawyers bolstered their position by relying on and supporting the private foundations in which they played major roles. Thanks to the US spoils system, they could avoid any competing reformist strategy that might arise through the autonomization of the state bureaucracies. The result was that they were able to preserve the profits stemming from their pre-eminent positions serving the world of business, while at the same time making temporary incursions into the world of state power, whether as a career strategy or as a response to times of crisis or war.

Historical and political circumstances, combined with professional dynamics, explain the relative success of these strategies of internationalization, but also their limits, as seen from the point of view of the Europeans whose work was introduced to the US market. Those successes included the creation of the Permanent Court of International Justice (see also Vauchez 2014) and the construction of the Peace Palace in The Hague funded by Carnegie. The limits, however, were especially evident with respect to the origins of International Justice. Only the US partners had the power to mobilize the substantial political and economic resources required for such a venture to succeed, and the Continental professors found themselves in an awkward position, since US law practitioners imported their work into the United States mainly for domestic purposes, to help legitimize the free trade aims of their clients as well as boost their own stature.

After the First World War, the United States generally pursued a politics of withdrawal from international alliances. The European professors were unable to rely on their own resources, which consisted mainly of still marginal academic capital and a dominated position within diplomatic arenas. The European professors as a result privileged a cautious strategy that essentially cantonized the institutions of The Hague, which they had developed with the support of US and Russian sponsors before 1914. In this way they formed a small, learned, cosmopolitan circle sustained by the support—financial and symbolic—of their US sponsors (Koskenniemi 2001).

The European professors' strategy of withdrawing into an ivory tower was also determined by the lack of opportunities for these European merchants of peace to act on the diplomatic or legal scene. These professors held dominated positions in the academic and diplomatic fields; it was the gentleman-lawyers of the United States who held the upper hand. Deteriorating political and financial conditions in Europe throughout the 1920s (as a result of hyperinflation and the rise of the Bolsheviks in Russia) accentuated the weakness—even impotence—of international forums for handling inter-state conflicts. This very weak position was exacerbated by a strategy that limited access to European positions in international law to a small group of professor-diplomats, a circle that was later expanded just enough to include a few learned practitioners who occupied diverse roles—which could be accumulated—including judge, lawyer, or producer of doctrine (Sacriste and Vauchez 2007). This peer group was able in this manner to accumulate the profits—which were essentially symbolic—of a small market while avoiding dissent, criticism, and even overinvestment that might damage the weak credibility of their offerings and underscore the impotence of what they were promoting in the face of rising political disorder. The result was the Permanent Court of International Justice as a kind of virtual forum, barely visible except for a few of the initiated, who were making every effort to believe—and foster the belief—that one day they would be able to contribute to the objectives of international peace as called for by the idealistic pronouncements of their founding fathers. The institutions of international law at The Hague also provided important symbolic capital for notables from the global South, who formed alliances with the more meritocratic but relatively marginal professionals who worked with them there (Dezalay and Dezalay 2017).

5

Social and Neoliberal Revolutions in the United States

The legal revolutions depicted by Berman involve a reinvestment in meritocratic scholarly capital—in opposition to conservative social and political capital—as well as strategic alliances with emerging political or social groups disposed to embed their movements in the law. In the United States, lawyer-brokers found ways to connect with international scholarly capital from Europe, huge corporations, social movements, and a new reformist politics. They upgraded legal scholarship and legal argument to serve and better legitimate the emerging coalitions, and they brought new and more meritocratic blood into the legal profession. The same set of events reinforced the hierarchies of the legal field with the rise of new professional organizations, more stringent educational standards, and challenges to the law schools that served immigrants and others not sharing the White Anglo-Saxon Protestant characteristics of New York's elite lawyers and their counterparts in other major cities.

A highly stratified market in legal education emerged, defined mainly by the elite schools' connections to the "upper hemisphere" of corporate law firms. Market competition reinforced hierarchies, since those who had social advantage were far more likely to gain entrance to leading law schools, but the relatively meritocratic competition between laws schools and within those schools also helped make the US legal field more responsive and porous than the European legal fields with respect to economic, social, and political change. That adaptability is apparent in relation to the various challenges and responses of the twentieth century—from the New Deal to the civil rights era to deregulation and global neoliberalism. There was a succession of relative busts and booms in the United States that saw the elite of the profession further open up, legal scholarship play an increasingly important role, and law professors gain a stronger position than they had held in the early twentieth century, when they were merely subordinate teachers and compilers of laws made by notable lawyers and judges. The booms and busts were less a function of diminished professional markets than of challenges or threats to the symbolic capital accumulated around the law.

THE LEGAL REALIST "COUP": FROM TEACHERS AND COMPILERS OF THE LAW TO FULL PROFESSORS AS ADVISERS FOR REFORMIST RULERS

The Great Depression and the New Deal brought a serious challenge to the established hierarchies of the legal field in the United States. At first, the corporate law firms on Wall Street echoed their clients' ambiguous relationship to the New Deal (Shamir 1995). They recognized that a crisis was at hand and acknowledged the need for bold action. But after a few years, client opposition to new regulations strengthened and corporate law firms exceeded their clients in their opposition. They saw administrative agencies and European-influenced notions about legal bureaucrats being independent experts as threats to their position, and they became more and more identified with resistance to the New Deal. Indeed, the agencies initially *were* a threat to lawyers, who, during the 1930s, were in danger of being excluded from the New Deal and of losing the access to courts where they could challenge administrative policies. Wall Street corporate law firms and their analogues in major cities had become too complacent. They had prospered through their tight relations with the major corporations and through practices that were conservative both politically and relative to the once forward-thinking expertise they employed. Now, during a severe economic depression, new social groups and the emerging social sciences were challenging the legal and economic establishment.

In the relatively open (as compared to Europe) US context, there were opportunities for entrepreneurial lawyers to forge strategic alliances both to push against established law and, ultimately, to rebuild the credibility of lawyers and the law from within. The scholarly challengers, identified with the legal realists especially at Yale and Columbia, denounced a profession that had become "the obsequious servant of business, tainted with the morals and manners of the market place" (Shamir 1995: 148). Through key brokers such as Harvard's Felix Frankfurter, lawyers placed their expertise in the service of the new bureaucracies of the New Deal by promoting "socially informed law" through "enlightened legislation" capable of solving social problems that were "too complex, too difficult to be handled by the average judge" (150). The legal realists thus took on the elite corporate bar and the appellate judiciary that supported its positions to promote an upgraded expertise that arguably needed to go around the law. At the same time, as Shamir rightly emphasizes, legal realism was a "collective mobility" project for legal academics who were at the time still relatively marginal in relation to the most powerful corporate attorneys and leading judges.

The academic challengers attacked the idea that the law was neutral and predictable, and they criticized the courts and the conservative legal establishment for resisting New Deal reforms. Law professors formed alliances with the emerging social science disciplines (Schlegel 1995) with the goal of applying the law to resolve social problems and enhancing the credibility of legal academic scholarship.

Key to all this was the meritocratic component of the movement as embodied by the New Deal and legal realism. Shamir notes that the movement brought Jews, Catholics, and the children of immigrants into legal positions to which they had previously lacked access (Shamir 1995; Dinnerstein 1983; Auerbach 1976). Roosevelt once declared: "Dig me up fifteen or twenty youthful Abraham Lincolns from Manhattan and the Bronx to choose from. They must be liberal from belief and not by lip service. They must have an inherent contempt both for the John W. Davises and Max Steuers [conservative corporate attorneys]. They must know what life in a tenement means" (Auerbach 1976). Accordingly, while "young Jewish attorneys in the 1930's" found few career opportunities in law firms, the New Deal was relatively open to them: it "needed legal talent, and Jewish lawyers needed the jobs that the New Deal provided" (Dinnerstein 1983: 464). To be sure, Jewish lawyers did not gain appointments to many judgeships or cabinet positions, but advisers like Benjamin Cohen and Thomas Corcoran, one Jewish and the other Irish Catholic—both Harvard graduates recruited by their former professor, Felix Frankfurter—were among the most influential lawyers in the New Deal (Dinnerstein 1983).

This challenge from within the legal field opened up places for a new generation of meritocratic lawyers and law professors, who would turn out to be central to the New Deal. Thus, the rise of the activist state in the United States was not accomplished by pushing lawyers aside, notwithstanding the complacency that had led to the political depreciation of the Wall Street elite. Instead, aided by a system of administrative law that gave the courts a significant role, lawyers again thrived within the system. This revitalized the legal hierarchy and buttressed the centrality of the corporate bar. One aspect of this was a clear increase in the status of the elite law professors. As Shamir (1995) writes, "legal academics offered a scientific rationale for the administration's policies, countered the bar's and the judiciary's resistance, and contributed their services to the governmental state apparatus. In return, law professors reached positions of influence and prestige that they had never enjoyed before" (152). This also led to a strengthening of existing hierarchies. As the professors and their disciples rose within the existing fields of power, the critical bite of legal realism diminished, as did any hints of a new administrative elite consistent with that realism (Schlegel 1995; Shamir 1995). The incentives to gain power and credibility by taking the social sciences seriously likewise diminished considerably. By the 1950s, with the advent of the Cold War, the new politics and the new social sciences had been converted into the legal establishment, with its accompanying programs of the new "legal process school."

Along the way, the corporate elite was revitalized through the rise of Washington law firms that had emerged from legal realism and the New Deal, epitomized by Arnold, Fortas, and Porter. These firms reestablished the legitimation strategy earlier developed by the Wall Street firms—a combination of public service and corporate representation, symbolized now by the revolving door in Washington, D.C., between the corporate law firms and the federal regulatory agencies and departments. These Washington firms too became more open. They recruited Jews and others who had not been welcome on Wall Street. As Auerbach notes, "the battleground was at the apex, where old and new elites clashed. When the dust kicked up by their professional rivalry finally settled, the old structure was greatly strengthened by its newest inhabitants, who were, by their presence, its newest defenders. . . . In service to power, lawyers made government by a legal elite the culmination of New Deal liberalism" (Auerbach 1976: loc. 4744).

With the increased prestige of the law professors, the place for academic "legal theory" grew substantially. But this did not change the hierarchy of power within the US legal field. Indeed, paradoxically, the emergence of the Washington law firms reinforced the strength and legitimacy of the corporate practitioners close to the state and to economic power. The legal academic market thrived through the alliances forged between the legal realists and those who had ascended into the government through the New Deal. They were able to criticize the legal establishment—especially the Wall Street lawyers—as overly formal and conservative; meanwhile, their success enabled them to rebuild and retool that establishment for an era in which the state and state regulation were increasing in importance.

THE CHALLENGE OF THE 1960S

The background for the challenges of the 1960s and later was the success of the coalition that governed after the New Deal. The Kennedy administration marked the apotheosis in power of the so-called foreign policy establishment (FPE), a group descending from lawyers like Elihu Root (see the previous chapter) that included a strong cohort of investment bankers as well as corporate lawyers. The history of the FPE and the Council on Foreign Relations, which came to monopolize the key positions in foreign policy from the 1940s through the 1960s, has been well-documented (e.g., Bird 1992; 1998). The elite circles linked to the FPE during those decades controlled the Ivy League universities, the major philanthropic foundations, the State Department, the CIA, and the major corporate law firms and investment banks. Geoffrey Kabaservice (2004) referred to the network around the FPE in the 1960s as the "liberal establishment."

A key individual was McGeorge Bundy, once a very young Dean of the Faculty of Arts and Sciences at Harvard. He became Kennedy's National Security Advisor in 1961 and remained in that post until 1966, when he left amid controversy over the Vietnam War to become president of the Ford Foundation, where he remained until 1979. Bundy was not himself a lawyer, but his father and brother were, and he was quite close to the elite legal world. Kabaservice's book on the liberal establishment focuses on McGeorge Bundy, Kingman Brewster, Cyrus Vance, Elliot Richardson, John Lindsay, and Paul Moore. Brewster, Lindsay, Richardson, and Vance were all corporate lawyers at one time or another. What united this social and academic elite was the belief that the establishment in its own interest had to expand opportunities for new groups in the postwar era. They served the government and brought together the resources of the elite universities, exemplified by Bundy's ties to Harvard and Brewster's presidency of Yale; the metropolis, with New York City Mayor John Lindsay in particular; the foundations, including Bundy at the Ford Foundation; and the corporate law firms, with Cyrus Vance of Simpson Thatcher in particular (Vance also served on the boards of Yale and the Ford Foundation).

The patrician social profile of this group helps explain the challenges that later emerged. As noted by Richard Barnet in *Roots of War* (1971), a book that laid out this challenge, "the temporary civilian managers who come to Washington to run America's wars and preparation for wars, the national security managers, were so like one another in occupation, religion, style, and social status that, apart from a few Washington lawyers, Texans, and mavericks, it was possible to locate the offices of all of them within fifteen city blocks in New York, Boston, and Detroit. Most of their biographies in *Who's Who* read like minor variations on a single theme—wealthy parents, Ivy-League education, leading law firm or bank" (49).

The politics of the academic investment that was central to the legitimacy of this Eastern establishment contributed to the questioning of the social homogeneity and implicit consensus that provided its strength. Ivy League colleges in the years after the Second World War broadened (in relative terms) their recruitment policies. As noted earlier, members of the liberal establishment sought to enhance the legitimacy of that establishment by opening it up to those who had been excluded (Kaboservice 2004). These new arrivals, however, were often less disposed to accept the prevailing orthodoxy and hierarchy. Unlike the preceding generation of so-called wise men, the newcomers had not, as a rule, passed through the prep schools of Groton, Lawrence, St. Paul's, Andover, or Exeter. They lacked the shared background that had allowed the preceding generation to acquire very early the social habitus that was at the root of their moderate political vision.

There was therefore a pronounced contest internal to the system. It emanated from the newcomers and the generation they represented. The critique by Richard Barnet, a graduate of Harvard and Harvard Law School and at one time an assistant to John J. McCloy, the so-called "Chairman of the Establishment" (Bird 1992), reflects the world view of this generation. The newcomers were quite conscious of the limits of the meritocratic ideology that formed part of their own identity. Tensions were found especially in the institutions whose task was to bring combat to the terrain of ideas, precisely because those institutions were situated where the field of power met that of learning.

The Vietnam War divided the liberal establishment between hawks who supported the war and doves who were against it – a split that enabled the election of Richard Nixon in 1968. More fundamentally, many among the younger generation who opposed the Vietnam War became radicalized and challenged the legitimacy of the liberal establishment and its leaders in the corporate bar. They also began to question the Washington bar, whose members had long occupied positions as both servants of business and so-called wise men deemed capable of governing in the public interest. They were perceived as hawks and as too close to business. The corporate law firms' links with the elite campuses were threatened by this loss of legitimacy and by movements on the left that attacked big business and those who served it. At the same time, the civil rights movement brought into question the moderate tactics of the corporate lawyer-statespersons. As we shall see, the corporate legal statespersons at the top of the profession were seen as increasingly out of touch with American society.

When given access to elite institutions such as the leading law firms, many in the new generation did not feel in sync with those in power. In addition, as the path from the Ivy League colleges to the institutions of Wall Street and Washington, D.C., became more crowded, the new generation had to invest in new spaces of professional practice. One set of opportunities was connected to the expansion of such areas as developmental assistance, including the Peace Corps and programs launched in the name of the Alliance for Progress in the early 1960s. Another set of opportunities was linked to the many projects of social integration that came into being under John F. Kennedy, later to be identified with the Great Society of President Lyndon Johnson. The War on Poverty encouraged many young idealist lawyers to work in programs offering legal services for the poor, and lawyers became more aggressively involved in the civil rights movement. Indeed, the civil rights movement is one example of how the generational divide surfaced.

As the civil rights movement heated up in the 1960s, elite lawyers and their allies in the federal government spearheaded a number of legislative reforms to try to get in front of these civil rights and anti-poverty issues. It was difficult to contain the civil rights struggle in the South, and it quickly became a challenge for the Kennedy administration. Thomas Hilbink writes that in the view of many activists, "the Kennedy administration proved not to have the moral commitment to the goals of civil rights as activists believed" (Hilbink 2006: 75). In fact, the elite lawyers around Kennedy were simply working according to the usual strategy of the moderate reformers, and that strategy was unable to accommodate the political turbulence. Hilbink's exceptional detail on the generational clash provides a unique vantage point on this process.

As Hilbink suggests, it is indicative that the lawyer selected to head the Civil Rights Division under Kennedy was Burke Marshall, a partner in the Washington,

D.C., corporate law firm of Covington and Burling—"a first-class lawyer who would do the job in a technically proficient way" (76), according to Byron White, then the Deputy Attorney General. The administration inevitably looked to elite corporate law firms for people with the stature and leadership to manage difficult problems at home and abroad. As Hilbink shows, Marshall and others in the administration were Ivy League gentlemen who wanted to persuade reasonable individuals in the South—their presumed counterparts—to open up the system to African Americans. They "*assumed* that the system maintaining their status was basically sound," but by then both sides of the civil rights struggle were pushing the bounds of civility (78). The advisers followed the strategy of trying to gradually expand participation, but this moderate strategy was not working in the South.

The "rule of law" by which this elite defined itself was being threatened by southern resistance and civil rights activism, and elite corporate lawyers pushed Kennedy to do more to handle the situation. The White House responded with an invitation to this corporate elite and some others to assess what could be done through law. The gathering brought 250 distinguished lawyers—"very elegant lawyers"—but notably excluded the leftist National Lawyers Guild. Kennedy called for the help of elite lawyers in keeping everything "calm" (78). Some of those there, including Father Robert Drinan, then the Dean of Boston College Law School and more on the side of activism, felt that the administration was too tepid in its commitment to civil rights enforcement.

The administration then formed a committee—the Lawyers Committee for Civil Rights Under Law (LCCRUL)—chaired by Bernard Segal, later president of the ABA and a corporate lawyer in Philadelphia, and Harrison Tweed, former president of the National Legal Aid and Defenders Association (NLADA), chair of the American Law Institute, and named partner in the Wall Street firm Milbank and Tweed. This committee was a prestigious group dominated by corporate lawyers known also for their public service. The natural order in their social world was that the lawyers would help solve the problem and at the same time reinforce the ideal of lawyer-statespersons serving both their clients and the public good.

When the famous Freedom Summer arrived in 1964, it presented a challenge to the players in this domain. The corporate lawyer–dominated LCCRUL opted to bring some volunteers to the South with a narrow mandate—to represent ministers and to try to persuade white southern lawyers to represent individuals arrested for civil rights activities. The more activist side of the liberal establishment went further. According to Hilbink, the NAACP resisted the participation of volunteers from outside—mainly to protect their own turf; meanwhile, the America Civil Liberties Union took an interest largely to "pre-empt" the Lawyers Guild (101). Soon after, the ACLU teamed up with the American Jewish Congress, the American Jewish Committee, the Congress of Racial Equality, Father Drinan, and others to coordinate activist lawyers and students who would be going to the South. Terming their alliance the Lawyers Constitutional Defense Committee

(LCDC), they sought to connect more to the new-generation activists. They recognized that genteel strategies were not working. But, as noted, they also sought to keep the Lawyers Guild at a distance.

After the Freedom Summer, the groups that had provided assistance recognized the desirability of a more permanent presence in the South. Making the case to foundations, the more activist LCDC emphasized its connections as well as its ability to "appreciate the political purposes and strategy of the operative civil rights organizations" (131). The more establishment Lawyers Committee (LCCRUL), by contrast, emphasized its connections to the federal government and its elite professional profile. When it came time to choose which group ultimately to support in 1967, the Ford Foundation opted only for the Lawyers Committee.

The story Hilbink tells provides detail on how the combination of professional prestige, connections to corporate clients, and connections to the major philanthropic foundations shaped the Kennedy administration's approach to the civil rights struggle. The administration naturally turned to its legal counterparts from the liberal establishment's social world. The elite lawyers they turned to also, not surprisingly, did not want to work with and provide legitimacy to those whom they perceived as outside the mainstream, in particular the National Lawyers Guild. The threat to the hierarchy in public service was also a threat to the position of the corporate lawyer-statespersons.

With respect to the War on Poverty and civil legal aid, the second director of the Legal Services Program, Earl Johnson, Jr., recognized that the elite law firms were being questioned and sought to build on that development. There was an opening, he saw, for idealistic law students who were not radicals but who also did not want to work in corporate law. Johnson promoted Reginald Heber Smith fellowships to try to recruit "the top rank of graduating law students," former federal judicial clerks, and young corporate lawyers, with the goal of creating an "elite corps of lawyers" who would make lawyers key to the War on Poverty. Johnson sought to create an outlet for "a group of talented young lawyers rejecting the rhetoric of revolution and signing up for a low-paying job that sought only peaceful, orderly change through established institutions" (Johnson 2013: 149). Legal services lawyers in the mid-1960s did indeed take up the call for legal activism, especially through test cases. Their legal activism, even if through the system, faced strong resistance at the end of the decade as conservatives began to fight back under Richard Nixon (Hilbink 2006).

The challenge from the left was also still there. Hilbink (2006) points out that notwithstanding the progressive activities of the relatively elite bar in the 1960s and 70s, "radical lawyering" that directly challenged the elite institutions was thriving. According to Johnson, leftist lawyers told those who joined the Reginald Heber Smith program that legal services could only "mitigate" conditions that required more revolutionary action. The most radical lawyers had very little faith in law and the legal system. They did not believe that solutions to social problems could come through the moderate legal reforms favored by the liberal establishment—in fact, law was considered a major part of the problem. The lure of radical lawyering (or just radical action) further undermined the position of law and its hierarchies—corporate lawyers, elite law graduates—in the US state and economy. More fundamentally, the credibility of corporate lawyer-statespersons was threatened—their social capital was depreciating.

The story Hilbink (2006) tells of the creation of public interest law early in the 1970s fits this account. The crisis felt by Washington law firms in particular was central to the emergence of public interest law as a solution to the more general problems facing the liberal establishment and the elite corporate lawyers within it. Ralph Nader's activities on behalf of consumers drew many elite law graduates toward activism against corporate misconduct, and Nader made clear that Washington lawyers were at the core of the problem. The revolving door between Washington regulators and corporate lawyers—once a marker of public service—was characterized in the environment of the late 1960s as illegitimate. The classic ideal, that corporate lawyers gained stature and credibility by helping write and enforce rules that to some extent moderated and at the same time legitimated the power of their clients, was not persuasive to the public, to elite law students, or even to a number of the associates in the leading corporate law firms. It was not enough, for example, that Lloyd Cutler, who represented the auto and drug industries through Wilmer, Cutler, and Pickering, was on the board of the Lawyers Committee for Civil Rights Under Law, nor that he had served numerous presidents. The critical climate was especially strong since the leaders of the firms under attack were classic New Deal liberals, including the partners of Arnold and Porter. In such a climate, the attractiveness of law school—and corporate law as an elite career—for talented and ambitious idealists was under threat.

The public interest lawyers who emerged in this era, according to Hilbink, represented "a cross-section of those typically found in the upper echelons of the American bar. They *were* the establishment" (309). In fact, they had the establishment credentials of elite law schools, judicial clerkships, and corporate law firm positions, but, as in the New Deal, they were not the WASP social establishment of the classic corporate legal elite and its accompanying circles. Charles Halpern, as profiled by Hilbink, exemplifies the change that took place in the appeal of the corporate lawyer-statesperson role. Halpern grew up in Buffalo, New York. He is Jewish, and his father was a law professor and judge (Halpern 2017). Halpern was relatively apolitical as an undergraduate at Harvard. He attended Yale Law School, went to work at Arnold and Porter after a federal clerkship, and imagined "a career of working at a law firm, doing pro bono work, and taking stints in government" (Hilbink 2006: 311). He embodied meritocratic success. His ambitions also reveal that he had internalized the hierarchies and incentives that put US corporate lawyers at the top of the legal field and brought them economic rewards, respect, and influence over public policy. He was looking to become an elite lawyer-statesperson.

In the late 1960s, however, Halpern began to feel increasingly attracted to activism and disillusioned with his work for Arnold and Porter, which included representing big tobacco. The career for which he had prepared himself had depreciated in value. He also did not find a natural fit at Arnold and Porter. As he wrote in his autobiography, "I had no skill at schmoozing with general counsels and chief executives in the clubhouse after a round of golf. I couldn't imagine bringing new corporate business into the firm. Ultimately, that's what the firm was all about. Lawyers who lacked that skill, no matter how brilliant, stalled partway up the ladder. The meritocracy that seemed to flourish in the law schools and in the first round of law firm hiring was replaced by a different meritocracy, one that was explicitly attuned to attracting corporate clients" (Halpern 2008: loc. 714). Working with others who shared his position, he came up with a proposal for foundation funding of a Center for Law and Social Policy.

Another key individual profiled by Hilbink, Carlyle Hall Jr., began Harvard Law School in 1963. After graduating, he took a detour, traveling to the Sudan and Uganda to do "law and development" work. Upon his return in 1969, he went to work for O'Melveny and Myers in Los Angeles, attracted by Warren Christopher, the most important partner and one who had "long combined private lawyering with public service" (315). Hall too was following the internalized program of the elite lawyer-statesperson. But he too became disillusioned with corporate practice, again reflecting the depreciation at that time of the traditional path to the elite. He joined with three others from O'Melveny to work on a proposal to the Ford Foundation for the Center for Law in the Public Interest.

These personal histories, in Hilbink's words, "demonstrate the connection of public interest lawyering to both the late 1960s and the movements that influenced and preceded it" (316). The connection to activism is evident, and it helped make corporate lawyers seem quite conservative. Both Halpern and Hall had been on a track to mimic the lawyer-statesperson roles they identified with the Washington, D.C., corporate elite represented by Arnold and Porter (in Halpern's case) and Warren Christopher (in Hall's case). As a new generation less endowed with social capital, they may have felt less at home in the corporate firms than they expected; they also were invested more deeply in the idealism they had thought accompanied the elite lawyer role.

The liberal establishment, including the elite universities, the Ford Foundation, and leading corporate law firms, had sought to handle the unrest of the 1960s through a partnership with the federal government as it promoted moderate changes in public policy. The changes sought to bring in groups that had been excluded from the benefits of American prosperity. The election of 1968—which divided the establishment over Vietnam—had led to Nixon's election, and problems of social unrest remained strong. The Ford Foundation and others sought to maintain their influence, bring progress that would curb the social unrest, and restore faith in the rule of law. Also implicit in the Ford agenda was a sense of the normal as one in which the elite lawyers were at the top of the legal hierarchy and the economic and political system that allowed the clients of those lawyers to thrive was viewed as legitimate. McGeorge Bundy, the president of the Ford Foundation, was a strong believer in legal strategies as a way to steer a middle ground between the left and the right.

Halpern sought out the Ford Foundation at the same time that individuals there, notably Sanford Jaffe and Gordon Harrison, were looking for ways to retool the legal profession in a time of political crisis. Harrison was then already in contact with a group of Yale students seeking to create an organization to address environmental legal issues. Harrison helped link the students to Whitney North Seymour, a prominent Wall Street lawyer with experience in environmental law. The moral enterpreneurs, the elite law schools, the liberal establishment, and corporate lawyers were in the process of coming together. According to Laura Kalman, Yale law professors Charles Reich and Boris Bittker helped facilitate a "forced marriage" between corporate lawyers and the Yale idealists (Kalman 2005: 223). As the Ford Foundation moved toward a new program, it naturally approached trusted advisers, such as David Peck of Sullivan and Cromwell, who favored the initiative. In March 1970, Jaffe and Harrison brought a proposal to the board of the Ford Foundation titled "Advocacy, Law, and the Public Interest."

The price of gaining the support of the Ford Foundation was a forced marriage with the members of the liberal establishment open to this reform. The program contemplated a very close relationship between progressive members of the corporate bar and public interest law. Jaffe and Harrison sought "the best professional judgment available concerning professional integrity, quality, and experience of individual and group applicants" (Hilbink 2006: 332). That meant the elite corporate bar. In particular, Jaffe put together a Public Interest Advisory Committee to "insure that the highest standards of prudence and professionalism characterize our efforts in this field" (333). The four members of the committee were William Gossett, former partner of Hughes, Hubbard and Reed (and married to the daughter of Charles Evans Hughes), ABA president, Ford Foundation general counsel, US Trade Representative under Kennedy, counsel to the Ford family, and at the time partner in Dykema, Gossett, Spencer, Goodnow & Trigg in Detroit; Orison Marden, partner in White and Case, former president of the NLADA and co-founder of the Legal Aid Society of New York City; Bernard Segal, a corporate lawyer in Philadelphia, former president of the ABA and former co-chair of the Lawyers Committee for Civil Rights Under Law; and Whitney North Seymour, partner in Simpson Thatcher, former president of the ABA, the Association of the Bar of New York City, and the Carnegie Endowment for Peace. As Hilbink notes, these lawyers unsurprisingly were committed opponents of radicalism and radical lawyers and believed that the system must be made to work better (337). Kalman in her study of Yale Law School in the 1960s aptly notes that the creation of high-prestige, foundation-funded, public interest law firms provided an outlet to the graduates of Yale and other elite law graduates that, as she stated about Yale, allowed "students and professors alike to see themselves as both members of, and rebels against, the Establishment." (2005: 226).

Public interest law expanded dramatically in the 1970s and was followed by analogous investments in the global human rights movement by the Ford Foundation and others (Dezalay and Garth 2002). This was part of a retooling and revival of elite law consistent with the capital embedded in the liberal establishment—large corporations, philanthropic foundations, elite law schools, and the state (Kabaservice 2004). The relative complacency of elite law in the 1960s had led again to a potential period of "bust" and a challenge from within and without that ultimately was absorbed and contained. Elite corporate lawyers served on the boards of the public interest law firms, hired some former public interest lawyers, and helped elite lawyers regain some distance from their clients through the efforts of the public interest law firms. The pattern from the early twentieth century of elite processes of moderate reform tied to philanthropic foundations and corporate law firms had regained its credibility.

Legal theory in the relatively homogeneous law schools was consistent with the prevailing balance of power. Mark Tushnet's observation about constitutional legal theory in the 1970s is revealing in this respect: According to Tushnet, "the typical constitutional law article today has a standard form. The author identifies a doctrine developed in recent Supreme Court cases, notes some difficulties in the internal logic of the doctrine, indicates that the doctrine seems incompatible with the results of other cases, suggests minor modifications in the doctrine to make it consistent with those cases, and concludes that the doctrine as modified—almost uniformly into a balancing test—provides a sensible way of achieving results without going too far." In this way, according to Tushnet, the author manages in the end to show that the cases can be "embodiments of principles of justice, defined as the standard political principles of the moderate-left of the Democratic Party" (Tushnet 1979: 1322). This kind of homogeneity and complacency was part of what opened up the legal academy to challenge as well.

The story of continuity in academic legal theory from the New Deal into the 1970s is one of lawyers and law professors holding on to the places they had secured through legal realism and the collective mobility project of elite law professors. Elite constitutional law and legal theory from the leading law schools occupied that high-status space, with the interdisciplinary work of law and society being done mainly outside those spheres, but they all fit well within the "liberal legal establishment" and the project of moderate social reform. The challenge from the outsiders on the left had been contained and channeled into institutions where the elite corporate lawyers dominated.

CHALLENGES FROM THE RIGHT

The challenge from the right to the US position linked to the liberal establishment, the leading role of corporate law firms, and the position of corporate lawyers in politics and the state was both similar to and different from the one from the left. While the weakening credibility of the liberal establishment was important here as well, the challenge from the right came largely from outside the Ivy League and the Eastern establishment. It was initially led by conservative social movements and neoliberal economists. Part of the story involved the mathematicization of economics, which enhanced its legitimacy as a science and fostered the recognition of meritocratic entrants to the field. A related part was the rise of neoliberal economics centered in the University of Chicago economics department led by Milton Friedman. There was a social dimension to the movement. Chicagoans had an antagonistic relationship with the liberal establishment different from that of the insiders who had become antiwar and civil rights activists in the 1960s (Dezalay and Garth 2002). Chicago professors tended to view the ruling elite of the east coast in terms of "us against them."

The 1960s reinforced this sentiment of exclusion in several ways. First, that period of economic growth had been credited to the Ivy League universities. Kennedy had invited the best-known Keynesians, in particular James Tobin and Paul Samuelson, to join his team of advisers. They recruited their students to Washington, where those students could gain more experience in setting economic policy. The Chicago outsiders' resentment with respect to the establishment that excluded them, despite their recognized scientific credentials, made the pioneers of pure economics the natural allies of those who promoted the conservative counterrevolution, which began to ascend in the 1970s (and included many businesses that felt that establishment organs—the New York Times and the Ford Foundation, for example—had become "antibusiness"). Second, they shared a hostility to the welfare state and—perhaps more importantly—to the Eastern establishment, which dominated the field of state power in part through its investments in the intellectual field. A learned counter-offensive—conducted under the banner of institutions such as the Hoover Institution, the American Enterprise Institute, the Heritage Foundation, and the Cato Institute—would provide these dominated theoreticians with the long-awaited opportunity to gain public recognition for their ideas.

James Buchanan, a disciple of Chicago who received the Nobel Prize for Economics in 1986 as the "father" of the new scholarship of public choice, contributed key theoretical tools for this counter-attack. Buchanan explicitly recognized his position of outsider, hostile to the establishment, as the source of his application of neoclassical economics to the analysis of political choices. His objective was to show that the holders of power were only following their own interests or those of the people who stood behind them. In addition to extending the imperialism of the neoclassical paradigm to new objects, this approach served to justify the postulates of the Chicago theoreticians who favored the market economy. The market could be justified as a way to avoid the inevitable rents associated with governmental intervention. Therefore, "in addition to providing a theoretical abstraction, public choice became a tool utilized above all to nourish and reinforce tactical arguments against monopolies, intervention, and state regulation" (Stone 1996: 156).

The reactionary think tanks were the principal instrumental users of this theory. The interests of "pure theory" thus coincided perfectly with the anti-establishment strategy of the populist right, and one reason was that each side occupied a very similar position in the field of power. One of Buchanan's students recognized this connection as follows: "We were all heretics who were excluded from the academic world by the pure thinkers. . . . We had to make our way in policy circles instead. That's why so many of Jim Buchanan's students turned up in the Reagan administration" (Craig Roberts, in Warsh 1993: 96). Policy think tanks like the Heritage Foundation and the Cato Institute were also full of these "heretics." In this ideological counter-offensive, these "outsiders" skillfully managed to gain support through marketing and media campaigns.

The liberal establishment had staked its credibility on a gradual opening up to new groups that had been excluded from the centers of power in the United States. Corporate lawyers, philanthropic foundations, and the academy were central to this project. But the economics of the 1970s that went with the oil crisis, increased global competition, and challenges to corporate profits made corporate America and institutions such as the *Wall Street Journal* ready to embrace the neoliberal challengers and their scholarly theories and to take on the liberal establishment and the moderate activism it had come to embrace.

Law was considered to be on the side of the activist state and thus was viewed as a target rather than a potential ally. The Reagan administration had come to power fortified by a conservative social movement and a coalition of neoliberal economists and corporations determined to make Washington, D.C., more favorable to business. There were lawyers in the administration, of course, but legal expertise was not of any great importance except for the practical purposes of deregulation and an attack on legal activism. Richard Posner and other leading scholars in the field were quickly promoted to the bench during the first Reagan administration. But this largely reflected a negative strategy aimed at shrinking the state and deregulating the economy. These moves were not associated with the elite law schools, which were still overwhelmingly liberal (except for the University of Chicago) (Duxbury 1995). In the early stages of this movement, little value was assigned to lawyers and law, both seen as too close to the welfare state.

THE PRODUCTION OF A "GOLDEN AGE" IN US LEGAL THEORY

There is a perception that the 1980s were a kind of golden age for legal theory in the United States (Hackney 2012)—a time when academic law played a major role in social debates. Law and Economics contended with Critical Legal Studies, Critical Race Theory, Law and Society, and Feminist Legal Theory, among others. From a sociological perspective, we can hypothesize some of the circumstances that produced this phenomenon. One was certainly an intensification of competition in academic scholarship within law, which related in part to the open-ing of the schools to more meritocratic entrants. Tenure standards tightened in law schools, and academic production became key to the growing lateral market in law professors.

Crucial to the story, however, was the political competition that fueled the academic production. The liberal establishment, despite efforts that responded to and contained the movements of the 1960s and 70s, had not prevailed. It had lost a good part of its credibility as the strategy of social inclusion ran up against resource limits, economic crises, and the conservative backlash. The loss of cred-ibility could be capitalized on by elite law professors importing critical theories from Europe (on Duncan Kennedy, see Hackney 2012: loc. 427). The legal scholars more generally offered competing theories to potentially connect with whatever political trend might next take over the country. Critical Legal Studies helped maintain the prestige and notoriety of the elite law schools and their professors with leftist critique—even though practitioners could essentially ignore it. Law and Society scholars thrived in part because they could maintain their alliances with dominated social groups, their commitment to social science technology (on Austin Sarat, see Hackney 2012: loc. 1986), and their defenses of the social state. The right's ascendant political movement directly against the liberal establishment found a place in the legal academy as "Law and Economics," which gained increas-ing influence in the 1980s.

CONSOLIDATING THE POWER OF THE RIGHT
AND REBUILDING THE LEGAL ESTABLISHMENT

The continuing vitality of much of the liberal establishment into the 1970s, despite the criticisms leveled at it, meant that the initial legal policies of the Reagan administration aimed at "defunding the left" to the extent it was embedded in law. As Steven Teles (2008) noted, "the most obvious strategy available to Reaganites for dealing with the organizational imbalance between legal liberals and conserva-tives was a vigorous attack on the financial foundation of liberal public interest law" (57). The Reaganites tried to take on public interest law and the Legal Ser-vices Corporation as one part of the strategy, but the legal establishment kept these programs alive. Another part of the Reagan program involved attacking "activist judges." At that point, indeed, elite law both within and outside the legal academy and the corporate bar was not on the side of the Reagan administration, and the conservative movement did not embrace elite lawyers and legal strategies. Teles labeled the situation "Grassroots without Elites: The Conservative Legal Move-ment Circa 1980" (57).

Put another way, as a parallel to the 1960s, the political activism of this time—conservatism—distrusted elite lawyers, whom it identified with a status quo it opposed. As Ann Southworth (2008) points out, it is indicative that "several lawyers talked about their unsuccessful battles to persuade their law firms to allow pro bono work for conservative causes" (120). The corporate law firms close to business clients did not even recognize the legitimacy of public interest law on the right. The legal establishment led by corporate lawyers was still one-sided in terms of its public service.

A key figure in remedying this was Michael Horowitz, a conservative, Yale-educated lawyer. Illustrating the strength of elite school ties, Horowitz was invited by his liberal Yale classmate, Charles Halpern, to a symposium on public interest law (Teles 2009: 64). Horowitz noted the ways in which those in government and those in public interest law firms worked in "profoundly collusive ways, where the government agencies would lose and the court would order expansion of government programs, in a sense mandating appropriations that Congress was refusing to give. . . . When I was at Charlie's conference, here were these general counsels of agencies saying my door is always open to the Environmental Defense Fund, and we plot and scheme. . . . We work it out. You make these radical demands on me and then I can look like I'm in the middle. So we can advance the ship that way. . . . I thought that was a wonderful model" (64).

Horowitz wrote a report for the Scaife Foundation just prior to Reagan's election. It was a strong attack on what then existed as conservative public interest law. Interestingly, liberal scholars now trace the rise of public interest law and aggressive legal strategies on the right to a memorandum that Lewis Powell, soon to become a Supreme Court Justice, wrote in 1971 to the US Chamber of Commerce. Among other things, he called for more investment in learned legal strategies to counteract the liberal legal establishment. Activist websites today state, for example, that "the Powell Memo was the precipitating event for the swift rise and astounding success of big business and its control of the United States, starting in the early 1970s. The memo presented a bold strategy for how the corporate law firm could take over the key portions of the system, without the other side knowing what was happening" (Thwink.org 2006).

As Schmitt (2005) noted, however, the Powell memo was not really discovered until 1993, after the legal counter-revolution had essentially succeeded: "Most histories of the right don't attribute any significance to the Powell Memo at all. Indeed, a biography of Powell . . . doesn't discuss it" (2). That memorandum was a pitch to broaden the legal establishment and promote more business-friendly rhetoric, but it was not very important at the time because the legal establishment was essentially irrelevant at that time to the conservative agenda.

Horowitz's report on public interest law attacked the existing conservative public interest law firms in part for the "privileged role of business in the movement," suggesting that they gave the appearance of being "nothing more than shills for conservative business interests" (Teles 2009: 68). Business funding did not help. The funding, he argued, should be mainly from the conservative foundations. They also needed to distance themselves from "party politics," and perhaps above all, they needed to recruit elite "idealists" and speakers "for such unrepresented parties as taxpayers, ultimate consumers, and small businesses" (69). Accordingly, they needed to recruit law clerks, law review leaders, and graduates from the most elite schools, who would be inspired by ideas and by standards of professionalism. They needed to develop close ties to the elite law schools and legal scholarship.

Horowitz joined the Reagan administration himself, but in the early days of that administration, he stated, it was difficult to find ideologically committed lawyers with elite credentials. According to Teles, "these were the days before the Federalist Society was really off the ground, so it was hard to find lawyers who had a conservative political outlook" (69). They were not just missing from public interest law. They also were not in the law schools or in the large corporate law firms. The legal establishment contained only a few conservatives at the time.

Key to the change that followed was a strategy of aggressive recruitment developed under Attorney General Edwin Meese during the second Reagan administration. After that administration, many more elite lawyers were available to move into the elite legal academy and the conservative public interest law firms, there were respectable scholarly theories for lawyers on the right, there were openings for conservative pro bono in large law firms, and it was easy to find conservatives who were "the next generation of Lloyd Cutlers and Joe Califanos who are prepared to run law firms and to assume major government positions" (Southworth 2008: 39).

Horowitz made a similar point about his work recruiting into the administration: "[I acted] as a career mentor and someone who encouraged people to come into government, or not to stay too long and go back into private practice and earn a source of independent income so that they would not be government junkies all their lives . . . to approximate the model of the Clark Cliffords and Cy Vances and Califanos and the others to move from their law firms back to cabinet secretaryships back to their law firms" (Teles 2009: 72). Horowitz quite clearly embraced the model of the lawyer-statesperson at the top of the legal hierarchy, but he wanted a place for political conservatives playing the same role as the liberals had in the past. Drawing on the same set of elite institutions—law firms, public interest law firms, foundations, law schools—that had sustained the liberal establishment, coupled with an alliance with neoliberal economists, he set out to rebuild the place of elite lawyers in the competition to produce solutions to social problems and enact the agenda of the newly configured establishment.

POSITIVE LEGAL THEORY, THE FEDERALIST SOCIETY, AND THE NEW CONSERVATIVE LEGAL ESTABLISHMENT

Meese and Horowitz embraced the Federalist Society to build their recruitment. The Federalist Society provided a group of young and ambitious law professors seeking to retool legal scholarship in alliance with the emerging political right—a version of the classic Berman formula for legal revolution. The Federalist Society had been established by Yale College graduates attending elite law schools in the early days of the Reagan era. They were acutely aware that liberals dominated those schools. These law students teamed up with the few famous conservatives close to the elite legal world, including Robert Bork and Antonin Scalia. Meese then recruited from among the few conservative legal academics, such as Gary McDowell and Federalist Society founders Steven Calabrese, David McIntosh, and Lee Liberman Otis, and focused on long-term scholarly thinking and planning.

At this point, finally, legal academics and legal theory entered the picture. One of the Federalist Society projects was to develop "originalism" as a constitutional theory. Originalism provided a legal theory—not just a political program—that helped secure prominent places in elite law schools for legal conservatives, and from those prominent positions they could provide tools for elite conservative lawyers and judicial allies to legalize the politics of the right (Hollis-Brusky 2015). There was a huge investment in the new legal theory. As Hollis-Brusky notes, the legalizing of the conservative agenda was quite remarkable:

> Law and Economics, Natural Law Jurisprudence, and Originalism—as recently as the early 1980s these strands of conservative and libertarian legal thought were considered by most in the American legal profession to be "off the wall" or, as Jack Balkin has more colorfully described them, "positively loony." . . . Within the span of two short decades, however, these ideas came to be accepted as "positively thinkable" and to being practiced as "good legal craft." . . . Each year, several hundred articles espousing these theories appear in the pages of the most respected law journals in the country, and these same ideas have been drawn upon by federal judges and Supreme Court justices to articulate some of the most important judicial decisions of the last fifteen years. (Hollis-Brusky 2011: 521)

Meese and his team thus connected with a heretofore marginal legal group and brought them into the core of the Reagan administration and the conservative political movement. They drew conservative law students into the same mindset— do they choose elite corporate law, government, or elite public interest law?—that liberal law students faced. One measure of their success is that conservative public interest law firms became one component of the academic, corporate law firm, and governmental strategy. Those coming out of the Reagan administration were perfect recruits, and "conservatives used strategic litigation to reshape perceptions that they were greedy, callous, captured by big business, and uninterested in the cause of racial justice" and also to "distance themselves from their existing constituencies" (Teles 2008: 279)—to serve them better in the long term.

Southworth examines what she terms the mediator organizations and the individuals within them, who serve as the core of this conservative legal establishment. They are the best-known individuals within the conservative legal community, and include Edwin Meese (who moved to the Heritage Foundation, symbolizing the move of elite law into the conservative policy movement once represented only by conservative economists), Ted Olson, and Kenneth Starr. Foundation money overwhelmingly goes to the groups associated with them rather than to other groups. Mediator groups also stress "the value of civility" (Southworth 2008: 81), as did the liberal legal establishment in the 1960s. They are "elite members of the broader legal establishment, concerned about maintaining their stature in that larger community and defending its values" (81). They defend one another regardless of politics (69). In addition, their connections to business and to corporate law ensure that neither conservative nor liberal law gets too out of touch with the corporate and financial communities.

The liberal legal establishment has shifted to absorb the neoliberal revolution, and that shift is well represented with the rise of behavioral law and economics, which is marketed as a supplement to neoliberal economics. The relatively more liberal, but still mainstream, economists who have pushed back on purer versions of neoliberalism, such as Joseph Stiglitz and Thomas Piketty, also offer ways for new legal theories to relegitimate a moderate social reform agenda in which elite lawyers can play a central role. The position of corporate law and allied public interest law is again relatively strong, now closely involved with both the liberal and the conservative establishments.

Elite law is divided, as is US politics, but elite law comes together within the key institutions of the legal field—law schools, the Supreme Court, corporate law firms (perhaps with some division of labor among more conservative law firms, such as Kirkland and Ellis, and more liberal ones, such as Arnold and Porter), and bar associations. The disagreements between the two sides mask the fact that both are closely connected to corporate power. The agreement extends also to certain issues of high profile for elites, such as gay marriage (Ted Olson and David Boies), and where elite corporate lawyers make common ground, such as when defending individuals detained at Guantanamo, disqualifying Supreme Court nominees who lack elite credentials, and a focus on the US Supreme Court as the key arbiter of politics (Southworth 2008). Indeed, making clear the pivotal role of the corporate bar today, Reuters published an article that reported that less than 1 percent of "lawyers who filed appeals to the Supreme Court" were involved in 43 percent of the decided cases between 2004 and 2012. And "of the 66 most successful lawyers, 51 worked for law firms that primarily represented corporate interests" (Biskupic, Roberts, and Shiffman 2014: 3).

CHANGE AND CONTINUITY

The rebuilding of the position of the legal elite in the United States is the culmination of the attack on the Eastern legal establishment from within and outside the institutions of the establishment. The story of today's divided elite is linked closely to the expansion of higher education in the 1950s and 60s, which produced a generation with elite academic credentials but also aware of the glass ceiling they faced because they lacked the social pedigree of graduates of the Eastern prep schools and the dominant leaders of the FPE. Their activism helped produce the counter-attack on the right, which also relied to a great extent on scholarly and meritocratic capital—beginning with neoliberal economics mobilized against the Eastern establishment of Keynesians anchored at Harvard and Yale.

The forces that brought about the conservative counter-revolution also fought on behalf of scholarly capital, especially neoliberal economics but also Critical Legal Studies and Originalism, against the mix of scholarly and inherited capital that had dominated the state since Franklin Roosevelt in support of the liberal establishment. The next part begins with a discussion of how law and development efforts abroad changed with respect to shifts within the United States. The first chapter in Part IV then discusses India, which in many ways is in between the two approaches to law and development emanating from the United States. On one side is the idealism of public interest law and retooled lawyer-statespersons; on the other is the powerful extension of the neoliberal revolution into the center of the legal field.

PART FOUR

From Law and Development to the Neoliberal Revolution

US LAW AND DEVELOPMENT PROGRAMS and initiatives have played an important role in legal reform in South and East Asia. There were significant efforts to export US legal approaches in legal education to India, South Korea, and Japan in the post–Second World War period and in China beginning in the late 1970s. Hong Kong is the only exception among the Asian case studies in this book, and it provides a nice contrast because of its unique openness to the market of lawyers and law firms. Importation of ascendant practices and technologies takes place there relatively easily. In each of the case studies, the processes of import/export, consistent with Berman's formula, involve surges of scholarly investment feeding into processes of potential regime change. The United States, of course, is not the only source of influence, but in legal education reform and the development of corporate law firms, the US influence has become the most significant such influence.

From the beginning of US law and development programs in the 1950s, the US approach has been to challenge the existing "guardians of the temple" outside the United States in the name of universals consistent with US hegemony. US philanthropic foundations and government programs sought to "modernize" legal elites to become moderate leaders in development and governance instead of conservative backers of a propertied class seen as resistant to reform. The projects were led by legal missionaries from the North. As David Trubek (2009) noted about his work leading a famous project in Brazil,

> there was a social dimension because after all there was a liberal democrat Kennedy administration. . . . We were offering an alternative to communist whatever, and this included the capability to have more rapid economic growth and in order to have

97

more economic growth you needed to have effective laws governing the economy and in order to have effective laws governing the economy you have to have lawyers who knew how to draft the laws, interpret the laws, implement the laws, so you can trace . . . the American interest in . . . back to this idea that we have to help Latin America to find an alternative to communism that would lead to satisfaction of basic needs and show that, that they didn't have to go in that direction. (33–34)

Reform projects sought to promote more meritocratic access to positions in the legal profession, more scholarly investment in law, and somewhat less reliance on family capital embedded in the law (in part through colonial processes). All of these potential reforms looked toward challenging familial "legal formalism" in favor of more strategic US-like lawyering that involved test cases, lobbying, and legal-political advocacy requiring more investment in technical legal arguments. Justice William O Douglas accurately captured the idea when he observed that lawyers in developing countries needed to learn the mix of skills identified with corporate law firms—that is, with "a first-rate metropolitan lawyer" (quoted in Gardner 1980: 37).

Some background on different colonial pathways is necessary to understand the processes associated with recent developments. Colonial legacies and histories, as noted in Part II, help explain and define processes of "modernization," including Americanization today. The different colonial paths have contributed to nuances in what we see today as denunciations of particular "guardians of the temple" as obsolete and reactionary. As stated earlier, the legal/colonial histories proceeded cyclically. Legal elites accumulated symbolic capital through credentials and links to colonial governance and then to independence. That legal capital could be inherited and transformed in countless ways, appreciating or depreciating depending on the circumstances. The variety of these different modalities is key to the current situations. Thus, for example, we see the legal elites behind India's Congress Party becoming the embattled and conservative senior bench and bar today. In Hong Kong, the expatriate and local brokers of the trading entrepôt converted themselves into a mix of democracy advocates and relatively complacent solicitors. Samurai in Japan converted their connections and status into the first generation of foreign-modeled lawyers in the Meiji period (Flaherty 2013). The legacies of these colonial histories, as we shall see, help explain the half-failure/half-success of the first phase of exported modernization that took place through law and development, as well as the later reinvention arising from importation by US-style modernists. We explore these differences in the chapters in this part.

The first era of law and development in the late 1960s and 70s can be seen as the final episode of a US-led program of moral imperialism. Modernizing elites were supposed to take up the cause of development and the creation of more open polities and societies, reducing the appeal of socialism or communism. The new era has drawn on the earlier agenda of legal education reform, but the driving force is no longer the Cold War and state-led development. The current situation is dominated by the global regime of law and global finance that emerged in the 1980s. That regime is fostering a new generation of publicly and privately funded elite law schools on the periphery that now play key roles in selection into elite corporate law firms. Legal education reform in the current context has contributed to the rationalization and legitimation of a grid of complementary "Magic Circles" of corporate law firms, which serve as bridges between global cities in the North, emerging economies, and countries that have developed through a variety of different models.

Throughout all these reforms, furthermore, the agents of the new legal/financial regime have taken advantage of a relative devalorization/obsolescence of legal education shaped by the former colonial powers and have sought to revive law schools through processes that combine import of foreign knowledge and academics, broader recruitment of students within more diversified social and business circles, and more competitive and selective scholarly training. These new schools appear to be in opposition and competition with the traditional centers for the reproduction of elite families, but they also contribute to the reinforcement of well-established legal hierarchies.

To quote from *The Economist*'s article on "Elevator malfunction," education today represents a "'marriage of meritocracy and plutocracy,' where the knowledge economy operates as a 'winner takes—almost—all' for 'superstars firms' in 'superstars cities.' . . . The meritocratic elite has proven remarkably good at hoarding opportunities. Successful people tend to marry each other. Couples devote themselves to giving the best education possible, starting in nursery. Private schools have also proved successful at adapting to the meritocratic spirit. Institutions that once turned out flannelled fools and muddled oafs are now obsessed with the exams results" (*The Economist* 2017).

India

Colonial Path Dependencies Revisited: An Embattled Senior Bar, the Marginalization of Legal Knowledge, and Internationalized Challenges

In the eighteenth century, at a time when the British Empire was being questioned at home and elsewhere for corruption and exploitation in India under the administration of the British East India Company, the rationale for empire moved away from trade toward the idea of "civilizing" India (Pitts 2005). With the termination of governance by the British East India Company in favor of the Indian Raj (1857), law and lawyers assumed further importance and became prominent embodiments of a co-optation strategy that went both ways. Part of the process involved forming, in Thomas Babington Macaulay's famous words, "a class who may be interpreters between us and the millions whom we govern; a class of persons, Indian in blood and colour, but English in taste, in opinions, in morals, and in intellect" (Ferguson 2004: 189).

The high courts were gradually opened to Indian advocates in the nineteenth century. Some were local advocates (*vakils*), but the vast majority had been trained in the English Inns of Court through an expensive process that lasted four or five years. Local Indian elites, including Brahmins from Madras especially and Parsis from Bombay (Sharafi 2014), became Indian versions of English gentlemen advocates. They prospered greatly through litigation and business representation, hence their characterization as "nabobs of the law." By the late nineteenth century they were a recognizable elite and the backbone of the Indian National Congress, founded in 1885.

This legal and social elite thrived. It maintained close relations with the Indian landowning class and used litigation to protect large landholdings in the nineteenth and twentieth centuries. Indian advocates also replicated the British system, which required apprenticeship with a senior advocate before gaining admission to the bar. In practice this meant that family ties were essential for entry into the upper reaches of the profession. Many of the leading practitioners tapped their legal expertise and social status, took their profits, and became the core of the Congress Party as it began to push for independence. The famous advocates who later became leaders in the independence drive included Motilal Nehru, his son Jawaharlal Nehru, and Mahatma Gandhi.

Because of the part it had played in the independence struggle, the legal profession enjoyed relatively high status at the time of separation from Britain. The legal elite was embedded in politics, in business, among the landowning class, and among India's leading families. At the same time, however, since the Indian legal aristocracy had been built through colonialism, the legal profession combined aristocratic status with a peripheral, dominated relationship with Britain. It also tended to be quite conservative except in relation to the independence movement, which had bolstered its position. It was not surprising, therefore, that the prestige of law and lawyers began to plummet as elite Indian lawyers used their power to fight the moderate socialist agenda of Jawaharlal Nehru (Williams 2020), who accused lawyers of "purloining the constitution."

The sway of family capital, the lucrative legal market, and the bunker mentality adopted by the traditional legal elite together helped weaken the prestige of law and legal careers. By the 1960s, law had lost still more prestige, compared especially to engineering, in part because the Indian Institutes of Technology were open to all who could excel on the entrance examinations. From the perspective of the Ford Foundation, which sought to build an idealistic law and development program in India to strengthen legal education and the profession (Krishnan 2004), law was "a second rate profession" (Dezalay and Garth 2010: 150) reluctant to embrace any change.

The legitimacy of law as a largely conservative, family-dominated profession was questioned; so was the law that the elite of the bench and bar produced. This came to a head in 1975, when Prime Minister Indira Gandhi, with the backing of her allied Supreme Court, declared a state of emergency to get around legal resistance to change. The state of emergency, because it went against entrenched legal norms, helped members of the elite of the bar win back their prestige by opposing Gandhi's position. For its part, the Supreme Court, which had supported the emergency, invested in public interest litigation to rebuild its credibility.

The development of public interest litigation in turn helped inspire in 1987 the creation of the first National Law School of India, which also was meant to help rebuild law's credibility by opening itself to more meritocratic students (in much the same way as the Indian Institutes of Technology had done). The fortuitous opening of the economy in the early 1990s then dramatically increased the number of solicitor positions in corporate law. This changed the orientation of the National Law Schools (NLSs); it also fueled their growth, for more lawyers were now needed to stock the corporate law sector. As shown below, that combination, mixed with international capital, helped renew and strengthen the challenge to the embattled elite of the bench and bar—the grand advocates—in the name of meritocratic standards and globally credible quality.

FAILURES OF LAW AND DEVELOPMENT
AND LEGAL EDUCATION REFORM

The difficulties of reforming legal education in India are well-documented (Krishnan 2005; Sood 2017). The Ford Foundation, consistent with the first era of law and development, was heavily involved in facilitating debates about legal education in India in the 1950s and 60s: "Policymakers at Ford Headquarters in New York as well as at Ford's New Delhi office believed that for Indian democracy to succeed, the country needed to have well-established, rule-based institutions administered by those educated in the legal principles of equity, due process, and individual rights" (Krishnan 2004: 448). Ford sent a host of leading US legal academics to study and advise Indian faculties of law: "Ford thus began spending millions of dollars and decades of energy working with Indians to create strong schools of law" (448). The advisers consistently lamented the level of legal instruction, the qualifications of law students, the part-time and poor quality of law faculties, and the weak libraries, among other problems.

One obstacle to reform domestically in India was the attitude toward the bar within the ruling Congress Party. According to advisers to the Ford Foundation, the lack of resources for law schools was a key problem for legal education, but it was unrealistic to expect a financial commitment from the central government: "Lawyers and Indian judges at that time were not favorably viewed by politicians. Politicians accused these two groups of impeding the state's ability to grow and carry out its economic and social policies" (452). The reactionary image of the bar made investment in legal education highly unlikely.

That skepticism about the role of the legal elite related to the colonial legacy. Krishnan reports observations by Harvard's Arthur von Mehren, a US adviser to Ford, suggesting the ambiguous implications of the colonial legacy imposed on them and echoed in the 1950 Constitution. The elite bench and bar tended to celebrate the colonial legal legacy, but at the same time, "lawyers and judges who worked within the legal system were viewed by the general populace as perpetuators of this non-applicable foreign species" (460).

The Bar Council of India (BCI), which had controlled legal education since the early 1960s, did not expect law schools to be more than places for teaching vocational skills (473). The BCI leadership at that time was focused on increasing the number of lawyers. Interestingly, those leaders were "not from the elite sections of Indian society nor were most of them upper castes. They believed that for too long ordinary Indians lacked access to the legal process, and to remedy this problem, the BCI approved the opening of hundreds of new assembly-line law colleges during the 1960s and 1970s" (473). This program did not challenge the elite bar.

There was, to be sure, intermittent discussion and activity in India with respect to the reform of legal education. Various Indian legal groups from the 1950s on, in particular, called for the reform of legal education (Sood 2017; Mustafa et al., 2018). As early as 1964, the Gajendragadkar Committee, chaired by the Chief Justice and charged with suggesting reforms for the University of Delhi, discussed the possibility of creating a "National Law School," "where the best students from all over the country would come together to study" (481). But the discussions had little impact. The Ford Foundation sought to play a role, but US professor-consultants were consistently disappointed, and the Ford Foundation had given up this effort by the early 1970s after a negative review of results.

Still, some domestic activity continued, centered especially on the University of Delhi. In particular, the idea of a new National Law School picked up support through the Bar Council's Legal Education Committee, chaired in the 1970s by well-known Supreme Court Justice Mohammed Hidayatullah (481). Upendra Baxi was central to that effort, circulating an influential paper on legal education (Baxi 1976; Mathur 2017). Baxi, India's best-known legal academic, had obtained an SJD from the University of California, Berkeley, taught in Australia, and then come back to the University of Delhi. He taught there from the 1970s to the mid-1990s, served as dean and in many other capacities, and then moved to the University of Warwick in the United Kingdom in the mid-1990s. His career was closely connected both to the rise of public interest law and to the development of the NLSs. He was involved at various times in the efforts to create a National Law School.

These committees and commissions did not bring much actual reform. There was criticism of the legal education system but little political interest in reforming it. The existing system basically served the elite of the bar—and the reproduction of that elite—even though its prestige had fallen dramatically. According to a recent study, until the mid-1980s "the instability of the political environment coupled with the legal fraternity's early resistance to the five-year, NLU type model . . . together seemed to have sounded the death knell for progress in this regard" (Sood 2017: 9).

The activities around the Emergency and the development of public interest litigation (PIL) strengthened the voices of critics who wanted to renovate the legal profession and upgrade the level of practice. But it took an unlikely combination of circumstances to bring the idea of a National Law School to fruition.

PUBLIC INTEREST LITIGATION AND THE EFFORT TO IMPROVE THE IMAGE OF THE BENCH AND BAR

The key top-down initiative after the Emergency was the Supreme Court's embrace of PIL. This was largely a defensive measure for a beleaguered bench and bar. As

S.P. Sathe noted, "the post-emergency judicial activism was probably inspired by the Court's realization that its elitist social image would not make it strong enough to withstand the future onslaught of a powerful political establishment" (2002: 107). PIL facilitated some alliances with the new urban groups and professionals who, after becoming mobilized for the protection of civil rights during the Emergency, turned toward social activism through NGOs. PIL also connected to the rise of public interest law and human rights advocacy abroad through the support of the Ford Foundation.

The Ford Foundation sought to embrace this moment and use it to open up the profession and improve its outreach to disadvantaged groups. The local office in New Delhi sought to support "groups who gave legal representation to people excluded or outside the system" (Int. India-21). The foundation hoped to emulate California Rural Legal Assistance, an activist organization serving California's rural poor. The foundation eventually awarded a grant to the Public Interest Legal Support and Research Center (PILSARC), set up in 1987 and led by Rajeev Djavan, a prominent Indian legal academic in Britain who had returned to India to become a Supreme Court advocate. This program's challenges related to the bar's reluctance to open up opportunities for advocates.

The Ford Foundation criticized PILSARC for being unable to help build "institutions on the ground" or "take risks" (Int. India-22). It did not build a grassroots legal advocacy group. It also did not provide a place to build a new generation of public interest lawyers outside of the elite group of Supreme Court advocates and other senior advocates.

It did, however, carry out some refurbishment of the elite of the bar, who now could—in addition to their lucrative private practices—identify with PIL, thus reinforcing the hierarchies of the bar (for a discussion of the highly stratified public interest bar and its relationship to prestige, see also Krishnan 2004). It also developed closer ties to the US legal and philanthropic world. PIL generally was consistent with a moderate and defensive response to continuing challenges to an elite bench and bar dedicated to maintaining its position.

The timing of PIL did, however, feed into nascent and intermittent discussions about the reform of legal education.

RELUCTANT LEGAL EDUCATION REFORM: THE FIRST NATIONAL LAW SCHOOL IN BANGALORE

N.R. Madhava Menon, a protégé of Justice Krishna Iyer, a leader of PIL on the Indian Supreme Court, ultimately became the leader of the first National Law School, founded in Bangalore in 1987. Unlike Baxi, Menon was not well-known at the time as a scholar (Krishnan 2004: 473). He had been inspired by his visits to US law schools and his teaching at Delhi University. He had worked on legal education reform in the 1970s, and that experience led the Bar Council of India to turn to him to work on a proposal for new law schools. He completed a proposal in

1982 and "began to showcase this idea to various constituents, including lawyers, law professors, students, and politicians" (473). Despite his best efforts, however, Menon met resistance from people in each of these groups (473). His former colleague, the relatively innovative dean at Delhi University, P.K. Tripathi, wrote an editorial terming the plans "unrealistic, simplistic, and unnecessarily radical." According to Krishnan, Menon "was unable to persuade even one institution in the country to experiment with his proposal" (479).

In 1983 he left the Bar Council and went back to the United States for a year, "where he reunited with inspirational allies at Columbia University who sympathized with his reform efforts" (479). Re-energized, Menon "lobbied various constituencies (including many of his critics) for moral, political, and financial support" (485). In 1985, he finally managed to get the Bar Council of India to support the founding of an independent law school. The council then negotiated with the southern state of Karnataka, which agreed to combine funds with the BCI to set up the National Law School in Bangalore (485).

This story is not exactly one of the elite of the bar fully embracing the reform of legal education. Menon had to fight every step of the way, and indeed Krishnan notes that it is hard to explain why the very conservative BCI ultimately supported him. Krishnan suggests that "the Council too had become disillusioned with the quality of law graduates over the past several years." Critical, however, was that "the Council had a relationship with Menon . . . [who had] worked with the Council from 1978–83. The Council respected and trusted Menon's judgment." Finally, the BCI saw that PIL was helping the image of the legal profession, and the National Law School was geared to build on that image by producing public interest lawyers (485).

The state and BCI support was very limited, however. Menon suggested that without more support, the institution would have closed very quickly. He emphasized the role of the Ford Foundation, which stepped in with an $800,000 grant "at a crucial time when the law school was finding it difficult to continue operations (i.e. 1989–1994)" (Menon 2009: 52). The Ford Foundation finally had a champion in India to improve legal education.

The five-year curriculum of the National Law School that opened its doors in 1987 was inspired largely by US law schools (Menon 2009) and was much more rigorous than the three-year BA of the existing law faculties. An international team that included Marc Galanter, William Twining, and Savitri Gunasekhere from Colombo reviewed the first few years of the school and concluded that it had "fully met the objectives of being a Centre of excellence that serves as a pace setter for Indian legal education" (54). The success of the National Law School inspired the creation of the National Law School in Hyderabad (officially named: the National Academy of Legal Studies and Research [NALSAR]), which opened in 1998. After that, the model really took off. There are now some twenty-one NLSs throughout India, with varying claims to affinity with the original model.

The National Law Schools have also influenced legal education, both public and private, outside of the NLS sector. There are now fewer three-year LL.B. programs, the most prominent holdouts being Delhi University and the Government Law College in Mumbai. Recently, the Pravin Gandhi School of Law affiliated with the University of Mumbai switched its emphasis to a five-year LL.B. program away from a three-year evening program.

The key to the NLSs' great success was a timely shift away from public interest law. In the early 1990s, just as the first class of NLS Bangalore was graduating, Finance Minister Manmohan Singh brought an end to the Indian "Licensing Raj" and opened up the economy to much more foreign trade and investment. These liberalizing economic reforms opened space for new and expanded Indian solicitor firms and for global corporate law firms serving India from outside the country. Law firms retooled quite dramatically as the economy was transformed (Nanda, Wilkins, and Fong 2017). They had to shift from land conveyancing and some banking relationships to transnational transactions and mergers and acquisitions.

Many NLS graduates joined these firms, and students in those schools reportedly now compete for slots at national and global corporate law firms (Gingerich and Robinson 2017). As Krishnan noted in 2013, the growth of law firms is relatively recent, reflecting the impact of dramatic economic changes (Krishnan 2013). Of the forty top firms named in a survey, eight started between 1991 and 2000 and fifteen after 2000. Interestingly, the bar now complains about the lack of interest among NLS graduates in careers in the bar (Int. 15–India).

The rise of NLSs and corporate law firms has been presented generally as a remarkable story of reform (although there is now an emerging literature on those schools' limitations; e.g., Sood 2017; Mustafa et al. 2018). Part of their weakness stems from the serendipitous circumstances that finally brought legal education reform to some fruition within a still complacent legal establishment. It is notable also that NLSs occupy a relatively tiny niche within Indian legal education. There are some 1.3 million lawyers in India, more than 1,200 law schools and faculties of law, and perhaps 45,000 law students. There were more than 40,000 applications in 2017 for the 1,500 to 2,000 positions in the NLSs (Mustafa et al. 2018: 17). The Common Law Admission Test, established in 2008, has facilitated this large number because, as with respect to the Indian Institutes of Technology, the results of one examination can be used for applications to most NLSs throughout the country.

Access is not wide open, however. The standardized tests used by the NLSs require English proficiency, and the tuition fees of about US$2,500 per year deter a great number of applications as well. A recent study of students at the NLS in Bangalore confirms that they come disproportionately from high incomes and high castes (Jain et al. 2016). That 2016 study also found that Brahmins were 26.5 percent and other upper classes 32.5 percent; the numbers likely would have been higher had they included those who did not report (28). Some 30 percent of

Bangalore students were from major cities, but that was a decline from 50 percent, suggesting a more provincial trend, although not away from urban settings. Most students had parents who are fluent in English (35). There were also a small number of students in the "reserved" group for "scheduled castes" and similar groups. The report on Bangalore, however, suggests that those with more advantage do better in school, participate more heavily in the moot court competitions, and land prestigious jobs upon graduation (35; see also Mustafa et al. 2018) As others have suggested, it is very difficult to come from outside the elites and excel in law school in India (see Basheer et al. 2017).

As is the case at the Indian Institutes of Technology, the caste elites in law are distinguished not so much by wealth or property but rather by their embodiment of the meritocratic values that result in their being selected for top positions. As a scholar of the Indian Institutes of Technology suggests, the caste elites "are able to inhabit a universal world view precisely because of a history of accumulated privilege, a history that allows them a unique claim to certain forms of self-fashioning. Whereas at an earlier moment, status might have been more explicitly tied to caste, the social bases of merit continue to be constituted in ways that allow the same social groups to inhabit merit as an embodied ideal" (Subramanian 2015: 206).

The legal press in India has reported on the high-prestige positions that graduates obtain on graduating from the NLSs. Recently the NALSAR in Hyderabad reported that out of seventy-four graduating students, fifty-eight who had participated in the campus recruiting program all got positions, largely with corporate law firms, followed by in-house positions. Some 10 percent were planning on attending elite graduate programs abroad (Reddy 2017). Some planned on taking civil service exams, and one was taking a judicial exam. Only two reportedly were planning on becoming advocates or clerking for a court. Similar results apply to the other NLSs (Gingerich and Robinson 2017). The dean of a more traditional law school noted that law firms preferred to hire from the NLSs (Int. 2–India) rather than from the traditional schools.

These data are somewhat misleading, however. First, many leave the law firms that have recruited them after a relatively short time. One observer stated that half of the graduates of NLSs leave the practice of law within ten years for other careers such as business, design, or journalism (Int. 3–India). A close look at the LinkedIn members identified with the NLSs in Hyderabad and Bangalore suggests that many are still with law firms but quite a few are now in business, in-house counsel, legal education, or alternative careers. The original National Law School of Bangalore has 5,848 alumni listed, which no doubt includes those who have participated in a range of programs. The leading employers of these people are law firms (led by Cyril Amarchand Mangaldas, at fifty-three), business consultancies, and the Supreme Court (National Law School of India 2020), but clearly these graduates have followed a wide range of careers, and more than 300 of them are in the United States. The list shows a number of them at the top law firms, but their numbers in relation to the number of graduates are not high. Krishnan's research on the over-all frequency of individuals leaving corporate law firms—"peeling off"—also sug-gests that graduates are not in general making their careers in the large corporate law firms—even if they are still in the field of corporate law (2013).

Lawyers leave in part because the leading corporate law firms generally are of two types, family-dominated or dominated by a few individuals. Interviews con-firmed that this situation persists, suggesting there are very few "true partner-ships" (Int. 4–India). The value of family capital has not diminished. One young lawyer in a law firm with his father in Mumbai notes that family-operated busi-nesses often feel comfortable giving their legal work to the children of a long-standing lawyer with whom they already have a relationship (Int. 5–India). The new firms started by many of those who leave tend then to replicate the structures they left behind (Krishnan 2013). Also, starting salaries are relatively low. A small firm might pay 40,000 rupees per month, a large one 50,000, and a few firms such as the two Amarchand firms pay some 150,000 rupees a month. In US dollars, that is between $7,500 to $30,000 (often augmented with bonuses).

Many who leave the law firms seek to gain a foothold at the bar by teaming up with an established advocate. Krishnan shows how difficult it is to make it that way and break into the hierarchical advocacy world (2013: 38). A frequent observation about the graduates of the NLSs is that, after almost thirty years of producing law-yers, no graduate has become a grand advocate or a judge (Int. 6–India).

The meritocratic criteria of the NLSs have yet to overcome the strong familial capital required for a career at the bar, which can then lead to a judicial appoint-ment. Indeed, as discussed below, advocates promoting their NLS-inspired exper-tise can be seen as "too modern for the court," or as "incapable of playing by rules" because lacking inside knowledge of them (Int. 7–India).[1] The relatively successful reform and enhancement of the legal profession in India has been the product of a confluence of events and a desire to rebuild the credibility of the bench and bar. But results of those reforms and enhancements remain consistent with the entrenched conservatism of the family-dominated elite bench and bar, a conserva-tism that pervades both legal education and the corporate practice setting.

THE ENTRENCHED POSITION OF THE ELITE BENCH
AND BAR: THE RELATIONSHIP TO CORPORATE LAW

The world of the elite bench and bar has had a very strong impact on both the law firms and the NLSs, which are deeply embedded in the world of elite advocacy and the higher echelons of the judiciary. The law firms can be divided into three general categories. The first is what *Legally India* terms the "Big Seven" (Ganz 2016). The big seven law firms gained prominence or were established after economic liberalization. As reported in 2016, they include Cyril Amarchand Mangaldas, with 601 lawyers; Khaitan and Co., with 485; Shardul Amarchand Mangaldas &

Co., with 430; AZB & Partners, with 375; Luthra & Luthra, with 336; J. Sagar Associates, with 302; and Trilegal, with 221. They are the most important corporate law firms.

Another group is the older firms built generations ago by expatriates, such as Crawford Bayley, established in 1830. Other firms in this category are Little and Co. and Mulla and Mulla (Nanda, Wilkins, and Fong 2017: 72–75). These were the most prominent firms prior to liberalization, but they did not move quickly to adapt to the new situation, and a very few partners dominate these firms and their profits. They have been eclipsed by the newer and more entrepreneurial firms, which have also attracted more new associates because of the promise—albeit not often realized—they would be more egalitarian in sharing the profits and partnership places. The rest of the corporate legal sector is comprised of many small firms serving some aspect of the corporate business, but for large transactions, what is now a big seven has a "quasi monopoly" (Wilkins and Khanna 2017:144).

All law firms must have access to the leading advocates in order to win litigation for their clients. One of the larger firms reported the importance of access to the "face value" of the fifteen or so advocates they utilized (Int. 8–India). Nanda, Wilkins, and Fong note that the firms from the colonial era have survived in part because they are strongly connected historically to the elite bar, which also explains their resistance to change. Their niche generally is the places where "old-line connections and prestige remain salient . . . for big Indian companies" (Nanda, Wilkins and Fong 2017: 74)—in particular, the real estate and regulatory sectors. Furthermore, "These firms also have long-standing relationships with many of India's top Grand Advocates and high court judges"—"when the matter is really sensitive and the CEO needs someone he can really trust to navigate the bureaucracy of the courts." (75).

There are other ways that law firms connect to the networks around the bench and bar. Two of the most prominent of the big seven law firms, each of which has very prominent women in key positions, illustrate familial embeddedness. Pallavi Shroff, a key partner in the Delhi firm of Shardul Amarchand Mangaldas & Co., is the wife of Shardul Shroff, who chairs that firm, having inherited it (with his brother). She is also the daughter of well-known retired Supreme Court Justice P.N. Bhagwati, one of the justices most identified with PIL. The Shroffs also link closely to the Gujarati community and Reliance, one of the major corporate groups (78). Khaitan and Co. similarly is closely connected to the Marwari community from Kolkata and the Aditya Birla Group (78). Furthermore, Zia Mody, the founder of AZB and partners, is the daughter of Soli Sorabjee, a famous Indian jurist, Parsi, and former Attorney General of India. She started the firm after ten years as an advocate. Reportedly she became tired of the male-dominated bar and took advantage of her Cambridge law degree, Harvard LL.M., and family capital to start what has become one of the most successful law firms.

The law firm sector has grown substantially since economic liberalization, but it does not appear to be expanding very much today. After an initial growth of the corporate legal services market under liberalization, the market appears to have stagnated—perhaps in part because of the limited local opportunities and products offered in litigation (Int. 9–India; Nanda, Wilkins and Fong 2017). The corporate law firms in varying degrees are linked up with the familial world of the very conservative elite bench and bar. As discussed below, a number of those in the corporate bar are pressing for change.

THE ENTRENCHED POSITION OF THE ELITE BENCH AND BAR: THE NATIONAL LAW SCHOOLS

The connection between the elite bench and bar and the NLSs is even closer. The governing boards of the NLSs are dominated by leading members of the bar and judiciary. More generally, legal education is regulated by the Bar Council, which is the organ of the advocates. The Bar Council prescribes twenty-six mandatory courses, limits teaching by practitioners, and limits class sizes to sixty (Gingerich and Robinson 2017). It also imposed an all-India bar examination in 2010. Leaders of the relatively marginal All India Law Teachers' Organization, which represents members of law faculties, argue that the Bar Council should have "no role" in the teaching program of the law schools, but there is no likelihood of change in that direction (Int. 10–India).

The hierarchical connection between the judiciary and the NLSs is even stronger. Key judges generally decide whom to hire as the dean or vice-chancellor of an NLS. One vice-chancellor spoke of meeting a key judge for dinner and then getting offered the position (Int. 11–India). According to one knowledgeable observer, potential deans "cow-tow to the local judiciary," forming a "small cabal" (Int. 15–India). The chancellor of each school is a judge, with the Chief Justice of the Indian Supreme Court the Chancellor of NLS Bangalore. One critic of the NLS vice-chancellors stated that once they are appointed, they spend all their time and energy trying to gain stature within the world of the elite bench and bar (Int. 12–India). The dependence of each NLS on the vice-chancellor's clout magnifies the importance of those ties. Faculties have very weak voices, which means that the schools are "personality driven" by the vice-chancellor (Int.15–India; see also Balakrishnan 2013). Interviewees noted that when a capable vice-chancellor left NLS Kolkata, for example, the school went back to the "dark ages" (Int. 24–India).

A critic of the NLSs speaks of their "judicialization," but it appears that they were highly judicialized from the beginning (Int 15–India). According to the interviewees, the ability to get local government funding depends on the work of members of the judiciary, who lobby their local governments—which must pay some attention, since their representatives appear frequently before those judges. It is quite clear also that the funding levels for most of the NLSs are not very high, which puts pressure on them to increase tuition. Finally, the more recently established NLSs tend to have substantial local restrictions placed on them (e.g., the number of students who must be local).

Very high teaching loads are the norm in the NLSs, with the major exception currently of NLS Delhi, which is very well funded and, under the current vice-chancellor, focused on significantly increasing research output. More generally, the spread of the NLSs has not substantially raised the prestige and profile of legal academics in India. Many interviewees noted that there is still no real career in legal academia. One law graduate in a social science PhD program noted that there is no real job as "law professor"—it is a "dead end" (Int. 12–India). The NLS phenomenon, others note, has not changed the faculty model (Int. 13–India). At NLSs, the "main focus is teaching," and the teaching is not that high in quality.[2] There is "not much time for research," and there are no "structures to build up" to promote a better position for faculty members (Int. 14–India). There is little focus on the "quality of faculty" or "research agendas" (Int. 16–India). The faculty of the NLSs tend to be relatively young, and many faculty members do not stay in teaching. The group includes many who did not succeed in litigation and a number who are not on the "tenure track" (Ballakrishnen 2009).

The long-standing effort to upgrade law teaching and legal scholarly research, supported by a number of Ford Foundation initiatives beginning in the 1950s, has so far had limited success (Dasgupta 2010). The best and brightest law graduates do not seek careers as law professors. Many we interviewed suggested that more legal academics are producing scholarly research, and the number of academic scholars today is much greater than in the past. But interviewees also report that the journals are "dead" and that the advances in scholarship and prestige are quite limited (Int. 17–India). While many people in India can name judges or senior advocates, legal scholars, with the exception of Upendra Baxi, who is also an activist, are unknown even in the legal profession (Int. 19–India). The NLSs, moreover, are the relatively elite tip of the iceberg. There are more than a thousand other public and private schools that pay their faculty even less—including private schools, many of which pay half of what the public schools pay (Int. 10–India). Only a few of the more elite private law schools, exemplified by the Jindal Global Law School (discussed below) and the well-funded National Law School in Delhi, appear committed to encouraging scholarly productivity.

The pressure for change is coming mainly from those who go abroad. Many become part of a brain drain, but the existence of a group of relatively young lawyers with elite credentials suggests that more are returning. One interviewee noted that "increasingly people are coming back," the legal academy is more "exciting" than in the past, and many see "teaching as a vehicle" for research. They hope for a "recapturing and reinvesting of the brain drain" (Int. 19–India). What they learned abroad and is valued abroad, however, is still unevenly recognized in India and at times actually devalued (Ballakrishnen 2012). We examine these groups below after the discussion of the bar.

The problem of the reform of legal education is directly related to the structure of the elite bench and bar.

THE ENDURING STRUCTURE OF THE BAR

The tightly connected elite of the bench and bar remains at the top of the legal hierarchy.[3] It is dominated especially by well-connected elites, including Brahmins and upper castes and the Parsi elite in Mumbai (Sharafi 2014; Int. 5–India, discussing the links between Parsi family businesses and Parsi family law firms). The "grand advocates" are at the top of the hierarchy. Galanter and Robinson point out that seniority is one aspect of that hierarchy (2017). Since judges face compulsory retirement at sixty-two (and Supreme Court justices at sixty-five), they are often younger than the senior advocates who appear before them. They may have looked up to or even learned their practices from the senior advocates. The elite of the bar and bench has a very strong impact on legal education, on the governance of the NLSs, on the hiring of the vice-chancellors who govern the schools, and on the funding of the schools; they also provide social capital that helps sustain the elite of the corporate law firms.

The bar has participated under very particular circumstances in initiatives such as the NLSs and public interest litigation, both of which have enhanced the legitimacy of the profession and opened it up to more meritocratic, higher-quality entrants. But it is a legal elite that is essentially inbred and highly restrictive in entry. NLS graduates have to date had little success in this sector of the legal profession.

The conservative nature of the bar is quite evident. Its attitude toward law professors is apparently much like it was traditionally in the United Kingdom. An interviewee professor noted that the faculty at one NLS sought to eliminate Saturday classes in part to encourage research; the governing board rejected the request because, in their opinion, "law professors don't work anyway" (Int. 15–India). One interviewee noted a "large disconnect between academics and practice," and indeed that each side thinks it is superior (Int.19–India). The narrowness of the prevailing view of law practice is captured by a lawyer in a social science PhD program who had trouble renewing the lawyer's bar license. The authority from the bar thought that interdisciplinary academic study about law was inconsistent with the activities expected of bar members (Int. 12–India).

The issue of the quality of the advocacy among the senior elite arose in a number of interviews (also Galanter and Robinson 2017; Wilkins and Khanna 2017). The litigation lawyers at law firms, as noted above, stated that for important cases, they needed the "face value" of the advocates they tended to use, but the lawyers at the firm also stated that the abilities of the elite bar are "lower and lower."

The problem in part is that the elite advocates handle too many cases. They also do not use technology in their arguments. They rely on "court craft," they have "no depth" (Int. 3–India), and they hold to a "blinkered vision of law" (Int. 18-India). There are, one noted, very few quality lawyers in the bar: the bar in general is "mediocre," and "80 percent were unprepared" (Int. 18–India). A number of the in-house counsel studied by Wilkins and Khanna supported these contentions, suggesting that there was "great frustration with the quality of these top advocates" (Wilkins and Khanna 2017: 146).

Well-trained lawyers armed with an Oxbridge or US law school degree, coupled with experience in international law firms, have found that they are "overtrained" for litigation in India (Int. 18–India; for a similar phenomenon experienced by Indians with LL.M.s from the United States, see Ballakrishnen 2012). One young lawyer reported that the senior advocates "don't have time" for complex points, and it is by no means clear that even if they did, the judges would embrace them. He left the practice of law because of this disconnect between what he had been trained for and what he could use in litigation in India (Int. 3–India).

Interviewees stated that there were some prominent exceptions among the bench and the bar. Most frequently named were two justices of the Supreme Court from prominent legal families. One is Justice Dhananjaya Yashwant Chandrachud, whose father Shri Y.V. Chandrachud was the longest-serving Chief Justice of India. Chandrachud graduated in economics and mathematics from St. Stephen's College in New Delhi in 1979 and went on to obtain an LL.B. from Delhi University in 1982 and an LL.M. from Harvard University in 1983. The other is Justice Rohinton Fali Nariman, a leading senior advocate who is a Parsi from Mumbai as well as the son of Fali Sam Nariman. The younger Nariman received his early education in Mumbai. He completed his LL.B. at the Faculty of Law at the University of Delhi and then obtained an LL.M. from Harvard Law School. He practiced law in New York for a year as well. In India he rose quickly, mixing family capital and merito-cratic credentials. The bar had to amend the rules to allow him to become a senior advocate at the age of thirty-seven. He reportedly is the first Harvard alumnus to serve as a Justice on the Supreme Court of India.

Family capital remains vital for careers in the bar and on the bench. The system for promotion into the judiciary is secret. It has been criticized but has not yet been changed. Selections to the high courts and the Supreme Court are made dur-ing closed colloquiums, and as one observer noted, the result is that long-estab-lished legal names are chosen that tend to be upper caste or from Mumbai's Parsi elite (as in the case of Nariman) (Int. 12–India). Moreover, the impact of selection to a high court or the Supreme Court endures beyond retirement, since retired judges gain many influential positions related to politics and the law after their service on the judiciary.[4]

The elite are somewhat aware of the bar's closed and insular nature. Interest-ingly, in a recent speech to the Bar Association in Mumbai, Justice Chandrachud raised some careful criticisms of the closed nature of the bar (Chandrachud 2016). After praising the learned nature of the bar—an "assembly line of brilliance"— he talked of "our outmoded way of working" and the "perception that the bar is closed." He lamented that talented individuals "never went to the Supreme Court" and argued that it was "an issue of grave concern" that there is "talent" with "no access to centers of power." He stated that it was important to "open up our bar to a true meritocracy." The muted nature of his criticisms suggests that he did not expect his audience to embrace the message enthusiastically.

The NLSs, as noted, have not provided an effective meritocratic path to the elite bar. One leading lawyer with a family firm in Mumbai noted that for the leading lawyers in his city, whether practicing in firms or as advocates, the likely choice of law schools would be the Government Law College (GLC), and the same would be true for Delhi with the Delhi Law Faculty (Int. 2–India; Gingerich and Robinson 2017). The reasons are twofold: the exam threshold is difficult to pass for admission to an NLS; and the networks around the GLC, for example, are essential to success at the bar in Mumbai.

Admission to the GLC is not easy. Many are turned down. But several locals noted that children of judges and elite advocates get in despite lacking the top credentials (Int. 12–India). One graduate noted that if one has "no connections," it is very difficult to find mentors at the bar one needs to succeed; however, a faculty member says that the GLC students without connections have the time and capacity to find them (Int 21–India). In any event, no one disputes the value of family capital in careers starting at the GLC.

Similarly, neither graduates nor faculty argue that there is any real teaching at the GLC. Classes meet from 7:30 a.m. to 10:30 a.m., and busy practitioners may not show up to teach if something else comes up (Int. 12–India). There is in any event "no need to attend classes" (Int. 12–India). The students essentially spend all their time apprenticing with the advocates who congregate at the Bombay High Court one block from the GLC. There are conscientious professors who help, for example, with a law review, but scholarly capital pales in importance to family capital. However, one faculty member reported that despite the lack of any systematic educational program, there were currently three GLC students at Harvard. One administrator noted that leading US schools recruit at the GLC and that as many as 25 percent study abroad—again, despite the lack of academic rigor at the GLC (Int. 22–India).

This portrait of the bar reveals a legal elite that is highly inbred and closed to outsiders. There is no way, in addition, to mix the legal milieus. The graduates of the NLSs have to find paths for making the most of their meritocratic achievements. And they will be different paths from the one taken by the small subset reproducing the national elite around the courts and advocacy.

The growth of trade, increased corporate activity, and growing investment within and outside India, however, are providing opportunities for a professional class that can offer the state and big corporations more "modern" expertise. The law firms, which rebuilt their approach after the era of conveyancing and banking relationships, are one place where some of this upgrading is taking place, but they are limited in this by a very conservative elite bench and bar. They may try to go around grand advocates, but the top advocates are still necessary for access to the higher courts.

CHALLENGES TO THE ELITE BENCH AND BAR: BATTLES OVER EXPERTISE AND EDUCATION

Pressure for change tends to come from the outside. As noted, at least one of the top Supreme Court justices, who holds multiple degrees from abroad, is seeking to modernize the system from within. But the highly internationalized and more meritocratic group of top recent law graduates is the more general source of the change. It includes many who have studied abroad, including a number with Rhodes Scholarships (*Legally India* 2019) or who have returned from the United States or from positions in the Magic Circle law firms (or variants in Australia). A good proportion of these returnees have advanced degrees from the United Kingdom, though in recent years the United States has become more attractive for study abroad (Ballakrishnen 2012). The voices of this relatively young group were audible in the litany of criticisms in the preceding section. A number of graduates of the NLSs hold teaching and research positions abroad. They too participate in these debates. It is indicative that a recent review article on law and social science research emphasized the work of those from India but working abroad (Sharafi 2015). Within India, there are now clear alliances between this internationalized group and businesses, philanthropies, and various government sectors promoting modernized "good governance" within India.

The leading internationalized law firms in India are part of the modernizing offensive (which includes enhancing opportunities for women [Ballakrishnen 2019]). One top litigation partner with experience abroad noted the impact of the bar's narrowness on law firm markets. The partner argued that in transactional work the leading law firms could grow and take advantage of foreign clients and their own local and transnational expertise (Int. 3–India). But in litigation they are still being blocked. They cannot deploy their expertise or their ability to draw on technological innovations. This mismatch also restricts the growth of the Indian legal market. Some firms are trying to build their own in-house litigation expertise to work with or go around the advocates, but the possibilities for this sort of bypassing are still quite limited.

Thus there is a new group of challengers to the traditional bar elite, with its own hierarchies and trappings linked to the NLSs, but for this group to jump anywhere past the limited positions that their relatively high status can offer (i.e., law firms, global organizations, think tanks, some in-house positions) or to jump into the mainstream legal elite will require different forms of capital—especially legal family capital. NLS graduates have profiles similar in this respect to the graduates of the Indian Institutes of Technology (Subramanian 2015), but they do not have the same opportunities in India to mix engineering, social science, technology, and law in the way that it is done in Silicon Valley, for example.

One potential remedy for the economic liberals would be to open up the legal services markets, but the bar has strongly opposed competition from abroad within India (Coe 2016). There is more momentum now than in the past for a limited opening, but there are still "snags." The opening would undoubtedly have an impact, albeit one that is hard to predict. On the one hand, it might weaken the power of the Indian corporate law firms, since the global law firms have advantages for large-scale transactions. As suggested by Wilkins and Khanna (2017: 147), "foreign firms were more likely to handle important matters involving M & A, and civil liability, and arbitration." The global firms might also facilitate challenges to the traditional bar generally—in part through their ability to attract more Indian nationals back to India because of the relative openness of those firms in terms of advancement (Nanda, Wilkins, and Fong 2017: 106). At the same time, the traditional firms founded in the colonial era by British lawyers "might actually be seen as more valuable" if the market were opened up because of their unique ties with the regulatory authorities, the grand advocates, and the courts—that is, the enduring value of their social and familial capital (109).

Many of those who go abroad become interested in research and teaching, and they are adding to the pressure for change within India. Many of these people stay abroad (Sharafi 2015). Krishnan names at least six who are teaching in the United States, the United Kingdom, and Singapore (email). But as noted earlier, quite a few of them have returned to India to "recapture and reinvest the brain drain" (Int. 19–India). They have overinvested in technical scholarly sophistication in part because of the challenges they face in India to break into a world dominated by the bar. Not surprisingly, they often aim their research precisely at the quality of the courts and the judiciary, seeking transparency as a way also to challenge the conservatism they encounter. As already noted, they have not yet succeeded in tearing down the walls. Scholarly research at the NLSs is very limited, including at the top ones, and the position of law professor is still not widely respected and does not offer an attractive career path.[5] The upgrading of faculty credentials so as to require a PhD in order to teach at the NLSs (thus emulating the British model) has not changed this situation.

Nevertheless, there have been some very prominent research successes, such as the research at NLS Delhi on the death penalty, which draws on empirical legal research approaches imported from the United States. Anup Surendranath, the law professor in charge of the project, is a graduate of NALSAR in Hyderabad with an Oxford PhD gained through scholarship assistance (Mandhani 2014).

Other examples are think tanks created by individuals returning from abroad and well aware of the limited opportunities to deploy their knowledge and expertise. The Vidhi Centre for Legal Policy represents a particularly notable example.

According to its website, it "is an independent think tank doing legal research and assisting government in making better laws. Vidhi is committed to producing legal research of the highest standard with the aim of informing public debate and contributing to improved governance. Vidhi works with Ministries of the Government of India and State Governments, as well as other public institutions, providing research and drafting support at various stages of law-making" (2020). Vidhi also conducts independent research, including what it describes as taking "a data-driven approach to suggesting reforms that address the problem of judicial delays."

More than thirty professionals working with Vidhi are listed on the center's website. The research director and one of the founders is Arghya Sengupta, a graduate of NLS Bangalore and Oxford, where he was a Rhodes scholar. His D.Phil. at Oxford was on the "Independence and Accountability of the Indian Higher Judiciary." The credentials of the Vidhi group are stellar: it includes members with degrees from the NLSs and US, British, and other graduate programs, who have experience that includes work with corporate law firms.

The group had its beginnings among graduate students at Oxford, who noted the "inadequate legal research" that formed the basis of the government's work on an Indian–US nuclear deal (Int. 19–India). The group that came together included two from Oxford, one from Harvard, and one from Delhi, who believed there was a "gap in the system." The government had high-quality input on economics and policy but not with respect to law. This group acted voluntarily to remedy the problem for the nuclear agreement, and they succeeded in gaining credibility and attention despite their youth (they were only in their early twenties). They decided to build on this work and create a think tank to conduct high-quality legal research. They perceived no problem in government litigation, which in any event was under the control of the bar, but noted that the quality of legal expertise generally needed upgrading.

They used their capital from their study abroad and the prestige of Rhodes Scholarships to seek independent funding. They succeeded in raising money not from the legal profession but from philanthropies, including substantial support from Rohini Nilekani, part of the Infosys community. On this basis, Vidhi was founded in 2013 as the "first legal think tank." It was able to tap into some appetite within India for an upgrade in legal expertise as part of good governance. Vidhi is very careful to avoid "advocacy" or other activities that might taint its members' "expertise" (Int. 19–India). The center has made it clear from the start that it is fully invested in upgrading scholarship. Vidhi also works with other disciplines and other think tanks, with some circulation among such think tanks as the Centre for Policy Research in New Delhi. It also has links to the NLSs and to the Jindal Global Law School. This group belongs self-consciously to a group that is challenging the traditional, conservative world of the bench and bar.

The Jindal Global Law School is the first high-profile private law school in India and also the first to focus specifically on academic scholarship (Kumar 2017). It is the brainchild of Raj Kumar, a representative of the diaspora reinvesting in India. He has degrees from, among other places, Delhi, Oxford (where he went as a Rhodes scholar), Harvard, and the University of Hong Kong. In 2009 he became the founding Vice-Chancellor of the Jindal Global Law School. Kumar was teaching at the University of Hong Kong and was convinced that the NLSs had not succeeded in bringing Indian legal education as far as necessary. In particular, he wanted there to be more emphasis on scholarly research. Drawing on US capital and US institutions for initial support, building also on the success of the private Indian School of Business, he went searching for philanthropy to build a $100 million private law school. He succeeded ultimately with support from the wealth generated through the Jindal steel empire. Still, tuition has had to be set quite high by Indian standards to handle the expenses of this new model for Indian legal education. Tuition is now around US $10,000 per year. The school offers a five-year LL.B/BA, a three-year LL.B., and a one-year LL.M.

Having begun with a law school, Jindal Global University now has a business school, a liberal arts and humanities school, a communications and journalism school, and a school of international affairs. Jindal in this way is seeking to build interdisciplinary connections around law that are missing from the traditional faculties of law and the NLSs. Jindal has numerous relationships with schools abroad, and the faculty includes a number of expatriates. Notably, some one-third of the faculty are graduates of one of the NLSs (Shrivastava 2017). Faculty salaries are relatively high for India, and there are centers focused on research. The teaching loads are not light, and the scholarly output is uneven, but the professors are well-integrated into the global and especially US scholarly worlds.

A third area challenging traditional legal knowledge is found not within the various law schools but rather in the social science departments, especially at the prestigious Jawaharlal Nehru University in New Delhi. There is a Law and Social Sciences Research Network (LASSnet), organized by the Centre for the Study of Law and Governance at JNU, and it has held a number of conferences. It draws on and challenges legal scholarly capital in several ways that complement the challenges from within the law. The key individual organizing this network is Pratiksha Baxi, a sociologist and, not insignificantly, the daughter of Upendra Baxi. This interdisciplinary work offers an option that law graduates may pursue to avoid the narrowness of legal scholarship and the precarity of the law professor position.

This terrain of expertise challenging the conservatism of the elite of the bench and bar is mainly a detour around prevailing hierarchies. It builds on foreign capital—especially from the United Kingdom and the United States—to push beyond the conservatism. This terrain provides some outlet for the hundreds or even thousands of individuals who have received good educations but have been locked out of the deeply conservative and embattled bar elite. These efforts have not touched the elite of the bar in a substantial way to date, but the aging elite of the bar faces a threat that may render their enduring conservatism and bunker mentality obsolete.

The challenge to the traditional bar is not simply about meritocracy versus inherited legal positions. The challengers leading this legal revolution have substantial resources from within current Indian society as well as from abroad. Jindal is funded by a large business, and many students rely on business-generated wealth to attend. It takes resources as well to succeed on the tests for admission to the NLSs and to be able to study abroad after acquiring an NLS degree. Most Indians do not have sufficient knowledge of English to study effectively in that language, but mastery in English is necessary to succeed in an NLS. The think tanks, in particular Vidhi, also connect to major businesses seeking to upgrade the quality of governance in India, including the quality of law. It took connections to that wealth and cosmopolitan capital—Oxford and Harvard degrees—to gain entry to those groups and build Vidhi. These approaches allow law graduates to branch out and to challenge the traditional elite, but they represent a palace war mainly among the relatively advantaged.

The senior advocates in India find themselves embattled. The grand advocates and high court and Supreme Court judges are facing challenges from those who are more attuned to globally ascendant expertise and technologies. But the elite remain able to assert their influence over many of the ostensible challengers within legal education and within the solicitors' firms.[6] The challengers are more meritocratic and less dependent on family capital, and they therefore provide a counter-movement to the traditional closed legal profession of India. But the challengers, as noted, do not represent the graduates of the more than one thousand law schools that now exist in India.

The stratification, which is now based more on resources that translate into meritocratic achievement, is consistent with the US-inspired legal (and educational) revolution. There is a huge gulf between the few who attend the NLSs, Jindal, and the other important private law schools and those who attend the great mass of schools. The training at private schools of law that focus on corporate law careers is quite consistent with US-style globalization. We see the kinds of alliances that we expect for the making of a legal revolution. The challengers are seeking to upgrade and revitalize legal research and scholarship as well as legal argument, so as to modernize the bench and bar as well as discourse about the law. They have found allies in business and philanthropy and among their international contacts. The experience of Vidhi, at least, suggests some openness in governmental circles. But to date the traditional elite, strong on family capital but relatively weak on meritocratic and scholarly capital, still controls the show.

Hong Kong as a Paradigm Case

*An Open Market for Corporate Law Firms
and the Technologies of Legal Education Reform—as
Chinese Hegemony Grows*

Hong Kong's historical status as a colonial entrepôt provides a major contrast to India. While the elite advocates and judges in India have resisted foreign competition and new approaches and technologies, Hong Kong overall has tended to embrace international influences. With the neoliberal revolution and the opening up of China to trade and investment, international lawyers and law firms gained strength quickly in Hong Kong and reshaped the balance of legal power there. It is a striking indication of the value assigned in Hong Kong to international legal capital that roughly half the spots in the training program for admission to practice in Hong Kong are kept open for graduates from outside the Hong Kong law schools (Standing Committee 2018). That group includes people from outside but also the children of Hong Kong elites, who study abroad to gain international credentials, which are still more highly valued than local degrees, despite the existence of three prominent law schools in Hong Kong. As of 2018, there were 9,475 solicitors with a certificate to practice Hong Kong law, working in 898 law firms; 85 of the firms were foreign, and 1,498 foreign lawyers were employed in Hong Kong (19). Eighty-two per cent of the solicitors were identified by the Law Society as ethnic Chinese (19). There are also about 1,300 barristers practicing in Hong Kong. Of these, 99 are Senior Counsel at the top of the bar (19).

Hong Kong thus provides a paradigmatic case of how a relatively open and internationally oriented entrepôt has shifted with the new global hierarchies. Hong Kong decades ago moved from its old colonial position serving the British Empire to a central place in the new global order. Its double position—within China but a separate "system" —has also strengthened China's impact on and/or opposition to US-style legal globalization. With respect in particular to *both* China and the

United States, as shown below, international capital associated with global power has led to influence and success locally in Hong Kong. The recent crackdown on dissent and the restrictive changes to the rules governing elections in Hong Kong, in fact, are consistent with Hong Kong's history of local shifts according to global balances of power.

This chapter begins with a brief review of the colonial history of the legal field in Hong Kong, tracing it from the handoff to China in 1997 to the shift in orientation toward US-style globalization even while China's economy grew increasingly powerful. We trace the transition to Hong Kong's current position in between competing and to some extent complementary powers.

We then turn to how this entrepôt position and openness to the changing world of corporate law has related to changes in legal education. At the time of the handoff, legal education was aligned with the British legacy—that is, with relatively low-status faculties (staffed mainly by expatriates) viewed, as in India, mainly as teachers rather than scholars. There was a hierarchy, with places in the bar and bench at the top, and below these a relatively conservative solicitors' profession fed mainly through profits from conveyancing. Expatriates educated abroad still held many of the top positions in the profession, including in the judiciary and at the top of the bar.

The current situation represents a fascinating story of a shift toward "global" practices in legal education and a greater attention to China. Training for corporate law has increased dramatically. At the same time, there is continuity in the relatively subordinate position of Hong Kong's faculties (which are still staffed mainly by expatriates, now in a different mix) and locally produced lawyers.

HONG KONG BEFORE AND AFTER THE HAND-OFF TO CHINA

The period in Hong Kong prior to US-style globalization and the 1997 handoff to China was characterized by a very small solicitors' branch and an even smaller bar. There were only a hundred members of the bar in 1970 (Int. 1–Hong Kong; Hsu 2020). Until 1968, legal education for admission to the bar required a sojourn in the United Kingdom to study for the bar, which only the privileged could afford (Int. 2–Hong Kong). Until 1986, those who qualified in Commonwealth countries were entitled to practice in Hong Kong solely on that basis (Hsu 2020). Expatriates took advantage of this openness, and British expatriates dominated the practice until the 1970s. It was possible for locals to qualify by taking the examinations of the Law Society of England and Wales in Hong Kong (Standing Committee 2018), but the numbers were small. The languages of practice were Cantonese and English, and lawyers could make careers practicing in English.

When legal education came to Hong Kong in 1968 and opened up legal careers to locals without the means to go to London, Hong Kong University (HKU) gained a quasi-monopoly in the local production of the profession. Today there are two additional faculties of law, at the City University of Hong Kong and the Chinese University of Hong Kong. They now compete for students and faculty, but as noted later, they all follow the same general approach.

As in India, there was a certain complacency in both branches of the small Hong Kong legal profession. Until the 1980s, the bar engaged mainly in criminal defense litigation, while the solicitors prospered through the profits from convey-ancing. The bar adapted to the rise of commercial litigation and arbitration, which brought more prosperity to the bar, and the booming Hong Kong real estate mar-ket continued to serve the solicitors well. Complacency was seen especially in the local attitude toward China. The local lawyers were not looking to the growth of the Chinese economy. Local Hong Kong lawyers looked down on clientele from mainland China, who were seen as "farmers and peasants" (Dezalay and Garth 1996; Int. 15–Hong Kong). The supply of lawyers was under control except, as noted above, for the ongoing openness to individuals qualified in Britain and its colonies—and later to global law firms seeking to take advantage of expanding international trade and investment (Hsu 2020). Hong Kong's peripheral position within the British Empire meant also that very important cases often brought Brit-ish QCs at the apex of the colonial legal order to argue in the Hong Kong courts (Dezalay and Garth 1996). Interestingly, according to Hsu, Hong Kong barristers worried less about foreign competition than about lobbying the British for the right to appear in British courts (Hsu 2020). They measured their own success in terms of success at the British core.

The solicitors' branch, represented by the Law Society, did not initially welcome the foreign law firms that, under pressure from the United States, the Hong Kong government allowed to enter in the late 1980s. According to Hsu, "the Hong Kong Law Society was strongly opposed: in an extraordinary meeting 97 per cent of members voted against this policy" (810). Yet in the context of Hong Kong, the result was not a policy of exclusion. Under rules that went into effect in 1994, firms could enter the market under certain conditions, and "after practising in Hong Kong for three years, foreign lawyers can be qualified as Hong Kong lawyers" (810). In 1995, "135 foreign lawyers from 12 jurisdictions sat for the first Overseas Lawyers Qualification Examination" (810). More than 1,800 lawyers have success-fully completed this examination over the past twenty years (Standing Committee 2018), and many others practice foreign law without a Hong Kong qualification.

Because of the relative openness of the Hong Kong legal market, coupled with the relatively free market for foreign trade and investment, Hong Kong makes evident the changes taking place in one way or another globally. The expanded business that came with economic globalization in the 1990s brought new oppor-tunities, especially involving trade and investment in China, that precipitated a shift in the orientation of the legal field in Hong Kong. Both sides of the profession in Hong Kong shifted toward the new players in the global economy, but they also had to compete with law firms and lawyers from abroad who could gain access to the Hong Kong legal market. Also, the firms from abroad were much more open than the Hong Kong local firms when it came to building a clientele within China.

The number of foreign lawyers increased and kept doing so until today it exceeds 1,500 (Hsu 2020). Hong Kong remains on the periphery in many respects, but the focus of Hong Kong has shifted away from the British center toward the United States and, increasingly, China. The pull of both powers is evident. In fact, according to Hsu, "Chinese lawyers . . . grew rapidly from 7 per cent in the late 1990s to 15 per cent in 2016, and the trend is continuing" (811). Hong Kong thus occupies a kind of in-between position that reflects both the joint interests of and some antagonism between Chinese, US, and other global approaches.

The new opportunities attracted a changing mix of legal skills, which now include knowledge of the civil law (for interpreting Chinese codes), of British and US commercial law (for global trade), of Mandarin (as the language of the mainland), of English (as the lingua franca of globalization in law and commerce), and of the United States and China (as the dominant imperial powers shaping the rules for the governance of the state and the economy). Financialization and the growing presence of investment banks and large corporate law firms were part of the transformation. The transformation has worked well for the bar, which participates in large-scale commercial litigation and in international commercial arbitration. It has worked less well for Hong Kong solicitors.

Hong Kong is now home to international law firms brokering trade between China and the rest of the world. It is also home to law firms from China playing the same role. Almost all international corporate law firms with strong Asian interests have a Hong Kong branch, and these lawyers bring with them the cutting-edge approaches at play in global commerce. Hong Kong also is a very prominent center for international commercial arbitration, again largely involving disputes between China and the rest of the world. The arbitrators include many of the world's most prominent, and prominent arbitrators who began in Hong Kong are now recognized and used more generally (e.g., Int. 4–Hong Kong). Hong Kong as an entrepôt—both legal and financial—continues to thrive, despite the political turmoil that has pitted locals against the Chinese government as it oversees Hong Kong.

The political turmoil in Hong Kong relates also to the traditional bar. Until the handover, the bar, as noted earlier, was not involved in politics. It was small, prosperous, and not threatened until the Chinese began to set the terms for the handover. An activist group emerged at that time, when a number of barristers not necessarily historically active in politics—including, most famously, the now arrested Martin Lee—took strong public stances in favor of Hong Kong autonomy, especially its legal autonomy. This group remains quite important and has found strong support among the Hong Kong public. The solicitors through the Law Society are not vocal, since outspokenness directly affects their legal practices (which is not the case with the bar). But when the solicitors vote secretly, they have supported the bar (Int. 2–Hong Kong; Lee 2017; Hsu 2020).

The Civic Party, established in 2006, has been a key player in these debates. It is in fact often called the Barristers' Party, for it includes leading barristers such as Audrey Eu, Margaret Ng, Elvin Kwock, and Allan Leung. This portion of the bar was active, for example, in the Occupy Central and Umbrella demonstrations that began in 2014—the clash between the so-called yellow ribbons of democracy and the blue ribbons of the Hong Kong establishment. The pro-democracy demonstrations and other activities gained adherents in the law schools, especially at HKU, where much of the bar attended law school. In several law schools, including HKU, classes were recorded to allow students to participate in the Occupy demonstration, for example.

Professor Benny Tai, considered the key organizer of the Occupy demonstrations, taught at HKU until he was fired for that activism in the summer of 2020. The dean prior to Michael Hors, who came from the National University of Singapore, was Johannes Chan, who is also associated with the democracy movement. Others, including the current dean and another former dean, Albert Chen, have taken a much more moderate stance toward China and issues such as elections. HKU's supportive relationship with the demonstrators had its costs. It also led to some retaliation against Johannes Chan, even though he had not participated directly. The Chief Executive of Hong Kong, Leung Chun-ying, who is the Chancellor of HKU (as a continuation of the colonial policy whereby the governor served formally as Chancellor of every university), reportedly retaliated largely because Benny Tai was a student of Johannes Chan. The result was that Chan was rejected after being recommended for a position as a pro-Vice-Chancellor of HKU (Int. 5–Hong Kong). The situation was highly controversial and led to more demonstrations and public outcry (Cheng 2015).

The bar is divided politically. One part of the bar has embraced China and the leadership role of the Chinese Communist Party. The larger group, however, identifies strongly with the democracy movement and the relative independence of Hong Kong and its courts from China (Lee 2017). The bar's pro-democracy activities do not significantly affect its members' prestige as advocates, but there are other impacts that interviewees noted (Int. 2–Hong Kong). Political alignment affects matters such as promotion to judge (or even temporary judge), appointment to governance committees, and even membership in the prestigious Jockey Club. The activist group has lost access to some of the traditional perks and prestige positions of the Hong Kong legal establishment.

The in-between position of Hong Kong has encountered some tension as a result of these developments. Most notably in recent years, the prosecution of police who beat an Occupy sympathizer—caught on video—who had poured water on a police officer generated considerable controversy. An expatriate judge sentenced the police officers to two years in prison, setting off a campaign among many (who

generated "vicious" Facebook traffic) to question these "white" judges and call for
their monitoring (Wong 2017; Leung and Cheung 2017). Chinese delegates at a key
national parliamentary meeting in China, for example, questioned the role and
judicial neutrality of expatriate judges (Huang 2017).

Chinese law professors also weighed in: "Beijing University law professor Rao
Geping urged a ratio be set to ensure more ethnic Chinese judges. 'Hong Kong
is not short of local talents,' he said" (E. Lee 2017: 3). Local professors responded.
"Simon Young Ngai-man, a professor at the University of Hong Kong's law faculty,
said the expatriate Court of Final Appeal judges included some of the most senior
and experienced judges in the common law world (4). "Their valuable insights
could enhance the Hong Kong courts," he said (4). He said law would become stag-
nant if all judges shared the same background or gender: "HK is still very much
an international city" (4). The numbers are not clear, but according to the Justice
Department in Hong Kong, "although the judiciary could not provide statistics
on the nationalities of the city's 157 full-time judges and judicial officers, it stressed
that 89 per cent of them were bilingual—English and Chinese. Only 6 per cent, or
about 10 by a *Post* calculation, are monolingual" (5).

One of the proposals offered by Chinese professors was to restrict the expatriate
judiciary, as in Singapore, to commercial cases. Interestingly, the debate did not
question the role of the English language in the high courts and in the teaching of
law in Hong Kong (3). And as noted, it did not question the propriety of expatriate judges trying commercial cases. Hong Kong remains in a delicate balance as
broker between different powers that converge with respect to commercial matters
but may diverge with respect to politics. The current demonstrations that began
over a new law on extradition to China have only heightened these tensions, now
further exacerbated by arrests and changes in the rules for eligibility for elections.
The leaders of the bar have gained a remarkable prominence in protecting the
courts and local governance. They have embraced the US and global legal revolution of the late twentieth century, and they are strongly resisting the increased role
China is asserting in Hong Kong law.

The *American Lawyer* noted that there is concern about the clashes in Hong
Kong but that global law firms cannot realistically leave: "As challenging as it is,
global firms can't stay away from the Hong Kong legal market. Of the 100 highest-
grossing law firms in 2017, 63 operated a Hong Kong office, and 44 of the top 50 are
in Hong Kong. Similarly, 48 of this year's Am Law 100 are in Hong Kong, mostly
concentrated in the top 50 (39 out of 50). Moreover, 25 of the 45 top-grossing Chinese firms are also in Hong Kong. Most of these firms focus on China-related work
in Hong Kong, and it's unlikely they will leave anytime soon" (Zhang 2019: 2). The
role Hong Kong plays for China makes it likely that, despite the increased political
pressure from China on the politics of Hong Kong, Hong Kong's unique economic
role is not likely to change.

The retooling of Hong Kong and its relations with competing powers can be
seen also in the institutions of legal education. Issues about legal education reform

in Hong Kong squarely reflect the pressures associated with the transformation now taking place. Reforms in legal education are inscribed with the British legacy but clearly show the mark of the emerging new global order of the United States and increasingly China. The impact of the that new order on the faculties of law and on the style of teaching and research is quite evident. We see both the impact of the legal revolution emanating from the United States and the growing influence of China.

LEGAL EDUCATION IN HONG KONG

Hong Kong's recent revamping of legal education began in 2001–2. It drew on the work of two Australian consultants, Professor Paul Redmond, Dean of the Faculty of Law at the University of New South Wales, and Christopher Roper, formerly Director of the Centre for Legal Education. Their focus was on how to keep Hong Kong's local graduates competitive in the global legal services market (Steering Committee 2002). The consultants noted: "The situation appears to be that the large commercial law firms are relying to a significant extent on law graduates trained in overseas law schools or they are recruiting qualified lawyers from overseas jurisdictions. Although there are no centrally available data, it appears that the large firms, whilst they seek to recruit those with the very best results from Hong Kong's law schools, rely heavily on those trained outside Hong Kong" (70). They noted "a perception that Hong Kong's law schools are not producing, or not producing enough, lawyers trained to a level that equips them for employment and practice across the full range of professional activity in Hong Kong" (70).

The review directly confronted the question of what should be done to train Hong Kong lawyers to facilitate legal services suited for US-style globalization and the increase in the importance of corporate law firms. Results of the reform agenda that emerged included the addition of one year of study, from three to four years, for the undergraduate LL.B. and a stronger emphasis on English-language proficiency (Jones 2009: 112). In addition, "all the law schools introduced some degree of United States-style credentials (such as JD programs), United States-style teaching methods, and United States-style law and business courses" (111). These reforms highlighted what the reviewers and the Hong Kong reform committee thought essential to produce lawyers able to compete for positions in corporate law firms.

The law schools in Hong Kong are not very different from one another in terms of programs and the students they serve, but they have a kind of division of labor in relation to the interests that shape Hong Kong. Hong Kong University is the oldest, the most British in orientation, and also the most focused on constitutional law and local issues around Hong Kong's relative independence from China (Int. 6–Hong Kong). As noted earlier, it is the faculty of law historically most strongly identified with Hong Kong and with the pro-democracy movement. The other schools—City University and Chinese University—stake out orientations more toward the contending powers, China and the United States. Again, however, they are all much more similar than different in their responses to the global influences pervading Hong Kong.

Since HKU's law school is relatively old, it has gained a stronger reputation locally and globally. It is also the most resistant to the changes arising with the new era of globalization and Chinese dominance of Hong Kong. Its graduates make up a large percentage of the bar, and indeed the bar is the first choice for graduates; by contrast, the other schools are oriented more toward the corporate law firms (Int. 6–Hong Kong). The LL.B. is the main degree sought by HKU graduates; the JD has become more important in the other two schools in response to recent reform pressures.

The research orientation at HKU is more traditionally British, and its hiring criteria fit the British system. HKU, for example, has long required that all professors have at least two *law* degrees, which excludes top scholars with a law degree and a PhD in the social sciences, as well as most US law professors, who have only the JD. The focus of hiring is on British-trained law graduates or individuals with existing ties to HKU. Still, HKU has hired expatriates from many jurisdictions besides the UK. It has more than sixty full-time academic staff, comprised of professors from the UK, Australia, Canada, Hong Kong, the United States, and China. Traditional HKU professors, we were told, see no reason to change the curriculum in relation to the changing context, preferring to stick with the traditional curriculum dictated by the Law Society (Int. 7–Hong Kong).

City University, the second law school established in Hong Kong, has historically been more open than HKU to middle-class students, and it has recently moved more to emphasize Chinese law. It boasts some thirteen Chinese law professors, reportedly the largest group of Chinese law professors outside of China. The research emphasis at City University is relatively recent (Jones 2009). There is considerable overlap with HKU, given that all universities are responding to the same changes. For example, one City U professor described the faculty as relatively "transient" and still mostly connected to the UK, despite the orientation to China (Int. 8–Hong Kong). And HKU itself has ten full-time Chinese faculty and emphasizes its strength in Chinese law.

Chinese University, the newest of the three law schools, having been founded in 2006, nods toward the emerging context, with a focus on globalization and especially global trade and economic law (Int. 9–Hong Kong). It is the most foreign-oriented of the three schools, and according to a professor at one of the other Hong Kong schools, it has done the best recent hiring in terms of research (Int. 7–Hong Kong). Its research is also more highly rated than that of the other faculties of law by the government-mandated Research Assessment exercise.

All three law schools compete for faculty with other globalized law schools that have similar orientations—in Australia and Singapore in particular. None of the three in Hong Kong have many locally trained faculty. Expatriates dominate the numbers, reflecting the continuing lack of local prestige for law professors and the relatively peripheral role of Hong Kong faculties that has continued through colonial to postcolonial relationships. Notwithstanding the recent emphasis on research, the historical model of law professor in the UK appears quite salient. While this is changing, the focus is still largely on the lower-status role of teacher rather than scholar.

The general reliance on expatriates as law professors has raised recruiting challenges. In particular, it is difficult to attract women and mid-career professors to Hong Kong—in contrast to very senior and very junior faculty. Starting pay for assistant professors is comparable to starting pay at US law schools (except for the elite US law schools). Assistant professors at one school reportedly made about HK $76,000 per month plus $11,000 as a housing allowance—about US $130,000 in total (Int. 10–Hong Kong). But it is very expensive to live in Hong Kong.

The approach of the law schools, with the relative division of labor, is a new version of the strategy of the past. They import expertise by hiring expatriates who cannot find places in their own countries for their cosmopolitan investments. Those expatriates include, for example, a number of Scottish academics facing limited places in Scotland, as well as others seeking adventure in Hong Kong or who do not fit into their domestic academic markets. The academics in Hong Kong are oriented toward scholarly markets outside of Hong Kong, as before, except the orientation is no longer solely toward Britain. They respond to the new scholarly hierarchies. As evident from the description so far, the situation is quite unlike what was seen in India, where strong barriers remain to the revamping of the legal market to align with the new global order. The relatively free market of Hong Kong has been able to make changes in the traditional colonial model without major difficulties.

The number of law students in Hong Kong remains small, and the number admitted into practice from that group is smaller still. The number of applications nevertheless remains very high, with law second only to medicine in terms of demand for places (Int. 11– Hong Kong). Control of local enrollment remains strong. The size of each LL.B. program is set by the universities, and those sizes range from HKU, which produces about 250 LL.B. graduates (most combined with non-law degrees), to City U and Chinese U, which range from 50 to 100 LL.B.s. HKU keeps its two-year JD program small, limited to 40, with City U at 115 and Chinese U at 200. All of the programs also offer LL.M.s. The move from LL.B.s to JDs has increased costs, which range from about HK $40,000 (about US $5,000) per annum for the LL.B. to over HK $300,000 (about US $38,000) per annum for the JD.

All graduates who wish to be admitted to practice in Hong Kong must go through the Postgraduate Certificate in Laws (PCLL) program that each law school runs (costing about US $10,000, though 100 students receive subsidies). In total, HKU graduates about 290 students seeking admission to practice; City

University about 150; and Chinese University about 280. The numbers have grown but not substantially.

The local law school total is therefore about 720 graduates annually. They compete for only about half that number of available slots in the PCLL programs of the three schools combined. As discussed below, roughly half of the PCLL slots are kept open for graduates from outside the three Hong Kong schools, although it appears that the number has gone down somewhat in recent years. In total, there are about 1,300 applicants for the 700 open slots. The overall supply remains controlled through numerical limits—in stark contrast to India, for example. Despite this control over supply, the power of local legal elites is much weaker than in India and in our other case studies. The focus of the reforms in 2001–2 on elevating the interest of Hong Kong corporate law firms in the graduates of the local law schools has not had much success.

CONTROL OF THE SUPPLY OF LAWYERS

There is some controversy today about what the number of new lawyers should be and who should determine it. First, there is the question of how many students from mainland China should attend the Hong Kong law schools and practice law in Hong Kong. According to one law school administrator, there was a perception at one time that one or more of the Hong Kong law schools was "lining its pocket with self-finance fees" of mainland Chinese, especially in the JD programs (Int. 9–Hong Kong). The more general problem was the sheer number of high-quality Chinese who might qualify for admission to the Hong Kong law schools, which could make it much more challenging for locals to gain places in law schools and in practice. As a result, the Hong Kong law schools now strictly control the number of Chinese admitted. HKU, for example, takes only five to seven undergraduate Chinese from some 11,000 applicants to the LL.B. program. Chinese University similarly limits the number of mainland Chinese undergraduates to at most 10 percent, and the number of JDs to about 15 percent. The LL.M. enrollments, by contrast, are as high as 60 percent Chinese, but these programs do not qualify for admission into the Hong Kong profession.

More controversial within Hong Kong is the control of the numbers admitted into the PCCL and accordingly to local practice. Since the time of the review of legal education in 2001–2, the Law Society has expressed concern about who controls that number. Since then, the number admitted into the PCCL has been determined through a committee representing the judiciary, the law schools, and the practicing profession. There is substantial tension, however, between the Law Society and the academy over this process. The President of the Law Society in 2012, in particular, sought to establish a common bar examination to be administered after the PCCL, and this issue links once again to the question of who controls the number of students able to enter practice.

The Law Society is dominated by the 70 percent of solicitors who practice in firms of fewer than five lawyers. They have not prospered in recent years, and their plight has led them to try to gain more control over the market, which includes seeking to expand their own potential market through rights of audience in the courts, which so far have not been extended. The boom in conveyancing ended in the 1990s, and these firms have not participated greatly in the expanding international business. Their language is Cantonese, whereas Chinese transactions require Mandarin, and as noted earlier, they did not move quickly to embrace Chinese clients in any event. Shrinking the numbers would appeal to many of these solicitors. Others, however, are unhappy for different reasons, including the difficulty of getting their children admitted into the PCCL. Some want rule changes that may make it easier for those who have job offers (which favors family ties) to gain entry into practice (Int. 12–Hong Kong). But the power of the Law Society and its agenda in internationalized Hong Kong is limited.

In 2013, the Standing Committee on Legal Education and Training set out to study these issues. The Law Society highlighted the problems of its membership in a statement to the consultants: "The increase of overseas lawyers and law firms, and those qualified through the OLQE [Overseas Lawyers Qualifying Exam] may fill the gap in legal services for specialized areas . . . but they also intensify the competition for work, and for the smaller local practices whose businesses and income may be more volatile to socio-economic changes, they may be put at a particularly disadvantageous position as they will inevitably be measured against their international counterparts in terms of experience, talent, network of offices, skills, specialization" (Standing Committee 2018).

The consultants initially were Woo Kwok-Hing, QC (Chair), formerly Vice-President of the Court of Appeal of the High Court; Tony Smith, Professor of Law at the Victoria University of Wellington, New Zealand, and a former Chair of the Faculty of Law at the University of Cambridge; and Julian Webb, Professor of Law and Director of the Legal Professions Research Network at the University of Melbourne, Australia. Following Woo's resignation in October 2016, the chair became Anthony Rogers, QC, Chair of the Clearing and Settlement Systems Appeals Tribunal, Hong Kong, and former Vice-President of the Court of Appeal. The group produced a lengthy final report in 2018 (Standing Committee 2018), which assessed the entire system of legal admission and admission into practice and came out against the Law Society's effort to impose an examination for all law graduates. In this respect, this international report sided with the law schools. The law schools noted that they were already upholding standards, with "no complaint on quality" about the graduates of the PCCL (Int. 5–Hong Kong).

The report was critical, however, of the quality of education in global terms: "It is not clear to us that Hong Kong is showing the same appetite for innovation that has been apparent in the US and, to a lesser extent, Australia. The relative lack of competitiveness in the domestic market may account for some of that difference (though that also brings advantages). . . . If the Hong Kong law schools are to maintain relevance and competitiveness in the global market, more needs to be done, not just to bring the academic curriculum and learning design into a '2020 vision' but to prepare the way for the law school of 2050" (Standing Committee 2018). The report then went into a lengthy discussion of the importance of the US-promoted idea of "outcome measures" to evaluate legal education.

INTERNATIONAL STRATEGIES AS LOCAL CAREER OPTIONS

The strategy of entrepôt brokering trade and relationships between China and the rest of the world continues, supported by Beijing and critical constituencies in Hong Kong, despite political controversy. The comprador role of double agency remains quite prominent. The law schools in Hong Kong have bent toward China with new programs and centers, a much larger group of professors from China, more students from China, more offerings of common law instruction for Chinese, and programs to promote more proficiency in Mandarin. But they also continue to teach in English, require proficiency in English for admission, and encourage non-Chinese expatriates not only to teach but also to serve as judges.

The expatriate professors also obviously connect to China, the West, and international and transnational law. They may use their Hong Kong experience to build their international capital and bolster their careers outside of Hong Kong. The subordinate position of Hong Kong in these relationships is apparent in the pull toward the West and China. Hong Kong has embraced the new legal order and its relationships with China, but complex relationships of core and periphery have long been associated with its peripheral entrepôt status.

One strategy, for example, has been to invest more in Chinese capital to make a career in and around Hong Kong and its issues. Another is to use Hong Kong expertise to make a career through China. The examples of professors and lawyers supporting the pro-China business establishment are obvious. But there are also more striking examples in legal education that potentially leave Hong Kong's local institutions in a relatively marginal position.

An early example after the handoff is Betty Ho, a professor at the University of Hong Kong in the 1990s who trained at the University of Toronto. She died in 2010 and was celebrated in a memorial issue of the *Tsinghua China Law Review* (Alford et al. 2010). She taught at Tsinghua from 2002 until her death. Prior to that she had practiced law in Hong Kong. She was also an active "Hong Kong animal" seeking to protect law, democracy, and the rule of law in Hong Kong around the time of the handover (Dezalay and Garth 1996: 266–67). Despite her prominence in Hong Kong, she left in 2002, "as she believed that she could make a greater impact by teaching the future leaders of China" in Tsinghua (as noted by J. Chan 2010: 6). She also later obtained a tenured position at the University of Toronto, and she continued to teach at both places. According to the then-Dean of the Tsinghua

University School of Law, Zhenmin Wang (2010), she played a role in China as a broker between the common law and China:

> Her last public speech at Tsinghua was: "Save the Country by Commercial Law." She told students, "the purpose to study the law is not for yourself, but to serve your country and your people." That's exactly what she had been doing. She once told Hong Kong friends that her research, her scholarship is for China. She translated all her books into Chinese and published in China, so that more Chinese people could afford to buy and read the books. In early 1990s, upon invitation from the Chinese government and the then Vice Premier Zhu Rongji, Betty helped China draft the legal framework and policies on listing Chinese State companies at Hong Kong stock market. She made fundamental contributions to the rule of law development in China. (14)

For Betty Ho, despite her activism in Hong Kong, the main event was in China, and she used the latter part of her career to invest in the globalization of the Tsinghua School of Law.

The strategy of investment in China is also evident elsewhere in Hong Kong. Hong Kong, as noted, is a prominent center for international commercial arbitration, and the Hong Kong law schools offer programs in arbitration and dispute resolution. Yet one arbitration specialist noted that the academic centers within Hong Kong do not really link to the core of the international commercial arbitration world. The teaching at HKU, for example, does not involve arbitration "big shots connected to business," but instead emphasizes mediation (Int. 13–Hong Kong). The same interviewee noted that perhaps the leading Hong Kong arbitrator, Teresa Chang, a Vice-President of the ICC Court of International Arbitration in Paris, is a recurring visiting Professor at the Law School of Tsinghua University. There she is the co-director of Tsinghua's Master of Law Program (LL.M. Program) in International Arbitration and Dispute Settlement (Tsinghua University School of Law 2020). Tsingua's relative openness to the outside, including Hong Kong, has facilitated this international strategy of orientation to China.

The opportunity to go around Hong Kong and its law schools for success in Hong Kong is evident in other ways. As noted earlier, half of the PCLL positions go to those who study outside the three Hong Kong law schools. In addition, many of those who attend the Hong Kong law schools are ethnic Hong Kong Chinese who went to high school outside Hong Kong. They reportedly have the opportunity to take a different entrance examination, which is not as competitive as the one for Hong Kong high school graduates.

As noted, many of the sons and daughters of well-to-do Hong Kong residents go abroad for their law degrees. One professor noted, for example, that after the academic year starts in Hong Kong, a number of students leave when they gain acceptance to a British program. With respect to the PCLL, one administrator notes the "traffic" abroad that comes to practice here (Int. 9–Hong Kong), and others note that the international law firms also bring in applicants from abroad for the PCLL, further diminishing the role of the Hong Kong law schools. External educational capital identified with the core of the currently internationalized legal field remains valued in Hong Kong, just as it was under the British Empire.

A recent article on law student mobility by Swethaa Ballakrishnen and Carole Silver highlights a revealing interview with a Hong Kong student with a Hong Kong undergraduate degree in psychology and politics:

> And at that time I was thinking, do I want to stay in Hong Kong for a legal educa-
> tion [with] a ton . . . of other people? So a lot of my friends, they attend LL.B. in
> Hong Kong, so they already have their law degree and their undergraduate study.
> And Hong Kong also provided JD programs as well, but I was thinking, you know,
> I received my undergrad location in kind of the best university in Hong Kong and I
> know how this education is like. And also if I receive a JD degree in the States I can
> always go back to Hong Kong if I want, because they really welcome to American JD.
> So, and if I'm lucky enough, I can stay in the US. So going to, to pursuing a JD degree
> in the US gives me more choices, and also I think that US has the best legal education
> so that's why I want to come here. (Silver and Ballakrishnen 2018: 62)

The student recognized the value of the US JD within Hong Kong and as a way to maximize options. The student had internalized the location of Hong Kong and its law schools on the periphery of the legal world.

Hiring is intensely competitive in Hong Kong, producing an "oversupply" of graduates seeking positions in the international law firms. Hong Kong law school graduates are not necessarily favored in the competition to gain entry into the international law firms in Hong Kong. One long-time partner in international firms in Hong Kong noted the inclination to look outside, to seek candidates with a broader knowledge than what those who studied law "to please mom and dad" possessed (Int. 14–Hong Kong). She further noted that the "best associates are not from here." The large firms typically seek graduates from Oxford and Cambridge and other leading British faculties of law, which often means individuals originally from Hong Kong who go abroad. The Hong Kong natives who study at the London School of Economics, from this perspective, "read better" in the words of a leading partner in an international law firm. In addition, the US firms reportedly do not do traineeships, so they wait within Hong Kong until year two or three of a young career before "poaching" associates (Int. 14–Hong Kong).

Many interviewees mentioned the issue of language. As noted earlier, with a few exceptions, the local firms, especially those practicing mainly in Cantonese, have not prospered in recent decades. And the attitude that the Chinese are "peas-ants and farmers" continues to linger (Int. 15–Hong Kong), even though the tide has turned in terms of economic power and Chinese firms have built alliances with Hong Kong firms (Liu and Au 2020). The linguistic requirements for the interna-tional firms are Mandarin and English, and as noted, "cultural competence" with the mainland Chinese is relevant. International firms especially recruit those who speak native Mandarin and have studied overseas.

Administrators noted that among the local graduates with JDs, which seems to be the preferred degree for the large firms, the preference is for individuals from the mainland with a Chinese undergraduate degree provided that the individual speaks good English (Int. 12–Hong Kong). Such an individual may use admission into Hong Kong as a way to gain a foothold in the international firm—perhaps at some point seeking to transfer to the Shanghai or Beijing office. The next preferred group is ABC or BBC (American- or British-born Chinese) who come to Hong Kong after education elsewhere. And the lowest preference is for Hong Kong "local–local" undergraduates and JDs. There are also Chinese law firms in Hong Kong who can now hire from China or Hong Kong (Liu and Au 2020). Finally, international law firms hire individuals who only work in English but have desired specialties, such as intellectual property.

As a result, the part of the corporate law firm market controlled by the Hong Kong "production of producers" is small. The Hong Kong global and Chinese-oriented corporate market has grown substantially, but the means for market control are not through the Hong Kong faculties of law, which have very limited enrollments, or through the professional training programs. Those trained closer to the core of the global hierarchy, which for those coming from Hong Kong requires considerable family resources and scarce linguistic skills, have advantages in securing coveted positions in Hong Kong. Cantonese-speaking, public school-educated (not likely to be in English), and locally trained individuals without the resources to travel and study abroad—or perhaps even to pay the fees for the JD—lack realistic opportunities to join the global law firms. And those trained abroad can come and compete in Hong Kong. Locals lacking family capital and linguistic expertise also have little chance to compete at the bar. Those most embedded in Hong Kong are therefore limited as to what practice settings they can aspire to.

INTERNATIONALIZED SCHOLARLY PRODUCTION

The position of the Hong Kong law schools in the production of expertise is similarly limited. Seeking to gain credibility in a global market in which their rankings matter as a means to attract foreign students to Hong Kong schools of law, new deans come in with a mandate to have a "stronger focus on research" and to "differentiate" themselves in the market (Int. 6–Hong Kong; Int. 12–Hong Kong). There is a mission now to "get more quality research out."

The collective efforts of these academies of relatively marginal professors on the periphery serve to promote the quality and importance of legal knowledge in the relationships involving China and Hong Kong and international businesses. But there are very few Hong Kong locals teaching in the law schools. The law schools do not attract (or perhaps do not promote) local recruitment into the academy. The challenge of promoting research is compounded by the fact that law professors in Hong Kong, despite the increased focus on research, remain more like British or Indian "teachers" than US "law professors." The expatriate professors serve as brokers of imported expertise, but the mainly young professors are uncertain what kinds of research and what kinds of publications and journals are best for their careers. The Hong Kong academy remains in a subordinate position between China and the academic capitals of the West.

CONCLUSION

Hong Kong presents a very different picture than India. It is not for the most part a matter of an old guard resisting the importation of new approaches linked to international law firms, financialization, and US-style globalization. The Chinese and international orientation of Hong Kong serves and reflects its position as a relatively open entrepôt. It is open to new balances of power and to scholarly learning that relates to that balance. In many respects, therefore, despite current turmoil, it is thriving as one of the major global cities in the world economy, and the services sector, including law, is part of that prosperity.

This globalization in Hong Kong also dramatizes a phenomenon seen in India, albeit less clearly. Because of the factors that have made Hong Kong a success in brokering relationships, elite careers in Hong Kong are disproportionately available to those able to bring valued foreign capital into Hong Kong, be it familial, linguistic, or cultural. "Chinese-Chinese" law graduates and those educated in Britain or elsewhere have substantial advantages in the peripheral Hong Kong market.

Furthermore, for both the Hong Kong–educated population and those educated abroad, the question of financial resources is much more important than in the past—reminiscent of the time when only education in Britain qualified one for practice. The costs of a legal education are one thing, the costs of getting a primary and secondary education that leads to fluency in English, much less Mandarin, are another, and the kind of travel abroad that leads to cultural competence in those external worlds represents a third way in which access to the top positions in Hong Kong is highly stratified—realistically available only to a very small percentage of potential and actual law graduates.

Finally, the position of Hong Kong as a relatively open entrepôt opens it up to participate in profitable global markets and global exchanges, and also to participate in hierarchical relationships of core and periphery. Scholarly agendas, faculty recruitment, and career strategies all are embedded deeply in the competing and complementary relations with China on one side and the US-style global core on the other. Unlike India, Hong Kong has in effect embraced the new legal revolution, but the beneficiaries are not necessarily the graduates of the Hong Kong law faculties.

South Korea and Japan

*Contrasting Attacks through Legal Education Reform
on the Traditional Conservative and Insular Bar*

India and Hong Kong are both former British colonies in which Britain made substantial legal system investments; yet they are also strikingly different from each other. Japan and South Korea, by contrast, look very similar in structure and approach as a result of Japan's colonial relationship with Korea from 1905 until the end of the Second World War. That relationship strongly marked South Korea's legal system and legal profession (and we find a similar story in Taiwan, also a former Japanese colony). Korean professors studied in Japan and taught with Japanese-language textbooks. The faculties of law and the legal profession were replicas of what existed in Japan after the Meiji Restoration. Legal scholarship was very much in the German tradition as replicated by the Japanese. The similarities make especially stark the differences in how each country has enacted and accommodated the recent legal revolution inspired by the United States. Both, to be sure, have absorbed much of that revolution, including a magic circle of corporate law firms, but in South Korea the very powerful Judicial Research and Training Institute (JRTI)—the fount of professional unity and conservatism—was ultimately dismantled through the reform of legal education.

HISTORICAL LEGACIES AND POSTWAR LAW
AND DEVELOPMENT EFFORTS

Historical accounts of lawyers in Japan usually begin with the Meiji Restoration in 1868, although Flaherty (2013) in particular points to important antecedents that made litigation a prominent social phenomenon much earlier in Japanese history. The explicit borrowing of Western institutions, including lawyers and judges as such, however, began in the Meiji period (Feeley and Miyazawa 2007). And as

Feeley and Miyazaya noted, that borrowing was consistent with the interests of those holding state power: "When Western-style law and legal training were introduced, they were imposed for purposes of state. Western-style law was adopted to head-off Western imperialism, and law schools were established to train government officials" (2007: 153). Hattori's history of the legal profession in Japan (1963) notes the predominance of training for government officials and relates it to the history of Japan prior to the Meiji Restoration. Law was to be in the service of state power.

Hattori also suggests that samurai rivalries in pre-Meiji times are also an important part of the story of subsequent developments. According to Hattori, "those who played leading roles in the Meiji Restoration were principally samurai of two of the major feudal fiefs, Satsuma and Choshu" (1963: 113). They understandably gravitated toward the executive branch and the military arm of the new government, "believing as they did that leadership in the executive and the military meant assumption of hegemony over the government as a whole" (113). In contrast, according to Hattori, "those who came from smaller and less powerful fiefs tended to enter the judiciary or take up other occupations within the administration" (113). His conclusion was that "movements for independence and strengthening of judicial power can be considered a reflection of opposition by the small clans to Satsuma and Choshu domination" (113). This historically weaker social position of those who went into the judiciary or private legal practice helps account for the sense of insecurity and embattlement that remains present within the judiciary and the practicing bar.

As it played out in the early years, according to Feeley and Miyazawa, the hierarchy kept those in the lower positions in check: "Ministry officials were quick to apply their influence on the judges" (2007: 162). The bar made arguments for more autonomy, insisting "that judges should be selected from among practicing lawyers and be wholly independent of the justice ministry" (162). Judges self-consciously pursued autonomy and independence (162), but they could not escape their subordinate position. They were careful to show deference to the state and to distance themselves from private practitioners.

Private practitioners faced a similar uphill battle and were looked down on by state officials. The first bar examination committees were "composed of judges, procurators, and some officials of the Ministry of Justice, but no lawyers" (128), reflecting the low status of lawyers. When some of the early law graduates gravitated toward private practice, the government quickly steered legal education away from Anglo-American approaches toward German-style ones, which were "thought to be more in line with strong state control" (Feeley and Miyazawa 2007: 161).

We lack sufficient data to complete this early history of the legal field, but it appears that the social hierarchies that preceded the creation of a Western-modeled legal field have structured not only Japan's legal hierarchies but also the politics of its legal field. The bar has retained an adversarial yet subordinate position vis-à-vis the state (160), and the judiciary—even after the 1947 constitution provided more formal independence and created a Supreme Court—has remained deeply conservative with respect to the state. That conservatism has been criticized for failing to protect individual rights but has also been defended as necessary to "ward off more aggressive political intervention into the affairs of the judiciary and . . . to assure the integrity and autonomy of the judiciary" (168).

It is not surprising that US influence in Japan in the years after the Japanese defeat in the Second World War involved efforts to reform Japan's highly German- and state-oriented legal education. The Ford Foundation in particular saw legal education as one place to revamp Japanese society so as to align it more closely to "modern" US values and approaches, including democratic ones. According to Levi, Dinovitzer, and Wong (2017), in 1954 the foundation granted $350,000 to promote the exchange of law students and professors between American and Japanese universities. The program began "with Japanese professors coming to the US, with institutions reflecting the legal academic elite of both countries: Harvard, Stanford, and the University of Michigan in the US, along with the Universities of Kyoto, Tohoku, Tokyo, Chuo, Keio and Waseda in Japan" (13). The foundation seems to have hoped that legal education would help build leadership in postwar Japan.

Levi, Dinovitzer, and Wong (2017) quote the foundation documents as follows:

> The need for cooperative research and study arises out of postwar changes in Japanese laws. Originally drawn largely from German sources, the legal system of modern Japan was extensively revised during the Occupation and now has a considerable deposit of elements of Anglo-American legal traditions, in addition to those of German and Japanese origin. The new Japanese Constitution embodies many of the democratic ideals and institutions found in the United States Constitution; there has also been enacted in recent years important legislation similar to that of the United States in such fields as criminal law and procedure, corporation law, labor law, antimonopoly law and tax law. (13)

In short, there was a place to build legal ties to the US and its educational programs.

As with virtually all law and development initiatives at the time, this program had little immediate impact. Its activities are summarized in *Law in Japan*, edited by Harvard's comparative law scholar Arthur von Mehren (1963) (who also played a role in India's Ford Foundation initiatives for legal education reform). The project in Japan may have influenced the reform proposals of the Provisional Justice System Investigation Committee, which reported in 1964 and focused on the legal profession. Foote summarizes that committee's work as follows: "The Investigation Committee called for increasing the number of judges, recruiting more judges from among practicing lawyers and prosecutors, increasing legal aid, placing greater emphasis on legal ethics, and taking steps to encourage lawyers to practice in areas other than the large cities. Most notably, the Investigation Committee also emphasized the need for substantial increases in the size of the bar" (Foote 2013: 384).

This may have led to a slight increase in the size of the bar, but as Foote also notes, "recommendations [for reform were] doomed in large part by failure to achieve consensus among the hôsô sansha [the term for the combined judiciary, prosecutors, and private lawyers]," which had the power to resist reform (2008: xxiv). The modernist agenda did not at that time move the institutions of the legal profession in Japan, which were able to protect their own relatively privileged positions, though they continued to be subordinate to the state.

The origins of the similarly conservative Korean legal profession are closely linked to Japanese colonialism. For South Korea, Jae-Hyup Lee (2009) chronicled this history in terms of law and development initiatives, with a focus on the founding of the Graduate School of Law (GSL) at Seoul National University. This was a local effort with some US law and development involvement. As quoted in Jay Murphy's *Legal Education in a Developing Nation: The Korean Experience* (1967), the 1963–64 Bulletin of the GSL argued that prior to Japanese annexation, "political factionalism, on the one hand, and corruption, on the other, paralyzed any effort at accomplishing an autonomous Korean law reform" (1967: 211). Reform in Korea would come only with the "occupying power, Japan, after her annexation of Korea in 1910" (211) and the establishment of two faculties of law. Japan's agenda regarding the legal profession was very narrow: "Japan was . . . bent on molding the young and able Korean lawyers into loyal imperial subjects" (211).

The Korean initiative to establish the GSL was supposed to help make lawyers more useful to democracy—to encourage them to move beyond their traditional subservience to empire (and state). The Bulletin of the GLS for 1962–63 made the following case: "We did not possess a sufficient number of lawyers prepared to assume the responsibilities of the legal profession in a democratic society" (211). That situation had been exacerbated by the Korean War, during which half of Korea's 400 lawyers died (212). Those who were left provided little to build on.

The GSL in Seoul tapped into US approaches to raise the level of legal education: "The need for raising the level of our law colleges generally from colleges of general education to graduate schools of law. Our law colleges at this time are not comparable to law schools in the United States. . . . The Graduate School of Law, then, is expected to be a true law school, providing our society with the type of lawyers we need in the period of social reconstruction." "[Another] reason lies in a need for reducing the wide gap now existing between the Bench and the Bar and between the judiciary and the academic law teacher." Finally, "the Graduate School of Law should be the hub around which the democratization idea of Korean law is channeled to the Korean legal profession and to Korean legal education" (216).

The picture that emerges is of a profession too closely identified with the Japanese, as well as narrowly trained and characterized by deep divisions between academics, legal practitioners, and the judicial branch. Law professors in particular were looked down upon by the rest of the profession as individuals not good enough to pass the bar. Consistent with US law and development programs and inspired in part by the US example, the GSL was meant to provide a much broader graduate education for all South Koreans who passed the bar. The faculty was to be a mix of academics, judges, and practitioners. Despite all the rhetoric, however, the reform brought by the GSL mainly provided an add-on to the education of the small number of bar passers; it was hoped that this would expand the horizons of the graduates and expose them to critical thinking. The GSL operated from 1962 to 1970 and produced 508 graduates. At that point, it was renamed the Judicial Research and Training Institute (JRTI), which would go on to become the dominant organization in the training of bench and bar.

Jae-Hyup Lee sees the GSL as a key example of locally inspired reform, one that presaged the current reforms in graduate legal education, discussed below (Lee 2009). The GSL "was the only institution established in a post-graduate level, in order to provide professional legal education with a full approval of the Supreme Court of South Korea. . . . It clearly demonstrates that South Korean experimentation of the post-graduate professional law school system in 1962 was not the result of external forces such as the globalization" (607).

To be sure, the local processes were not inconsistent with the linkages to US law and development, as Lee notes. Jay Murphy of the University of Alabama, with funding from the Asia Foundation, came to South Korea in 1963 as a visiting professor to study legal education there. Murphy's book stemming from his research (1967) perfectly reflects the idealism exported by US legal academics at the time, who included the Dean of NYU Law School, Russell Niles, and Yale's Myres S. McDougal (1967: 183). The United States' idealistic ambitions for the South Korean legal profession in the 1960s were not very different in broad outline from what local reformers supported.

The GSL did not realize its ambitions, however. Lee notes that the its rhetoric about democracy fit what were then the political ambitions of many South Koreans—a number of whom resurfaced later and helped galvanize new reform efforts. But the political support for those reforms was not strong enough in the 1960s, and Park Chung-hee's declaration of martial law in 1972 greatly impeded any democracy agenda. Probably not coincidentally, the shift from the GSL to the JRTI, which cut law professors out of the process, helped solidify Park's authoritarian control. The events suggest that President Park felt that the Supreme Court could be counted on not to make waves against his regime. That court's innate conservatism and its history of subordination to the Japanese empire played well with the authoritarian regime. According to JaeWon Kim, "following the Japanese model, the only path to becoming a licensed lawyer was through the Judicial Research and Training Institute (JRTI), directly controlled by the Supreme Court, which did not respect or trust law professors and did not want to surrender control over the production of lawyers" (2020: 790). The legacy of the Japanese system had overcome the idealistic US- and democracy-inspired reform of the 1960s, consistent with US support of Park's authoritarian government.

The continuity of the transformation from Japanese empire to South Korea can be seen in family biographies. Hong Jin-Ki was one of the very few Koreans who had passed the Japanese-language bar exam under colonialism. He came from a well-off family identified with successes on the earlier Confucian administrative exams (Int. 13–Korea). He attended Keijō Imperial University, graduating with an LL.B., and passed the bar examination, one of only fifty-seven Korean bar passers during the thirty-five years of Japanese control. He became a judge of the Jeonju District Court in 1943. Though he had worked with the Japanese, the first South Korean president, Syngman Rhee, believed he needed such individuals to govern and build the legal system. Hong Jin-Ki was named Deputy Justice Minister in 1954, Justice Minister in 1958, and Home Office Minister in 1960. He then resigned, and was later prosecuted for his activities in quelling an uprising in 1960. That uprising led also to Rhee's resignation.

The rest of the story of continuity is also instructive. As a private citizen, Hong Jin-Ki linked up with his friend, the founder of Samsung, Lee Byung-chul, to build the largest South Korean media company, Joongang Media. His son, Hong Seok-hyun, who had earned a Ph.D. in economics from Stanford, took over in 1994. Among other high-profile activities, Hong Seok-hyun was Ambassador to the United States. He resigned recently from Joongang for his son, Jeongdo Hong, to take over. Hong Seok-hyun's sister, Hong Ra-hee, is the wife of Samsung Group Chairman Lee Kun-hee, South Korea's richest person.

THE SITUATION PRIOR TO THE RECENT REFORMS

Both Japan and South Korea possessed small independent legal professions (and a much larger legally educated civil service). Bar passage rates for many years were at most 3 to 5 percent of those taking the examinations. Passage of the exam led to admission to the JRTI in South Korea and to the Legal Research and Training Institute (LRTI) in Japan. There the graduates learned practical skills, with a focus on crafting judicial opinions; they also absorbed the expectations and values that underpinned the legal profession. At these institutes, they forged a quasi-familial solidarity and absorbed patterns of behavior that brought them great prosperity if they later turned to private practice, typically after careers in the judiciary or prosecutors' offices. They did not make waves for the government or the national economic powers. They resisted any change that might endanger their status and prosperity.

Until 1981, the number of bar passers each year in South Korea was only 100. The number of those admitted to the bar each year slowly rose, reaching a plateau of 500 for Japan and 300 for South Korea. In the 1990s each country expanded to more than 1,000 (Ginsburg 2004). South Korea as of 2001 had around 6,900 licensed lawyers, including 1,400 judges, 1,200 prosecutors, and 4,300 practicing attorneys—all for a population of 46 million (Kim 2001: 46). In Japan as of 2001, there were fewer than 19,000 practicing lawyers for a population of more than 130 million (Foote 2013). The very small numbers ensured that those who passed the bar in both countries earned substantial monopoly profits and garnered elite status.

In each country, prompted in part by the Asian financial crisis of 1997 and more generally by the rise of global financial capitalism, interrelated proposals emerged for radical changes in legal education and the legal profession. Legal education reform became a key battleground for a number of contending groups. The first initiative was in South Korea; it was defeated before any reforms were actually carried out. Japan then embraced the three-year JD and an increase in the number of newly admitted lawyers, at which point South Korea followed suit. As we shall see, reform in South Korea has been much more successful than in Japan. We begin with a study of South Korean developments and then contrast them with those in Japan. In both countries the bar was quite conservative and sought to protect its position; only in South Korea did substantial change take place.

We focus on three dimensions of legal revolution. The first is the increasing power of the new global hegemonic state, the United States, relative to Europe, including Germany. That hegemonic power was especially felt in South Korea and Japan because of the close links between those countries and the United States during and after the Cold War. The second is the financialization and marketization of the economy, promoted strongly within Asia especially after the 1997 financial crisis. A greater role for law and especially corporate law firms is a part of what we have called the neoliberal legal revolution. The third is the emerging combination of meritocracy and exclusivity that has shaped the new winner-take-all economy. Legal education and the legal profession well exemplify this stratification and growing inequality. In each case, we see the efforts of an entrenched, quasi-familial legal elite to hold back the legal revolution.

THE LATE TWENTIETH-CENTURY MOVES FOR CHANGE TOWARD LAW SCHOOLS IN SOUTH KOREA: THE RESISTANCE OF THE LEGAL ESTABLISHMENT

The alliance that originally promoted reform in South Korea in 1995 included groups supporting more investment in the globalization of the South Korean economy and a legal profession serving the new democracy. These activities took place during the first civilian government in South Korea in thirty years, led by a long-time leader of the opposition, Kim Young Sam. These years of recent democratization coincided with the emergence of "civil society organizations" in South Korea, notably the Citizens' Coalition for Economic Justice (CCEJ) and People's Solidarity for Participatory Democracy (PSPD), which helped build the momentum of related groups of pro-democracy and human rights lawyers (Dezalay and Garth 2010: 238–42).

The key lawyers' organization was Minbyun—Lawyers for a Democratic Society—founded by fifty-one lawyers in 1988, one year after the collapse of the military government. Among its members were Roh Moo-hyun, who in 2003 became the sixteenth president of South Korea; Park Won-soon, principal founder of the PSPD and the mayor of Seoul from 2011 to 2020; and Moon Jae-in, the current president of South Korea. Park Won-soon, according to a source close to him, saw after he passed the bar that prosecutors in South Korea had the power to promote justice, but that in actual practice they promoted law as simply a "tool of the dictatorship." He thought that law needed to be a vehicle for "democracy" and for the people to claim their "rights" in the post-authoritarian period (Int. 1–Korea).

This alliance for reform, which supported the creation of new graduate JD programs and a strong expansion of the bar, represented a relatively small group from among the civil society organizations and human rights organizations that had abandoned radical opposition in the name of rights and anti-corruption through legal reform. Inspired in part by civil society activism in the United States, they sought change through law and professional initiatives. The PSPD, for example, used shareholder derivative lawsuits as a means to control corruption linked to the *chaebols*—the large, family-owned business conglomerates in South Korea (Ohnesorge 2003). The civil society groups provided credibility and a legal program for an emerging and overlapping political group seeking to take on both the *chaebols* and remnants of the authoritarian regime.

Park Se-Il, a founder of the CCEJ (with Reverend Kyungsuk Suh), was a key figure in these developments. From 1995 to 1998, he was President Kim Young Sam's senior secretary for policy planning and social welfare. In that position he was instrumental in developing the first initiatives to establish law schools for the Commission on the Promotion of Globalization (Kim 2001). A professor of economics and law at Seoul National University, he had studied globalization, and he had just returned from a sabbatical at Columbia Law School. Among his allies at the time were "critical jurists" of the South Korean Law and Society Association, identified with "campaigning for democracy and the rule of law" (Lee 2014). The idea of legal education reform, as Chulwoo Lee stated, was "packaged in globalization discourse," which gained support even in the conservative press despite the fact that "businesses were indifferent" (296). The idea, as noted below, initially failed, but it did result in a concession to increase the number of bar passers to 1,000.

The failure of this initiative was the result largely of the power of the entrenched elite in the legal profession at that time, represented especially by the Korean Bar Association. That association had evolved toward a reputation supporting human rights lawyers in the 1980s, which in fact had led the government at one point to double bar passage from 100 to 200 to try to weaken the bar's prestige (Dezalay and Garth 2010: 239). But the mainstream of the bar through the 1990s was deeply conservative and reluctant to change a system that had been very good to its members. It was far from embracing a new legal revolution.

According to JaeWon Kim, the opposition was uniform among "Korea's legal establishment, including the Supreme Court and the Korean Bar Association" (Kim 2001: 66). The details of their opposition are instructive. The bar and the judiciary emphasized division and hierarchy within the profession. They insisted that "Korean law professors were incapable of producing lawyers through the proposed graduate law school system" (66). They looked down on law professors as not good enough to pass the bar and therefore not good enough to be entrusted with the real preparation for practice. Furthermore, as JaeWon Kim also notes, the obvious self-interest was clear: "Practicing lawyers feared a dramatic increase in new lawyers and equated the proposed graduate law school system with a loss of control over barriers to entering their profession. The legal establishment saw themselves as members of a privileged small group threatened by a potential increase of lawyers" (66). The judiciary's opposition was also linked to their desire to retain the opportunity to retire from the bench into positions as highly paid litigators in a market of scarcity (Ginsburg 2004).

Law professors acting through the Association of Korean Law Professors also did not favor reform. They joined the opposition despite the potential increase in status that the law schools might bring. One argument was that "the education system of a common law country would be inappropriate for a civil law country like Korea" (Kim 2001: 66).[1] They were also seeking to protect their turf: "The overwhelming majority of South Korean law professors who studied abroad have done so in Germany. They seemed to worry that a shift to the American law school system might relegate them to second-class status. Their nightmare was of being subordinate to the few law professors educated in the United States" (67).

The opposition to reform from the interlocking parts of an entrenched legal establishment thus began with its strong commitment to maintaining a very low bar passage rate, which gave great stature and ultimately economic rewards to those who passed the bar. The traditional story was that bar passage brought three keys arranged by a marriage broker—to a house, to an office, and to a car. The unity of the bar arose also from social homogeneity. Many of those who passed the bar exam had attended the same high schools, and typically they had also attended one of the handful of schools that offered the best chances of bar passage, above all Seoul National University (SNU). SNU produced about 50 percent of the successful bar passers. The intense regime of study and attendance at the two-year JRTI—taught by judges and prosecutors—cemented their bonds through shared experiences and approaches. Again according to JaeWon Kim , "the South Korean Supreme Court supervises the JRTI, whose faculty is composed of judges and prosecutors. The training focuses on developing litigation skills to produce future judges, prosecutors, and trial lawyers. Undergoing the unified training course has built a military-like hierarchy among South Korean lawyers. This kind of hierarchy has been reinforced by the Confucian tradition in which seniority carries great privileges" (Kim 2001: 48).

According to a prominent graduate from the 1990s, the members of the bar were homogeneous in "values, methods, goals, and in excellence," and they were "most proud of being smart," as evidenced by success on the bar exam (Int. 2–Korea). Being smart meant excelling in memorization, which required one to in effect "memorize all the textbooks and theories" (Int. 3–Korea). As noted above, the JRTI was central to this familial relationship. As Yong Chui Park states, "the JRTI has been heavily criticized as the cradle of the 'legal mafia' in which students of the JRTI bond together more closely than any group of other professionals" (2018: 180).

The result of this formation process was an entrenched and complacent legal oligarchy that was reluctant to change and closely connected to governance by an authoritarian regime and the economic power concentrated in the *chaebols*. Also, the concentration on criminal and civil litigation left little room for the development of linguistic skills or business expertise, which led the relatively few corporate law firms to rely considerably on non–bar passers with US degrees. That group included some who were native South Koreans and who had studied in South Korea; others were "American-born Koreans" educated in the United States. A study used in support of reform found that 70 percent of South Korean corporations said they would pick foreign over domestic law firms (Int. 4–Korea). The *chaebols* in any event did not rely very much on law and lawyers within South Korea to shape their relationships with the state. According to JaeWon Kim, "under the circumstances, cordial personal relationships, not convincing arguments or technical legal skills, play a major role in legal practice. Heavy reliance on such personal connections has undoubtedly contributed to unethical practices within the South Korean legal community" (2001: 49).

Despite the activities of a few human rights lawyers, there was little incentive for members of the legal profession to challenge activities of the state or the *chaebols*. Those favoring the reform of legal education thus sought to transform what they considered to be "justice" based on the "elitism" of a small, complacent, and homogeneous group in favor of a more open and competitive legal system linked to a more legalized regime of governance. They also made very pragmatic arguments, for example, pointing to "the lack of qualified international trade lawyers during the Uruguay Round and professional corporate lawyers specialized in M & A" (Lee 2009: 611).

This pro-democracy and rights-oriented group of reformers tended also to be those most likely to oppose neocolonial policies promoted by the United States, such as an aggressive stance toward North Korea. Many of these individuals had long opposed the US support of authoritarian but anti-communist regimes in South Korea. Nevertheless, they supported US-style law schools and a US-style legal profession as a means to take on the remnants of the authoritarian regime.

They joined with those who sought to modernize the profession in relation to corporate law and globalization.

The role of law professors was largely secondary. They had not gone through the JRTI mainly because they had not passed the bar. In this context, there was "little exchange between the practicing bar and academia," and "very few university law professors were admitted to practice" (Int. 3–Korea). Accordingly, before the reforms, "the lawyer, judge or prosecutor eclipses the law professor in status" (Miyazawa, Chan, and Lee 2008: 352). A handful of US-educated professors supported the proposed move to the US law school system, but they were in the minority, as noted earlier.

The legal academy in the South Korean context sought to build on its connections to Germany (originally through Japan), studying German legal theories focused on the civil, criminal, and commercial codes. The style of research was highly theoretical, working toward the publication of books and especially treatises, not articles. With respect to German and Japanese law professors (Feldman 1993), hiring was generally a matter of selecting protégés from among the students (Int. 5–South Korea). Unlike the German professors, however, the South Korean professors did not have sufficient status to be called upon to issue legal opinions. The law professors, who were focused on their formal theories, also had no interest in hiring practicing lawyers experienced in the transactions identified with the expanding corporate law firms and the more open and competitive economy. In the words of a corporate law partner turned professor after the law schools were founded, "practice experience was discounted" in relation to "pure academics" (Int. 3–Korea). As stated in a recent article by Yong Chui Park, "law professors used to be a group of people . . . with a higher purpose of making monumental academic landmarks and teaching their great works . . . [and whose] teaching is irrelevant to preparation for the Judicial Examination" (2018: 182).

The almost uniform opposition of the relevant groups was sufficient to kill the original reform proposal. The idea, as noted, then gained traction in Japan (Chan 2011). There appeared to be a new emphasis on the rule of law and some weakening of the *keiretsu*— counterparts to the South Korean *chaebols* but different in that the Japanese business conglomerates are more bank-dominated as opposed to family-dominated— and the Japanese legal establishment at the time wanted to expand in part because corporate law firms were drawing from the talent pool available for the judiciary (Int. 1–Japan; Ginsburg 2004: 438). Japan then moved to establish law schools in 2004, as discussed below. We return now to the story in South Korea.

THE NEXT EFFORT, WITH A STRENGTHENED POLITICAL COALITION

The idea of substantially reforming legal education, including by moving to the JD graduate degree, was reimported back to South Korea in part because of the apparent success in implementing the reform in Japan. The reform then became law in 2007 under President Roh Moo-hyun, the former human rights lawyer and a long-time pro-democracy reformer. His government picked up the mantle of Kim Young Sam. This time, some progressive judges joined in support of the movement (Lee 2014: 296; Kim 2020). At that point, the emerging and overlapping political groups, according to one observer, reached "a critical mass on both markets and democracy" (Int. 4–Korea). They could now take on the alliance that had long existed among the *chaebols*, the authoritarian government, and a legal profession that had long stayed out of the way while profiting handsomely. As Chulwoo Lee stated, "at least partly, the legal education reform marked a struggle between a rising 'progressive elite' in various corners of South Korea and the traditional legal elite" (Lee 2014: 297). It also represented an alliance of legal groups who may not have agreed on political strategies but were united in their challenge to the "hegemony of dogmatic jurisprudence of Japanese and Continental origins" (299).

The South Korean reformers learned from the difficulties in Japan caused by the continuation of the undergraduate legal education system (see below). Despite their success in getting the reform passed, however, they faced continued opposition from the legal profession and especially the South Korean Bar Association. The result was a combination of law schools and undergraduate programs. Unlike in Japan, however, the reforms clearly shifted the center of legal education to the graduate law schools and the JD degrees.

There was thus strong competition to establish law schools. Twenty-five of them gained approval—twelve in Seoul and thirteen outside of Seoul. Universities without law schools could continue to offer undergraduate law courses, but the critical idea was to phase out the judicial examination in favor of a bar exam for law school graduates.

At the core of the attack on the legal establishment was the idea that the postgraduate, three-year law school system should replace the JRTI—the key institution in sustaining the conformity and conservatism of legal actors. Law school eligibility under the reformed system depended on the completion of a four-year undergraduate degree, and admission depended in part on one's score on a legal education eligibility test (LEET). Jae-Hyup Lee notes that "on its face, the South Korean law school system is modeled after the U.S. law schools, with two important exceptions" (2009: 611). One is that "a quota of total number of students (2,000) is set and strictly enforced by the Ministry of Justice" (611). The other is that "existing law undergraduate programs are eliminated in exchange for the establishment of the law school" (611). But "the curriculum, the method of teaching, and any other aspects of the internal operation of the law school are supposed to follow the U.S. model" (611). Legal education was supposed to promote global exchange, English-language courses, practical experiences, and interdisciplinary hiring and scholarship (611). Meanwhile, faculty/student ratios became much more favorable—set to be 1:15—and this led to substantial new faculty hiring.

The allocation of maximum students per law school depended on the reputation of the school. SNU accordingly gained the most law students, 150, and some schools were limited to only 40 students (611). One reform, ostensibly created to foster competition and to challenge the oligarchy of the three elite schools, SNU, Korea University, and Yonsei (known as the SKY schools) but especially SNU, prevented the law schools from enrolling more than two-thirds of their students from their own undergraduate universities.

Compared to Japan, the reform has been a success. One disappointment is that the percentage of bar passers has not stayed at 75 percent, as reformers originally sought. The recent rates have hovered around 50 percent. There are roughly 1,500 bar passers admitted each year compared to the 2,000 annual graduates, but repeat test takers reduce the bar passage rate. The signature accomplishment is that, despite some controversy, which continued until very recently (Yeo 2015), the Judicial Examination has been phased out, which in turn has meant the end of the role of the JRTI in training and socializing new admittees. Those opposed to the new system continue to assert that the openness of the Judicial Examination was key to social mobility, since anyone could take that exam. They ultimately lost the debate, and the numbers of those allowed to enter the profession through the Judicial Examination followed a downward pattern, with the last examination held in 2017. From then on admission was from the bar exam and law schools only.

The long-standing opposition of the Korean Bar Association has formally ended. The leadership elected in the spring of 2017 supported the law school reforms, and the numbers suggest that support will continue. As one interviewee noted, 9,000 out of the 20,000 lawyers in South Korea are now graduates under the new system, and this has shifted the balance of power toward the JDs and the new system (Int. 5–South Korea). It seems that the corner has turned. Indeed, the alliance in support of the law schools consolidated after the recent impeachment of President Park Geun-hye, herself linked not only to corruption but also to the military dictatorship. Interviewees referred to her impeachment as the "culmination" of legal reforms in South Korea, and the current president is a strong supporter of the reform agenda (Int. 5–South Korea).

IMPACTS OF REFORM

The gradual shift toward law schools has had a number of impacts. With respect to the question of shifting hegemony and a revolution in legal expertise, we can point to differences in the faculty and the courses that are taught. The number of faculty members increased immediately after the shift, especially at the law schools with larger quotas of students. The SNU law school expanded its physical facilities substantially and increased the faculty by 50 percent (Int. 5–Korea). SNU and other law schools hired professors who could teach in English as well as teach courses linked to large law firm practice and public interest law. SNU, for example, hired two leading partners from Kim and Chang, one of the top law firms in Seoul. This never would have happened prior to the establishment of the law schools, for the heavily code- and academic-theory–oriented teaching had no place for courses on mergers and acquisitions, for example. The prestige of the law professors also increased, in part because of the moves into teaching by senior partners and important members of the judiciary.

The heavily German-trained faculty is now much more US-oriented. SNU is described now as moving from "German heavy" to "more from the US," with roughly one third holding South Korean PhDs, one third US-trained, and one-third from other jurisdictions (mainly Germany). US training is especially relevant for constitutional law, commercial law, and financial and economic law (Int. 5–South Korea). Another faculty member said that the German influence was "less and less" (Int. 6–South Korea). No longer are faculty protégés hired as in the past. There is a much more open and competitive hiring process. More individuals with dual degrees are found now in the South Korean law schools than were on the undergraduate law faculties. And faculty positions are strongly desired, even though the pay—which is linked to salaries in the humanities and social sciences—is much less than corporate partners make (Int. 5–Korea).

The publications of faculty members reflect change as well. No longer is there an overwhelming emphasis on books and especially treatises. The focus is now on articles, and there is some emphasis on publishing abroad in English in "impact journals." Research and scholarship are not as internationalized as in the social science departments in the universities, but the situation is considerably different than it was in the pre-reform faculties of law.

The qualifications of the students match the shift in the kind of expertise valued within the legal field. Law firm partners in particular noted that they seek law graduates with experience and degrees in the sciences, accounting, economics, pharmaceuticals, intellectual property, and other areas (Ints. 7 and 8–Korea). They are less concerned than before about how well someone performed with their grades or on the bar exam. They also value "cultural experience" and skill in languages, especially English (Ints. 7 and 8–Korea). The law school graduates fit the needs of the large corporate law firms better than the products of the old system (Int. 9–Korea). One interviewee suggested that the graduates today are better because they give "different answers" in their work instead of the answers "they were supposed to have" (Ints. 6 and 10–Korea). Also, the large firms have changed their hiring practices. They now make offers to first-year students after their first-year internships (Int. 11–Korea)—at least at SNU—rather than waiting until bar passage. As in India with the creation of the National Law Schools, corporate law firms were not leaders of legal educational reform, but their growing presence, the specter of more competition from international law firms setting up shop to Seoul, and their association with US-style globalization meant that the system evolved to suit their needs.

There are still complaints from legal traditionalists. Critics lament a decline in the quality of the bar, distinguishing between the recent law school graduates and the "real lawyers" who passed when the standards were much tougher. One way to depict the criticism is to note that in the past, 1,000 students studied for seven years before entering practice. They had four years of law school, at least one year in bar prep, and then two years in the JRTI (Int. 4–South Korea). Now there are 1,500 students who study "only" for three years before entering practice. This is bound to make a difference, according to one professor (Int. 4–South Korea). Another partner of a corporate law firm suggests that there has been a decline in preparedness at least for those planning to go into litigation (Int. 12–Korea). But the corporate law firms notably are not concerned, according to our informants. They prefer the mix of qualities of today's law school graduates.

The bar examination is not so different from the prior judicial examination. It still requires a great deal of memorization, and the result has been a weakening of the law school system in several ways. First, the courses relevant to the new expertise, such as mergers and acquisitions or corporate governance, are not tested on the bar exam. There is a strong tendency for students as they move on in their law school careers to focus on bar passage and on courses that address the bar exam material (J.T. Lee 2017). According to one critic, "the law schools have become merely 'cram' schools for the bar examination preparation, and not places for innovation of legal discussion" (Park 2018: 178). Indeed, the focus on bar passage means that many students spend their time taking private cram courses while in law school. Students also tend to avoid courses taught in English, for example, or clinics, or courses about such matters as corporate governance, since they are not instrumental for bar preparation (Ints. 4 and 10–Korea). One professor noted that it was necessary to work doubly hard to recruit students to clinics, for example, by providing pass/fail grading to induce students to sign up. Another noted that students who started law school with excellent English would often see a decline in their skills over time while in law school (Int. 10–Korea). Professors, in addition, were being pulled toward the traditional lecture system by the incentive of the bar exam.

STRATIFICATION AND HIERARCHY AFTER REFORM

One ostensible goal of the reform was to foster competition in the legal profession and among the law schools so as to challenge a deeply conservative oligarchy that was reluctant to challenge the government or the *chaebols*. The "elite justice" criticized by the reformers was seen as controlled by a homogeneous group of individuals, a large portion of whom had graduated from SNU. Part of the effort of reformers was to open up the profession and diversify the backgrounds of those who would obtain law degrees and pass the bar. The requirement that no law school could have more than two thirds of its students from the same undergraduate university as the law school was meant to further this process (Int. 5–Korea).

In fact, the hierarchical structure remains intact despite a number of modifications under the new system. One criticism raised frequently today amounts to a new version of the criticism of the legal elite: only the rich can attend law school because of the increased tuition and the three years that have been added to a legal education. Law school tuitions—which averaged about $14,000 in 2015—reportedly are three times the tuition at other graduate schools (Lee 2018). Tuition is increasing in part because of the low faculty-to-student ratio (Kim 2020). According to JaeWon Kim, "Public opinion about the new law schools has been generally unfavourable. They have been ridiculed as 'money schools' for the rich, a label the mass media constantly repeat" (2020).

Entrance into law school depends now on more than test scores. This can introduce biases in favor of those able to travel, learn languages, and acquire experiences that gain the attention of admissions departments. Most students appear to be "upper middle class" (Int. 6–Korea). Reportedly the scholarships that are offered tend not to attract the more disadvantaged South Koreans. It is "hard to find students for full scholarships" (Int. 4–Korea). Even so, the romanticization of the prior system of open access to the judicial exam appears misplaced.

The South Korean version of the US "After the JD" study of lawyer careers, organized by Jae-Hyup Lee of SNU, compared students taking the different routes to passing the bar. The study has noted that there is little difference in terms of socioeconomic background between those who relied on the cram courses and those who attended law schools (J.H. Lee 2019). The reason is that it takes considerable resources for any individual to take the time, secure proximate housing, and pay the money required to pursue the cram courses. In any event, access to legal careers today is not very open to those without resources (S. Kim 2014), and the law school system has certainly raised the cost of that access.

There is also a very strong division between the elite law schools and the rest (Kim 2020). Those who are not admitted to one of the fifteen law schools in Seoul have much less chance of passing the bar than those who gain entry to the Seoul schools. The non-Seoul schools, a number of which maintain very low enrollments, purportedly attract only those who cannot gain admission to a Seoul law school. Law students also cannot transfer. The first-time bar passage for the Seoul schools is reportedly around 70 to 75 percent, while the figure for those from outside Seoul hovers around 50 to 55 percent at best (Ints. 6 and 10–Korea). Also, the very top schools, including the SKY schools and Sungkyunkwan University Law School, are closer to 80 to 90 percent in bar passage.

The top schools also perpetuate the undergraduate hierarchy even though they must take one third of their students from off-campus. They simply recruit from one another (Int. 11–Korea; Park 2018: 193). The division between elite schools and the rest also relates to the resources available to the schools. The *Korea JoongAng*

Daily reported in 2014: "According to data submitted by 13 of 25 total law schools—including Ewha Womans University, Konkuk University and Kyungpook National University—to Rep. Kim Jae-yun, from the minor opposition Unified Progressive Party, five schools had a deficit of 22.6 billion won between 2009 and 2011. The situation was tougher for these 'mini-law schools,' with less than 80 students enrolled in classes" (S. Kim 2014). The law schools acting through the Korean Law Schools Association maintain a united front in support of all twenty-five law schools, but there is discussion about raising the overall bar passage by reducing the number of students in the lower-performing law schools (Int. 12–Korea; Park 2018: 192). If that happens, the schools that admit those likely to be from less advantaged backgrounds will become weaker and weaker.

Most tellingly, the position of the SKY schools and above all SNU law school remains unchallenged. The winner-take-all economy is especially evident here. SNU's dominant position is clear from the fact that it has no Korea Law School graduates on its faculty—one is from Yonsei Law School and two from Ewha Women's University (Int. 11–Korea) The hierarchy is intensely felt. Professors at Korea Law School, for example, criticize SNU for mainly hiring its own graduates. Meanwhile, KU brags about the number of its own graduates on the KU faculty.

The hierarchy is strongly evident in the allocation of elite jobs. The most desired careers remain in the judiciary and in the prosecutor's office, and those careers can be converted later into teaching positions or lucrative positions in law firms. Those seeking careers in the judiciary can no longer go directly into those positions, but they typically will still begin with a judicial clerkship and return to the judiciary after a few years' experience. The number of elite positions totals about 400 annually, according to interviewees from the law schools and law firms. That number includes fewer than 100 serving as clerks for judges and a similar number for prosecutors. It also includes about 200 annual hires into the "big six" Seoul law firms—Kim and Chang,; Lee and Ko; Bae, Kim and Lee; Shin and Kim; Yulchon; and Yoon and Yang—that comprise the elite of the corporate bar. Among those going into these elite positions are reportedly one third of SNU law graduates, who constitute one quarter of new hires (Ints. 2, 6, and 10–Korea). The corporate law firms are still not large by global standards: "As of 2017, 11 Korean firms had more than 100 lawyers: Kim & Chang (654), Lee & Ko (454), Bae, Kim & Lee (414), Shin & Kim (325), Yoon & Yang (272), Yulchon (257), Barun Law (192), DR & AJU (146), Dongin Law (135). Jipyong (125) and Logos (111)" (Kim 2020). In-house legal departments are also now increasing their hiring, providing another relatively elite position.

Data compiled by Jae-Hyup Lee show the dominance of SNU and the SKY schools (2017). The big six hired 159 lawyers in 2014—73 law graduates from SNU, 25 from Yonsei, 24 from Korea University, and then 13 from Songyunkwan—leaving a total of 25 from the other law schools. Furthermore, with respect to the undergraduate university attended, 88 were from SNU, 21 from Korea University, and 18 from Yonsei, with only 32 from elsewhere (Lee 2017). Partners at the firms report hiring predominantly from the SKY schools, and this is certainly borne out by this study. Associates reportedly start pay at about US $90,000, substantially more than in other legal positions.

At the same time, the market is much more competitive generally. One newspaper article stated that more than 3,300 lawyers were unemployed in 2014. Starting salaries generally are not what they once were, and even those who get into the big six are no longer guaranteed support for an LL.M. in the United States. There is also little evidence that the increased competition has led to more access to justice for individuals. One scholar (Int. 4–Korea) stated that 70 percent of civil cases involve *pro se* representation. He contrasted this with the position of the *chaebols*, which, he said, have learned to use the law as a "legalized arsenal" against critics, including through criminal "defamation" actions with the aid of top prosecutors still "more friendly to corporations and the rich" (Int. 4–Korea).

At the same time, there has been considerable growth in pro bono and public interest law. Thirty hours of pro bono—termed "public interest activities"— were made mandatory in 2000, although without apparent penalties for noncompliance. Increased pro bono activity led to the creation of foundations by the big six law firms to coordinate and encourage pro bono, a notable example being the Dongcheon Foundation created by and housed at Bae, Kim and Lee.

The story of the small but growing public interest law sector is part of the story of legal education reform. First, the public interest law sector is an outgrowth of the same people and constituency promoting legal education reform to challenge the entrenched elite. One expert reports, for example, that the leaders of public interest law all met through Mingbyun and "all know each other" (Int. 10– Korea). Gonggam, one of the most important public interest organizations, was founded in 2004 by Park Won-soon. He was earlier a key founder of the PSPD and Minbyun, and he later founded Hope and Law (Int. 10–Korea). The budget of Gonggam is around $800,000; of Hope and Law, around $400,000. A substantial portion of the budgets of these organizations comes from individual donations. Students are also pushing the market by searching out nonlegally oriented NGOs and offering to provide a legal component to their work.

Second, there is a connection between the pro bono foundations, the law firms, and public interest in part because many of the important partners in law firms today are members of the '86 generation that demonstrated for democracy (Int. 10–Korea). They are inclined to support their friends in public interest law and to encourage pro bono. Third, the law schools, through their clinical programs and professors, build relationships that encourage pro bono and public interest. Finally, although this is not easy to document, it appears that the leading pro bono and public interest organizations, such as the elite law firms, are disproportionately linked to the graduates of the most elite law schools. It is indicative that seventy graduates of one class at SNU law school got together to fund a position for

advocacy for transgender rights (Int. 10–Korea). The increase in numbers in public interest law sustains a more diversified professional practice in some respects,
though not necessarily in terms of the lawyers who staff the leading organizations.

Finally, the global shift toward a new legal hegemonic relationship has brought
other challenges in South Korea. The Ministry of Justice, under pressure from
Europe and the United States, is gradually opening its markets to international law
firms. As of 2017, the Minister of Justice had authorized 145 Foreign Legal Consultants: "109 from the US, 23 from the UK, eight from Australia, and one each from
other countries like France, Scotland, New Zealand, Singapore and China" (Kim
2020). Among the global law firms active in Seoul are Baker McKenzie, Clifford
Chance, Latham and Watkins, Ropes and Gray, Sheppard Mullin, Skadden Arps,
and White and Case (Int. 10–Korea).

At least one interviewee stated that the domestic big six are increasing their
hiring to compete with the international law firms (Int. 12—South Korea).
An ex-partner opined that these international law firms were likely to favor
American-born South Koreans in order to gain bilingual fluency. To some extent,
therefore, there is the possibility here too—as in Hong Kong—of individuals
bypassing South Korean legal education but still gaining a strong position in corporate law practice in South Korea. The relationships of core and periphery are
more present to the extent that the market is more open.

Legal education in South Korea has substantially retooled itself to align more
with the expertise valued and current in post–Cold War global legal practice. It
has transformed the traditional legal oligarchy and the criteria for gaining admission. There are also strong continuities. Prosecutors and judges remain at the top
of the hierarchy and still are mostly quite conservative. The same schools dominate
the legal profession as in the past. And the students focus much more on bar passage than on clinics and business courses. We turn now to the situation in Japan,
which is similar but so far with a very different outcome.

THE JAPANESE CONTRAST: CO-OPTATION
AND RESISTANCE

The Japanese initiatives for the reform of legal education began after the financial
crisis of 1997, when the cabinet established a Justice System Reform Council in
1999 (Rosen 2017: 267). The "main initiator," according to Kay-Wah Chan, was
the "business sector" (2011: 185), which then as now "exerted a powerful influence
on the Liberal Democratic Party (LDP)" (186). In the wake of the financial crisis,
there was also a weakening of the *keiretsu* and the banks with which they worked,
as well as a growing call for more regulation by law and lawyers (188). Corporate
interests "began to agitate for more and better lawyers," both for negotiations with
international businesses and their lawyers and for "locating lawyers who know
anything about the substance of their businesses" (Rosen 2017: 271). As in South

Korea, lawyers qualified for the bar by knowing only what it took to pass the bar exam.

There were also arguments against the "close ties within the iron triangle, comprised of the ruling Liberal Democratic Party (LDP), the bureaucracy, and big business" (Saegusa 2009: 367). Rosen refers to "an orthodoxy that perpetuates the status quo" and "lays the groundwork for the 'extreme form of positivism and passivity of most judges in Japan'" (2017: 282, citing Miyazawa 2002). Legal scholars educated in the United States in particular also supported the change (368). According to Saegusa, among those she interviewed about legal education reform, "there is a taken-for-granted assumption that Japan should look for American models when reforms are discussed" (375).

At that point Japan allowed 1,000 bar passers per annum, leading to a 2 to 5 percent passage rate. The 1,000 reflected a gradual increase from the 500 per year between 1960 and 1990 (371). Big business and the state had not taken an interest historically in increasing the number because, as in South Korea, the small and homogeneous bar was deeply conservative and unlikely to hinder corporate or state interests (373). But now they argued strongly that the number should be increased to 3,000 per year (391).

The Justice System Reform Council established in 1999 had thirteen members, only three of whom came from the legal profession. Three were law professors and seven came from other sectors of Japanese society. The council argued for a strengthening of the legal profession both for ordinary people and for business. It seized on initiatives suggested by US-oriented law professors (Saegusa 2009).

There was resistance to the reforms. As in South Korea, "civil law professors tended to express stronger resistance to the law school proposal than professors of other disciplines" (386), fearing the Americanization of legal education. Furthermore, "professors at elite universities were reluctant to endorse the new system, but at the same time it seemed to them a good opportunity to eliminate many lower-status universities" (386). Law professors generally were skeptical but did not speak out because they did not want to alienate the Ministry of Education (387).

The prevailing arguments among supporters were for a "more diverse, internationalized" set of lawyers (Rosen 2017: 272), new expertise in such areas as technology (272), more competition leading to more lawyers locating outside of Tokyo and Osaka (273), and more engaged students and teaching. In Rosen's words, the argument for Americanization was that "American-style law practice and lawyers had become the default for global legal practice in the twenty-first century. American lawyers were everywhere. Their standards, to a great extent, had become the global standard. If Japanese lawyers were to hold their own in this environment for the benefit of their clients, they needed to know how to operate" (277). The law school plan for "twenty-first century global practice" became law in 2002 (275).

The timing coincided with an expansion of corporate law firms in Japan (Murayama 2020). Indeed, an initial impetus to expand the number of lawyers from 500 in 1990 to 1,000 in 1996 came after, in response to US demands in 1982, the Foreign Lawyers Act (No. 66) was enacted in 1986, "allowing lawyers licensed to practice in a foreign country to practice in Japan but not litigate. Because the Japanese economy was expanding rapidly, large Anglo-American law firms began to open offices in Tokyo. Most international transactions were out-bound as Japanese companies invested in the US and Europe" (755).

Then, facing international competition, "Japanese law offices specializing in international transactions began actively to recruit graduates of the Legal Training and Research Institute (LTRI) . . . Although those Japanese law offices were relatively small, with 30–40 lawyers, they tried to recruit the best graduates by offering a high starting salary. As a result, SC [Supreme Court] and in particular MOJ [Ministry of Justice] began to have problems recruiting enough judges and prosecutors and sought to increase the number passing the bar examination" (755).

At that time, as a result of the deregulation coincident with the Asian financial crisis in the late 1990s, foreign investors could buy Japanese companies more easily (757): "Unlike out-bound investment, in-bound capital required Japanese lawyers. Responding to increasing demand for corporate and cross-border legal work and, especially, the ability to handle M&A, Japanese firms specializing in corporate law and finance began to merge, growing to more than 100 lawyers. The *Big Four* [elite of Japanese corporate law] were created by such mergers between 2000 and 2007. A gradual increase in the number passing the bar exam in the late 1990s also helped them expand" (757).

CO-OPTATION AND THE HYBRID LAW SCHOOL SYSTEM

The new legal education system, as a compromise with the legal establishment, allowed the undergraduate law schools to continue their operations, but it also established sixty-eight new law schools, which began operating in 2004. Undergraduate law majors would enroll in a two-year JD program and non-law graduates in a three-year program. The compromise still purported to make major change and to open up legal education and the profession. There was considerable optimism at the time (e.g., Foote 2008).

From today's perspective, however, we can see the limits of this "legal revolution" in Japan. As Saegusa pointed out in 2009, the "legal establishment" from the start controlled the specifics of law school reform for their own benefit. First, she noted, "the law school system is supervised by the Ministry of Education, which, in the hierarchy of Japanese public agencies, is less powerful than either the Supreme Court or the Ministry of Justice" (388). That meant that legal education could not get too far away from the centers of power in the profession and the Ministry of Justice.

Second, control of the number of admittees was kept in the hands of the Ministry of Justice, which meant that, even if the reform council had suggested 3,000 new admittees a year might be too small, it would be the Ministry of Justice that controlled the actual numbers on grounds of "quality": "the Ministry of Justice has not exhibited full trust that the new law schools will sustain the quality of legal education, so it maintains the strict bar exam as the essential check on the law schools" (389).

Finally, and most importantly, "the introduction of the law school system could have jeopardized the existence of the Institute [LRTI]. However, representatives of the Supreme Court on the Reform Council emphasized the excellence of training that the Institute offered and insisted that the Institute remain responsible for practical training, even after law schools were established" (388). Saegusa quotes a Supreme Court official who stated that this was necessary because of the "uncertain quality of education in the law schools" (288). The institute remains the key to the socialization of the legal profession into the traditional roles that have helped hold together the political and economic elites. It is staffed not by law professors but, as was the case in South Korea, by the judiciary and prosecutors. According to leading Japanese scholars, it is very clearly in place to preserve traditional roles and approaches against the potential influence of law school faculties (Ints. 2 and 3–Japan). This situation is quite different than in South Korea.

Nevertheless, the beginnings were relatively auspicious from the perspective of reformers, with a diverse student body and many new courses focusing on non-bar topics relevant to global legal practice. But the bar passage on the first exam was 48 percent, declining the following year to 40 percent (Saegusa 2009: 278). The number of non-law majors entering the JD programs also declined.[2] The opposition then grew even stronger against having even the 3,000 bar passers, and the numbers were reduced (279). The current number is about 1,500. As in South Korea, the "declining quality" argument had strong adherents among the members of the bar and the Ministry of Justice. There were also fewer job openings than had been anticipated (279).

In addition, unlike in South Korea, the existence of the undergraduate schools along with the law schools, as well as the availability of the bar exam to non-law students (who now must pass a preliminary exam to qualify for the bar exam), undermined the law school system and the importance of law schools more generally. Bar passage declined to under 23 percent in 2016 (6,899 sat and 1,583 passed) (Rosen 2017: 283). Even University of Tokyo graduates passed at only a 48 percent rate (283). The 2017 results were even worse. Keio University produced the most passers in this category, at 144. The University of Tokyo came in second, with 134. Chuo University had 119, Kyoto University 111, and Waseda University 102. The following year, five law schools saw none of their test takers pass (*Nikkei Asian Review* 2017).

Even more troubling for proponents of reform is that individuals who took the alternative route through the cram schools and preliminary exam did much better on the bar exam: "Those going through this program and passing the exam increased 55 on the year to a record 290. This subgroup's pass rate came to 72.5%, and the applicants accounted for about 18% of all passers" (283).

Skills training, elective courses, courses in English, and even classroom attendance gave way to bar courses and especially to a focus on the cram courses outside of the law schools (Rosen 2017: 283–86). The trend now is for even those enrolled in the law schools to drop out and take the alternative route to bar passage. All of these trends challenge the role of any new expertise taught in law schools.

The political will for reform also evaporated. According to Murayama (2020), the "rapid increase during a short period provoked a strong reaction against further increases, and the new law school system began to disintegrate under lawyers' harsh criticism." In 2007, furthermore, "some LDP members, including the Minister of Justice, declared they would reconsider the lawyer population policy" (759). Then

> in 2009, a group of Diet members across party lines also demanded a drastic reduction in the number of law schools and students. In 2010 a lawyer who opposed increasing the lawyer population was elected JFBA president. At the end of his term in 2012, JFBA proposed reducing the number passing the bar exam to 1,500. That year the Ministry of Internal Affairs and Communications (MIC) officially endorsed the opposition. . . . It bitterly criticized the quality of professional education at the new law schools and argued that allowing 2,000 to pass the bar examination had created an oversupply of practicing attorneys. (761)

Lawyers across parties backed away from further expansion.

Finally, law school applications have gone from 73,000 in the first year to fewer than 10,000 now (Rosen 2017: 287). There is also discussion about cutting funding or defunding the schools with low par passage (287). The number of law schools is already dramatically down from a high of seventy-four. Only thirty-nine law schools enrolled students in April 2018 (Int. 4–Japan; Murayama 2020).

STRATIFICATION AND THE CURRENT LEGAL MARKET

The promise of dramatic expansion in access to Japan's legal profession has certainly not been realized. There has been an increase in the number of lawyers. The bar expanded from 23,117 members in 2007 to 37,680 in 2017 (Int. 1–Japan). That has meant there are more lawyers now in places that had very few of them prior to the reforms. But the market has not expanded in the ways that were predicted. As noted by Nakamura (2014: 104), "due to the introduction of the new system and an increase in the number of lawyers, competition among lawyers increased. The average income dropped from 17,010,000 yen in 2000 to 14,710,000 yen in 2010.

Since lawyers no longer enjoy privileged status and have difficulties finding jobs, the number of applicants to law schools dropped from 72,800 in 2004 to 13,924 in 2013." There are roughly half the number of law schools today than at the peak period after the reform.

The increase in the size of the corporate law firm sector has been substantial. In 1990 there were some 756 lawyers in business law firms, representing about 9 percent of the bar; the number in 2017 was more than 3,000 in firms of more than 100 lawyers (Int. 2–Japan; Murayama 2020). There were eleven firms with more than 100 lawyers and five with more than 350. The number of foreign lawyers permitted to work in Japan was 407 as of 2017. Foreign firms since 2005 have been able to hire local Japanese attorneys, but they have struggled to compete within Japan (Brennan 2013).

A big four—now big five—law firms in Japan make up a Magic Circle. The number of lawyers they hire annually is still not large. One recent study found that about 6.7 percent of the graduates of 2004 remain in "big law" in Japan, defined in terms of law firms of more than seventy lawyers (Int. 5–Japan). The big five offer high starting salaries, "around 12 million Yen (about $110,000) per year, the best fringe benefits, and opportunities to study abroad, often in the U.S." (Murayama 2020: 763). The number of offices of international corporate law firms has gradually increased, and the number of Japanese partners and associates had more than doubled by 2017. Large international corporate law firms have also formed partnerships with Japanese firms, although the largest ones have remained independent.

The stratification is strongly evident today. According to Rosen, "those that are doing well are, by and large, those that were on top in the old system: big-name institutions in large cities" (2017: 288). A study of large law firm hiring found that the tendency to hire from only the top law schools has increased since the law schools were founded (Nakamura 2014). According to Nakamura's research, which masked the actual names of the law schools, "school prestige did affect the size of one's first firm, and this effect is increasing, but in an unexpected way." The difference only "occurred between a limited number of elite individual institutions . . . versus the rest" (2014: 120).

In particular, one law school was at the top: "University A [likely the University of Tokyo] was the most striking example, where its graduates are overrepresented as new entrants to very large institutions, and this trend has increased" (120). Nakamura quoted a partner on the increased importance of the school attended: "Due to the introduction of the new bar exam system, the role of alma mater has increased. Before the judicial reform, a very limited number of people passed the bar. The fact that someone passed the bar could provide assurance of her/his ability. However, as the number of lawyers increases rapidly, passing the bar in itself can no longer ensure the ability of the person. Thus, school prestige became more important at the time of hiring as an index for ability" (120). One scholar reported, in addition, that many of the non–law school graduates who pass the bar are individuals who have left the more elite law schools, again suggesting the same stratification (Int. 5–Japan).

One result of the reforms, therefore, is that stratification, ostensibly based on merit, has increased. Furthermore, only a very few law schools and a very few law firms occupy positions in Magic Circles of the elite. At the same time, however, we do not know the extent to which the recent legal revolution has taken hold within the Japanese legal profession. The "failure" of the law school system in Japan, documented extensively in recent scholarship (e.g., Foote 2013; Rosen 2017), suggests that the purveyors of the new expertise did not find sufficient allies within emerging political movements. The relatively diminished role of the law schools even in supplying bar passers is an indication that new modes of teaching and new kinds of expertise are not at this point central to legal practice.

It is not clear whether there has been a major change in hiring within legal education or in the scholarship that is produced. Law professors at the time of the reform mainly "had come up through the graduate schools, which grant master's and Ph.D. degrees and primarily are devoted to training scholars, not lawyers" (Rosen 2017: 276). As noted earlier, they typically gained their positions through their relationships with a mentor-professor (Feldman 1993). The number of Japanese professors who are active in the new Asian Law and Society Association, organized by the many law professors who supported legal education reform, suggests a greater openness to interdisciplinary work oriented toward US approaches. The *Asian Journal of Law and Society* provides an outlet for that research. Japanese scholars state that the influx of new law teachers is "changing legal education" from inside (Int. 2–Japan). But certainly the situation is quite different from the Korean experience.

CONCLUSION: CONTRASTING STORIES BUT CONTINUING PROCESSES OF CHANGE IN BOTH SETTINGS

There has been no dramatic legal revolution in Japan in the sense that we saw in South Korea. Reformers initially used the Asian financial crisis to argue against the world of personal relations among the so-called iron triangle and the corruption it engendered. But the Iron Triangle did not draw the same kind of political opposition seen in South Korea. The *chaebols* in South Korea were linked to an authoritarian military regime, as were many of those in power within the legal field. The reform efforts and the politics behind them in South Korea did not face as strong opposition as the alliance among the state, the *keiretsu*, and the LDP in Japan. There is no strong and emerging political group united with the broader reform agenda in Japan. Political families in Japan do not have the links to authoritarianism that undermined the opponents of Roh and Moon. After the initial reform in the wake of the financial crisis, it is not surprising that the corporate initiators backed off and allowed the traditional oligarchy of the bar—which coexisted well with the Iron Triangle—to undermine and co-opt any movement for major change.

This conclusion, however, is not inconsistent with gradual shifts within the *keiretsu* and the Liberal Democratic Party. We need to know much more to see whether there is a more subtle legal revolution taking place that is consistent with global political and economic hierarchies. Turning to the legal profession, however, we can see some signs of movement despite the apparent failure of legal education reform.

A meeting of the Asian Law and Society Association in Taiwan in 2017 provided two perspectives on change within the profession. Atsushi Bushimata of Fukuoka University reported on a study of law graduates in Japan and found little evidence of change. He suggested that the practice of law today remains overwhelmingly in the long-standing core fields of traffic accidents, family, wills, and criminal defense—all components of a litigation emphasis. He found much less evidence of mergers and acquisitions, international business transactions, and corporate law, suggesting that the "corporate effort" is much smaller in Japan compared, for example, with what is found in the United States. He concluded that the "long-standing characteristics of the Japanese Bar still persist" and that the "structure of the Japanese Bar remains undifferentiated and homogeneous." (Quotations from notes taken at the conference by Bryant Garth.)

Daniel Foote of the University of Tokyo, a strong critic of the legal education reforms as they were implemented, suggests some paths that indicate change. Without disputing Bushimata, he emphasized the role of in-house counsel, which Bushimata left out of his sample. The bar after 2003 relaxed its restrictions on *bengoshi* working in for-profit companies. The number has grown from only 66 in 2001, working for 29 companies, to some 2,000 today—5 percent of registered lawyers. There are also relatively more women in this setting—almost 11 percent of women lawyers work in-house, versus 3.7 percent of men. There are also a number of non–bar passers in-house, and many are involved in issues of compliance that have a strong legal component. Of particular note is that some 45 percent of those completing the LTRI went in-house.

He also noted a great increase in lawyers in firms working essentially in government (since published as Foote 2018). Again, *bengoshi* were precluded from government employment until after 2000, and they are still limited to service for fixed terms, but Foote noted a major increase in lawyers building their careers in part through government service of one to three years. To Foote this suggests that there has been a shift in the nature of practice consistent with a greater legalization of business–governmental relations. In contrast to South Korea, however, Foote found no lawyers working in the not-for-profit and public interest sectors.[3]

There is thus evidence of a slow process of change consistent with the preservation of the basic practices and hierarchies of the Japanese bar. But, as noted before, there is not the drama of the more pronounced legal and political transformation that took place in South Korea. The ability of the entrenched legal elite to withstand the push for change was much stronger in Japan than in South Korea, largely because of the different relationship of the legal field to movements for political change. There are similarities, however, especially in the increased stratification that came with the apparent expansion of opportunity. In each setting the corporate law firm sector expanded notably—while still providing jobs for a relatively small group. And the actual changes that accompanied the reform of legal education were consistent with the increasing inequality of access to the legal profession generally and especially to the top positions in the profession. The cost of legal education is much higher, leading law schools are rewarded disproportionately, and the schools that serve the relatively less privileged gain fewer resources, face great challenges in bar passage, and are even threatened with closure.

Legal Education, International Strategies, and Rebuilding the Value of Legal Capital in China

Co-authored with Zhizhou Wang

As with Japan and South Korea, the founding of faculties of law and a Western-style legal profession in China came part and parcel with imperial pressures late in the nineteenth century (Kronche 2016: 67–68). Prior to that time, China provided the dominant model for national governance in the region. Indeed, between 1368 and 1841, China, Korea, Vietnam, and Japan had "maintained peaceful and long-lasting relations with one another" (Kang: 2010: 3), with China "clearly the dominant military, cultural, and economic power in the system" (3)—a "hegemon . . . operating under a presumption of inequality, which resulted in a clear hierarchy and lasting peace" (3). Kang terms this a "tribute" system. It involved travel, educational exchange, and gifts, and the other countries "consciously copied Chinese institutional and discursive practices in part to craft stable relations with China" (3). As a result, "there was no intellectual challenge to the rules of the game until the late nineteenth century and the arrival of the Western powers" (3). China's rules dominated. As Zhang notes, "although the Qing had plenty of interactions with foreign law, it approached these interactions from a period of political and intellectual strength" (2019).

Western power became much more salient after that time. With the decline of the Qing dynasty late in the nineteenth century, some among the Chinese elite acquired Western educations or influences and essentially sided with the imperialists against the traditional Chinese system, which was hostile to law and emphasized mediation and dispute resolution by traditional Confucian elites. While the Japanese in the Meiji period drew on Europe and especially Germany, Koreans operated within the imposed Japanese system, and Indians built on their English legal education, Chinese elites internationalized in multiple directions, playing double games in their own interests, and pushing aside Confucian learning and governance. An internationalized legal elite was built at that time.

This new elite evolved into a blend of pro-Japanese, pro-American, pro-German, pro-Soviet, and state or commerce-oriented law graduates. They became a kind of legal oligarchy akin to the others we have examined in this book. This group and those following its habitus have reproduced and endured into the present day. They played a strong role in Republican China, and as Tiffert shows (2015), they continued to be important in the People's Republic of China (PRC). The challenges they have faced have been enormous, but after much pain and turmoil the descendants of this group are thriving in China today. Unlike the traditional bar in India, this group has adapted remarkably well to changes in Chinese society and changing global hegemonies. This makes it exceptional among the case studies. Of course, many of this group stayed with the Kuomintang military government in the 1940s and moved with it to Taiwan after the communist takeover, but clearly there was a group that stayed behind.

The greatest challenge to this group's existence was a strand of Maoist Communism linked to cadres mainly of peasant background, who sought to minimize their role and the cosmopolitan and international influences they represented (Tiffert 2015). After many individuals from the cosmopolitan elite spoke critically of the government during the "thousand flowers bloom period" in China, they were severely attacked during the "anti-rightist" campaign that followed in the late 1950s. The Cultural Revolution beginning in the 1960s was the zenith of power of the radical Maoists, with devastating consequences for the cosmopolitan elites.

The revival of law after Mao's death in 1976, and the development of legal education and legal institutions after the Cultural Revolution, is a remarkable testament to the resourcefulness and resilience of this group. Elite and globalized legal education, corporate law firms, and even the "rule by law" policies of Xi Jinping only make sense in relation to the persistence and reproduction of this elite. The story of the past forty years is not about increased liberalism or democracy, as the West had hoped in the 1990s, but rather about an increase in the domestic value of internationalized legal capital, which had suffered a dramatic decline during the Cultural Revolution (Zhang and Ginsburg 2019).

LAW, INTERNATIONALIZATION, AND CHINESE INTELLECTUALS PRIOR TO COMMUNISM

As elsewhere in Asia, the imperial powers of the nineteenth century that forced China to open up to trade and influence also exported and even imposed their Western legal ideas. Strong local elites in China, as elsewhere, began to invest in and promote foreign models of modernization. In particular, as the Qing dynasty declined and Japan ascended, Japanese influence became important. Li, Li, and Hu focus especially on the impact of China's defeat in the Sino-Japanese War (2018: 251). Zhang points to a combination of factors, including changes in Confucian ideology to favor more pragmatism and materialism, the Boxer Rebellion, and signs of material weakness, as undermining traditional Chinese values. As a consequence, "the goal of political and eventually social reform became, more or less, to be like the West" (2019: 231). Nationalists increasingly viewed the foreign concessions in China as a "major embarrassment" and pointed to them as "one of the major justifications for legal reform" (234). The incentives for foreign legal intellectual investments were strong: "During the last fifteen years of the [Qing] dynasty, the promotion of Western law and political institutions became a kind of calling card through which new faces could open up the gates of power at the center" (235). Zhang argues that this group of Chinese intellectuals was unique in its embrace of Western models: "Chinese elites came to condemn and vilify their own sociopolitical traditions with a zeal that has few parallels, if any, in Asiatic history" (230).

The elites adapted to the new context. The legitimacy of the Confucian intellectual elite had been built on academic achievement and, prior to the Republican period, performance on the imperial exam. Studies indicate that this legitimacy was not inconsistent with the fact that access to the elite was not equally available. According to Wu, "those who succeeded in passing the merit-based examination came from only around 300 large families in selected regions during the Ming and Qing periods" (Wu 2017: 8). The mechanisms for reproducing this elite included the linkage of the exam contents to particular social worlds, in addition to more mundane ones such as the cost and expense of preparation (8; Elman 2013). Access to foreign ideas and education was similarly unequally distributed in favor of an elite that was able to capitalize on those assets (and many of them were undoubtedly descendants of the Confucian elite).

Reformers looked especially "to Japanese renderings of positivist German *Staatsrechtslehre*" (Tiffert 2015: xii; Zhang 2019), partly for convenience and partly because that approach to law was serving the Japanese state. Tiffert, like Zhang, emphasizes the radical nature of this shift away from Confucianism: "In imperial China, adjudication was part of a bursting portfolio of administrative responsibilities borne by local magistrates. . . . Consummate generalists, they cultivated humanistic erudition and received no systematic legal education, as China had none to offer them" (10). A functioning criminal/judicial field had taken shape around the Mandarin scholar-bureaucrats, but it operated mainly to build up the relatively marginal position of those seeking to moderate strict criminal sentences handed down by powerful local bureaucrats (Bourgon 2000). These kinds of local materials could be used and built upon within major transformations. But according to Tiffert, who emphasizes the break, "Confucian ideology frowned upon lawsuits. . . . The state restricted access to the courts, suppressed those who sought to facilitate litigation, and shunted most disputes to local elites and social organizations for mediation" (10).

From Tiffert's perspective, the radical change to a new judicial system "wrecked that model and the relations of knowledge and power imbricated within it. . . . This was nothing short of a Big Bang in the universe of Chinese law," which, he argued, "went beyond even the 1949 revolution. . . . The entire infrastructure of legal education and judicial training had to be built on the fly while the courts and the law took shape around them" (11). That effort—and other foreign borrowings—had very mixed results over the course of the nineteenth and twentieth centuries, but all the while, the internationalized elite thrived.

Legal education as such began in China, with the most important influence "from the last years of the Qing Dynasty to the first years of the Republic of China" being the Japanese system (Li, Li, and Hu 2018: 252). Indeed, "legal education in China then was merely a copy of that of Japan" (252). Professors also came from Japan: "From 1897 to 1909, law schools in China altogether hired 58 Japanese law professors" (253). This early tilt toward Japan (and derivatively toward Germany) was evident in the fact that, for example, "in 1915, the number of Chinese students in Japan exceeded 4,000. Most of them chose the majors of law, politics and economics" (254). At that point very few studied law in the US—reportedly only sixty-one in 1918 (254).

Under the Republic of China, founded in 1912, law was pursued by students mainly because of the opportunity it provided to join the government bureaucracy (253). The Chaoyang Law School in Beijing, established early in the twentieth century, for example, was the best-known private law school and focused on training for the government, especially the judiciary (Kronche 2016: 121). Public law schools also produced mainly government officials.

The investment in foreign legal models was not limited to Japan. Macdonald's work on Chinese legal education, published in 1980, provides interesting detail on how internationalized the law department was at Peking University, founded late in the nineteenth century on the European model. In the 1920s it was "divided into French, German, and English sections. Students elected to study in one of these sections and became proficient in the corresponding language" (Macdonald 1980–81: 316). The Japanese influence was still strongest, but the emphasis on the "international" rather than the particular country is telling.

The impact of the United States began to be felt in the 1920s "with the worsening of Sino-Japanese relations" (Li, Li, and Hu 2018: 257). The international legal influence on the Republic of China was evident in the fact that of the 2,448 qualified professors and associate professors recognized by the Ministry of Education between 1941 and 1944, more than 1,900 had studied abroad, including 934 who had studied in the United States (257). There was a "transition from the Japanese-style legal education to the American-style legal education" (257).

The private school in China most influenced by the United States was the Comparative Law School of China, established in 1915 near Shanghai by American missionaries as the law school of Soochow University (Connor 1994). The name itself reflected the internationalization of the legal field. That school focused on producing private lawyers and maintained close ties with the United States: "Most of its instructors came from the University of Michigan, and the majority of students sent abroad went to New York University . . . [but] spread around the globe" (Kronche 2016: 121). More than 1,200 students had graduated by 1946, and "72 of them took teaching positions in various Chinese universities (four of them took the position of dean), 21 became judges and 72 worked for the government" (Li, Li, and Hu 2018: 257).

The US influence also increased the size of the private bar in the major cities, including a commercial and corporate bar, especially in Shanghai, where the graduates merged with foreign counterparts that had begun to cluster around trade and the Mixed Court of Shanghai (Kronche 2016: 175). Also important was the relationship between the United States and the Kuomintang. Building on the long relationship between US missionaries and their lawyer allies with China, a number of influential individuals and groups in the United States saw the KMT as the great hope for building the rule of law in China (175–77). Chinese actors to some extent manipulated that faith, playing to US missionaries while not rocking the boat with the KMT, whose activities were more politically instrumental. Kronche notes the US approaches were kept alive also by a group of Chinese lawyers whose "personal capital in China was based on" their foreign (specifically US) expertise (176).

The picture is of a still quite small legal field coexisting with and evolving with foreign influences prior to the communist takeover. Some of the best-known members were foreign-educated, and they influenced others in the Western-oriented legal field of the Republican era. Foreign legal capital helped build careers, academic programs, and reforms even if the reforms were relatively superficial and the legal field had little autonomy. Since social capital was not invested deeply in legal capital, the orientation of the legal field could shift relatively easily in response to political changes. This flexibility has been key to the survival and success of this internationalized legal elite.

LEGAL ELITES AND CHANGE UNDER COMMUNISM THROUGH THE CULTURAL REVOLUTION

The communist victory in the Civil War brought another major shift. All preexisting law was abolished, and many of those central to the legal system fled with the KMT to Taiwan. This time the shift was toward the Soviet Union and its version of Marxist law. The new government under Mao Zedong in 1949 promoted the policy of "learning all from the Soviet Union" (Li, Li, and Hu 2018: 254). According to Li, Li, and Hu, "law was regarded by the ruling party of China as an important instrument to realize its socialist modernization. Therefore, the communist government decided to redesign its legal education based on the former Soviet Union model and to reconstruct its law schools and departments" (255). Here were the latest foreign-inspired recipes for modernization.[1] Tiffert in fact relates this embrace to the "habit to transplant first and sort out later" that began in the nineteenth century (2015: xii).

The Law Department of Renmin University was the most prominent facilitator of the move toward Soviet-modeled law. There were four teaching units: "the Unit of State and Legal Rights Theory, the Unit of State Law, the Unit of Criminal Law, and the Unit of Civil Law. Each unit consisted of Russian experts, translators and Chinese teachers" (Li, Li, and Hu 2018: 255). Renmin's graduates were "the main source of teaching and research staff in all other universities and research institutes" as well as teaching materials (255). Importantly, the government also retained law departments at six universities: "Chinese People's University [Renmin], Northeastern People's University, Beijing University, Wuhan University, Fudan University and Northwestern University" (Han and Kanter 1984: 546). By 1956 there were reportedly "2,824 new law students . . . ten times the enrollment figure in 1949" (548).

Institutes of Political Science and Law, modeled on the Soviet Union, also became central to legal education in the 1950s. In 1952 and 1953, a number of such institutes combined to form the East China Institute of Political Science and Law, the Beijing Institute of Political Science and Law, the Central Southern Institute of Political Science and Law, the Southwestern Institute of Political Science and Law, and the Northwestern Institute of Political Science and Law (Han and Kanter 1984: 546).

The descendants of the cosmopolitan legal elite had a strong presence. The Soviet Union's new influence did not fully displace other influences in classrooms. Li, Li, and Hu quote a graduate from that time saying that "points of different textbooks were contradictory to each other. . . . They used the Russian textbooks which were full of the descriptions of class struggle. Some others might have been labeled as 'extreme rightists' as they admired the constitutional politics, democracy and the rule of law, including the independence of the judiciary of western countries, without any criticism" (2018: 256).

Tiffert argues that one reason for this continuity was that the Communist Party prior to the victory had sought legitimacy linked to the intellectual elite long valued in China (2009). The Chinese Communist Party thus "assiduously courted intellectuals, appealing to their self-image as successors to China's imperial scholar-officials, their patriotism and their frustrated ambitions to undertake national salvation. . . . It welcomed them back into politics with promises to revitalize China and to usher in an age of multi-party New Democracy" (10). Many (we do not know the number) did go to Taiwan with the Kuomintang, but a significant number remained in the PRC.

As a result, "even high-ranking officials and judges of the former regime with no apparent leftist sympathies, such as the brilliant Yang Zhaolong, head of the Criminal Section of the Republican Ministry of Justice and protégé of Roscoe

Pound," joined to "contribute to the building of 'New China'" (10). This had a strong impact on the writing of the constitution of 1954. Leading participants, according to Tiffert, included "Shen Junru, the first President of the Supreme People's Court of the PRC, who earned the highest jinshi degree in the Qing imperial examinations of 1904, studied law in Japan, was a Republican era leader of the Shanghai Bar and the China Democratic League" (4). Another was "Qian Duansheng, Harvard Ph.D., close friend of John Fairbank, and a leading Republican-era constitutional scholar who served as the first post-1949 Dean of the Beijing University School of Law and founding President of what is now the China University of Politics and Law" (4). Finally, he points to Wang Tieya, discussed below, who was a student of Harold Laski and a renowned scholar of international law (4).[2]

Tiffert's recent work seeks to generalize further (2015). He argues that the PRC was "an heir (rather than . . . an antithesis) to Republican judicial modernization" (xxvi). Communist legal history thus amounted to "a dynamical system composed of shifting equilibriums" that allowed the PRC to tap into "an unheralded wellspring of diversity in PRC legal policy and practice" (xxvi). The Communist Party from this perspective was a mix of peasant cadres and members of the intellectual class, and one consequence of this mix was that legally trained elites from the Republican era were part of what constituted the Communist Party as well as the state. Those elites had adapted to promote the position of law through the importation of socialist legality into the new PRC.

Some of the literature suggests that individuals from the pre-communist legal profession began to face purges early in the communist period. But there are also many suggestions of continuity; for example, "lawyers, mainly holdovers from the previous regime, began to practice in state-run legal advisory offices" (Gelatt and Snyder 1980–81: 1). Noteworthy here is that Qian Duansheng became the first president of the China University of Politics and Law. Certainly, there was tension "between law-trained specialists (many of whom were trained in the West) or intellectuals and new cadres who 'lacked legal skills and knowledge,' but were ideologically reliable" (Han and Kanter 1984: 549; Li 1980). Such tensions generated conflicts from the start, but the early period gave an influential place to the intellectuals.

The Maoist emphasis on mediation became one source of tension, both symbolically and in practice. Ironically, according to Tiffert's research, the emphasis on mediation was one example of a party staple that evolved out of practices set in motion by the Nationalist-trained legal elites. The shift in mediation practices toward a more communitarian approach, partly to allay court congestion, came through Li Mu'an, "one of China 's earliest modern graduates and procurators, and a pioneer in the establishment of the Republican Bar" (2015: 51). According to Tiffert, Li Mu'an's 1942 reform as president of the high court of the Shaanganning border region opened the way to "popular mediation." This was initially promoted as a "new institution of border region judicial policy for educating the people to listen to reason and to do good, preserving peace among humanity." Later, "party rectification radicalized the atmosphere and inflamed class struggle." Prior to Li Mu'an's reform and its adaptation, "mediation occupied a small and neglected corner of CCP judicial practice" (59).

Mediation came to symbolize the divide between the legal reformist elites. Communist peasant cadres were suspicious of the cosmopolitan intellectuals. They tended to take an anti-intellectual stance against elites, whose minds were supposedly too corrupted to adapt. Mao, who tended to favor this group, supported this party-organized mediation against the legal programs favored by the Republican-trained elite (Tiffert 2015). While very different from traditional Chinese mediation, it served as a symbol of local approaches taking the place of Western-oriented law.

The position and value of the now Soviet-inspired law shifted with the political breezes, with the Cultural Revolution the culmination of the rejection of law and the zenith of the attack on, among others, the internationalized legal oligarchy, however flexible its members sought to be. According to Tiffert, "in the domain of law, the CCP bore multiple, competing visions of the revolution simultaneously, and as the balance of forces in the surrounding environment shifted, different equilibriums among these visions emerged, tracing a convoluted, sometimes violent course that reaches the present day" (2).

It is instructive to apply this perspective to an article in the *American Journal of Comparative Law* co-written by Han Depei and Stephen Kanter in 1984. It is written partly in the first person by Han Depei, who is discussed in more depth below. Looking back from 1984, the article defends the earlier work of the legal profession: "By 1956, then, a legal educational system basically suited to the needs of New China had been established and had achieved initial success" (1984: 548). The embrace of the Soviet model was deemed a success: "In reforming the old legal educational system and establishing the new during this period, our guiding ideology was clear, our principles and policies were comparatively correct, the measures adopted were reliable, and consequently the results were satisfactory. The graduates that came out of the institutes and departments of political science and law during this period have become the backbone of our country in politics, law and legal education" (548). The position of law and legal training was relatively strong at that moment. Indeed, Gelatt and Snyder (1980–81: 45) refer to the period as a "legal renaissance," Jerome Cohen termed it a "golden age" of law in China (quoted in Gelatt and Snyder 1980–81), and more recently Tiffert called it a "brief flowering of law" (2009: 25). All of this suggests that this flexible elite group of intellectuals felt able to thrive in a new legal context, this one modeled by the Soviet Union.

But the renaissance ended quickly: "By the late 1950's, however, everything changed. Legal scholars and practitioners had been among the first to take advantage of Chairman Mao Zedong's call in the spring of 1956 to 'let a hundred flowers bloom.' They had demanded more independence in their work and had gone as far as to challenge Party direction of the legal system. However, their outspokenness led to a quick backlash. Denounced as bourgeois rightists, many of China's small corps of legal experts were transferred to the countryside to be 'reeducated through labor'" (Gelatt and Snyder 1980–81: 42). A number of law professors spent "ten or more years [working] in the fields of village communes" (Murphy 1982: 51). The anti-rightist campaign led to the Cultural Revolution, at which point began the further persecution of legal intellectuals.

Han Depei, the co-author of the article on the changes in the aftermath of the Communist takeover, was part of that reform process after the revolution. He exemplifies a certain type of cosmopolitan intellectual of the time. He was born in 1911 in Jiangsu province, graduated from the law department of Nanjing University in 1934, and obtained a master's degree in law from the University of Toronto before taking up studies in international law at Harvard Law School in 1942. He became a professor in the Law Department of Wuhan University in 1945 and later the dean of the that department. As the co-authorship in 1984 indicates and as discussed below, he among others was active in the law revival of the late 1970s. He reportedly led the task of restoring academic prowess to the law department at Wuhan University in 1979 (Academy of Humanities and Social Sciences 2020).

Han describes the impact of the leftward shift in the late 1950s as follows: "Our department, one of the few law departments retained after liberation, was merged in 1958, together with the Central-Southern Political and Legal Cadre School, into the law department of Hubei University. Most of our teachers were transferred to other posts and some of our books and reference materials were taken away. The enrollment figures of students in law departments registered a sharp decrease throughout the country" (Han and Kanter 1984: 551). The situation then got worse: "In 1964 classroom studies were replaced by participation in the 'four clean-ups' movement (a movement to clean things up in the fields of politics, economics, organization and ideology), and law courses were soon abolished. By then it had already been announced that class struggle must be stressed year after year, month after month, and day after day" (552).

Even prior to the Cultural Revolution, then, "most of the professors who had studied old laws had been driven down from the rostrum, while newly trained teachers of law were forced to change their profession. Teachers and students who had been labeled 'Rightists' in the Anti-Rightists struggle bore continuous oppression. Law graduates were mostly assigned to posts in out-of-the-way places, unable to apply what they had learned. The youth of this period regarded law study as a dangerous road to take and naturally stayed away from it" (552).

Legal education came to a halt during the Cultural Revolution: "All the institutes of political science and law were also shut down, with the single exception of Southwestern Institute of Political Science and Law, which survived in name only. School buildings were seized and books and reference materials were divided up"

(554). Han and Kanter emphasized the remarkable devaluation and destruction of legal capital: "Advanced legal education, which had contributed to the training of law experts for our revolution and construction, suffered extremely serious damage. A thousand-strong contingent of law teachers built up painstakingly after liberation was dispersed and only a little over a hundred were left." (554).

REVIVAL AFTER THE CULTURAL REVOLUTION: THE RETURN OF THE LEGAL ELITES AND INTERNATIONAL STRATEGIES

As the Cultural Revolution waned in impact and higher education returned, "the law departments—not surprisingly in view of the particularly suspect classification of legal workers during the 'period of turmoil'—were the last to reopen their doors after China's educational hiatus" (Gelatt and Snyder 1980–81: 45). Peking University reopened its law department on a limited basis in 1974, two years after other undergraduate departments opened up again (44). By 1980, Peking law department enrollment had grown substantially, to about seventy (45). What is significant is that, as with respect to Han, most of the faculty were scholars who had studied law in China or abroad before communism, "participated in the legal renaissance of the 1950's and suffered the hardships of the anti-rightist movement and the Cultural Revolution" (45).

In 1978–79 the situation changed more dramatically. The four modernizations proclaimed at that time by the party did not include law but provided an opening for law. This renewed interest in developing the legal system reflected a new faith "that successful rapid modernization would be impossible without such a system" (Han and Kanter 1984: 556). At that time, there were very few professors available to teach law. According to the same article, "most highly qualified legal educators are elderly and are presumably nearing the end of their active careers" (561). Han, for example, was then seventy-three: "China is therefore in a race with time to train a new generation of law teachers, researchers and legal workers before the current fragile core of expertise disappears" (561).

The creation of the new law department at Wuhan University, for example, involved these relatively few pre-communist holdovers. Narrating again in the first person, Dean Han stated: "It was restored in August 1979. Surmounting all kinds of difficulties, we enrolled sixty undergraduates in the summer of 1980 as law majors, another fifty nonresident students in a branch school, as well as two graduate students of international law. . . . In 1981, we recruited 100 undergraduates as law majors and 32 as international law majors. In addition, thirteen graduate students were enrolled. The Department now has over fifty teachers and scientific research workers" (561).

At Peking Law School, according to one interviewee, there were classes on Western laws and legal systems, taught by Gong Xiangrui; as well as a course on comparative constitutional law, taught by Shen Zonglin; and another taught by Wang Tieya on public international law. These were offered as plain introductions to laws and legal studies in the West, and they allowed students to see China from a new perspective that inspired interest in the West (Int. 12–China). According to the same interviewee, the individuals who took up these teaching positions as the law schools reopened were valued for their educational capital—for their experience of studying law abroad and for the comprehensiveness of the legal education they had received (Int. 12–China).

By 1980, then, those legal elites who had survived the Cultural Revolution, including Dean Han, had become leaders in the revival of legal education in China (Li 1980: 226). Tiffert in fact notes that the cosmopolitan group that was influential in producing the 1982 constitution overlapped considerably with those who had worked on the 1954 constitution: "Much as they had twenty-seven years before, the Party's political elites again engaged constitutional specialists, Qian Duansheng among them, for guidance on how to cement this shift, restructure the state, and lay the foundations for stable economic growth" (2009: 25). The 1982 constitution, he writes, "provided the space for jurists such as Chen Shouyi, Jiang Ping, Li Buyun, Qian Duansheng, Wang Tieya and Zhang Sizhi—all of whom had either participated in the drafting of the 1954 Constitution or came of age in the brief flowering of law it spawned" (25). Tiffert cites their role in helping "to restore the legal and legislative machinery of the state, to reconstitute the legal profession, rebuild legal education and, in time, to reopen suppressed debates on marketization, democracy, the rule of law and human rights" (25).[3]

The revival included the universities as well as the larger law departments of the Institutes of Politics and Law, which had closed in the 1970s. A Chinese professor who has studied the revival of legal education after the Cultural Revolution noted the high quality of this first group of senior professors (Int. 2–China): "They were 'really good' with legal education from places like 'Harvard and Paris' and expertise in, for example, 'Roman Law.'" A number of them, as noted earlier, had international reputations prior to the Communist Revolution. This group trained the new generation of professors who would staff the law schools in the 1980s and '90s. Since the first law Ph.D. in post–Cultural Revolution China was awarded only in 1986 or 1987, the early faculty members from the new generation possessed only LL.B.s. Teaching materials were scarce. According to the same source, the early faculty typically knew German from their studies and Russian from the post-Revolution period, but their English generally was not strong (Int. 2–China). Many of the books they used were copies of Taiwanese texts that brought a mix of US and German/Japanese influence (Li, Li, and Hu 2018: 254).

As had their predecessors, these professors promoted international strategies that fit their own experiences and the need for allies in support of legal education and the legal profession. Jerome Cohen, for example, writes that "from the very start of the Open Policy in 1978–79, Chinese people have been eager to study law in other countries" (2010: 274). There was considerable exchange with the United States during this period. We have a good account of the relationship with Columbia Law School (Edwards 2009). Columbia began focusing on China in the early 1970s under the leadership of R. Randle Edwards, hired in 1973 on the recommendation of Jerome Cohen, then at Harvard and a key figure in US–China academic and professional relationships. Edwards traveled to China in 1978 under the auspices of a friendship program, and he reportedly met three law professors at Peking University—Wang Tieya, Rui Mu, and Guo Shoukang (Edwards 2009). He described their enthusiasm for an international program:

> The professors told us that the law faculty had just been reopened, after being closed for twelve years during the Cultural Revolution. They expressed keen interest in establishing exchanges with Columbia Law School and other American law faculties, when I broached the subject. On my return to Columbia, I followed up with invitations to all three of the Peking University law professors I had met on my first full day in China, and all of them visited the Law School more than once in the coming years. I discovered that one of them, Professor Rui Mu, was an "old friend" of Columbia, having held the status of Visiting Scholar at Columbia Law School from 1946 to 1948. (6)

The faculty members whom Edwards met initially exemplify the contribution of the already internationalized legal elite to the post–Cultural Revolution revival of law and legal education and the internationalization that went hand in hand with that revival (Minzer 2013: 351). One result was that, in the 1980s and 90s especially, Chinese legal academia once again became highly focused on the West—specifically, in this period, on the United States. This influence extended from preferred models of graduate legal education to the specific content of legal academic research.

The careers of the three professors whom Edwards met are interesting and informative. Rui Mu went on to revive his distinguished scholarly career, as summarized below:

> Born in a wealthy merchant family in Shanghai, he studied in the most modern "Western-style" school at that time. He was eloquent in English, French, and German, and proficient in Russian and Latin. After getting his Master of Law from the University of Paris and his doctorate from Frankfurt University, he went back to China serving as a law professor at National Southwest Associated University, later as deputy dean of the Peking University Law Department, and founding director of the Institute of Economic Law and the International Economic Law Institute. Though being marginalized during the "Cultural Revolution" (1966–76), he was immediately filled with energy after the reform and opening up, and laid the basis of two disciplines—economic law and international economic law in New China. (Peking University 2011)

We have an entry on Wang Tieya in Wikipedia that suggests a very similar background:

Wang Tieya was educated at Tsinghua University and the London School of Economics. He began his career as Professor of International Law at the National Wuhan University (1940–1942) and National Central University (1942–1946). In 1946, he moved to Beijing University. After 1949, he became one of the leading authorities on international law in China along with Li Haopei, one of his classmates in London. Wang was legal advisor to the PRC delegation to the United Nations in 1950 and the Third United Nations Conference on the Law of the Sea in 1979. During that time, he was Chairman of the Political Science Department (1947–1952), and Head of the Section on International Law at the Faculty of Law (1956–1983). In 1983 Wang became the founding Director of the International Law Institute of Beijing University. (Wang 2020)

Guo Shoukang was born in Tianjin in 1926. He graduated from the Peking University law department and became a professor in the 1940s. He became the leading intellectual property scholar in China after the 1970s. He had studied at Columbia University, Georgetown University, the UCLA School of Law, and the Max Planck Institute for Industrial Property. Reportedly, "he is also the sole expert having participated in drafting the three important IP [Intellectual Property] laws, *Patent Law, Trademark Law* and *Copyright Law*, and is widely acclaimed as one of the founders of IP legal system of new China" (Nie 2010).

Taking advantage of their foreign contacts and newly established exchange programs, this generation of professors sent a number of their top students to study abroad. Several notable legal scholars in China today were early graduates of Peking University's law school. One is Zhu Suli, who has served as Dean of the Peking Faculty of Law. He is the importer of Posnerian economics into China (Int. 3–China) and "probably the best-known Chinese legal theorist in the West" (Seppänen 2014: 85). He is considered the founder of neoconservative legal theory in China (89). He graduated in 1982, obtained a Ph.D. from Arizona State, and attended an LL.M. program at McGeorge Law School. He reportedly was a soldier and a civil servant prior to enrolling in the Beijing law program (Peking University School of Law 2020). Despite his international background and expertise, he is known as anti-Western and as a leftist in the Chinese context (Upham 2005).

Another is Ji Weidong, who graduated in 1983 and planned to attend graduate school in the United States. Instead he went to Japan, where he earned a doctorate from Kyoto University. He served as a professor at Kobe University before returning to Shanghai to become Dean of the KoGuan Law School, Shanghai Jiao Tong University, in 2008. He was involved in the reform of legal education in Japan, and his scholarship has embraced a strong law and society dimension. He is the editor-in-chief of the *Asian Journal of Law and Society*. His writings today focus on legal proceduralism (Seppänen 2016: 125–27).

A number of graduates of this period are leaders of the state today. They participated in the same educational environment. For a notable example, Li Keqiang, the current Chinese premier and the second most powerful individual in China, studied law at Peking University from 1978 to 1982 before obtaining a Ph.D. in economics. According to Cheng Li, a scholar who studies China's ruling elites,

> during his college years, academic and interdisciplinary study groups were very popular at Peking University, which had a long tradition in liberal arts education. Li actively participated in various public lectures and debates organized by these groups and studied under Professor Gong Xiangrui, a well-known British-educated expert on Western political and administrative systems. Li was particularly interested in the subjects of foreign constitutional law and comparative government. Li and his classmates translated important legal works from English to Chinese, including Lord Denning's The Due Process of Law and A History of the British Constitution. (Li 2016: 128)

At that time Peking University was deemed the center of liberal legal studies, with Renmin its conservative counterpart, but individuals at these schools and the institutes of political science and law did not always conform to the image of their respective schools (Int. 12–China). For instance, studies of civil law thrived in Renmin under the leadership of Tong Rou, who advocated for increasing the focus on civil society and private law. By contrast, at Peking Law School, in economic law Rui Mu focused on a more vertical state/market relationship (in opposition to the horizontal relations among private actors). Similarly, Wang Jiafu, who was in charge of the Law Institute of the Chinese Academy of Social Science (CASS)—an official think tank serving the ruling party—was well-known for his advocacy for a legal system that concerned itself solely with the civil/private relationship. And Jiang Ping, the former president of the China University of Political Science and Law (CUPL), which had been founded to train party cadres as well as legal officials who were loyal to the regime, made the school one of the most liberal in the country—its students joined in the Tiananmen Square movement in 1989 (Int. 12–China). Our list is of course incomplete, but we do want to show that this pluralism within institutions was consistent more with the legal field's overall focus on internationalized legal learning than on the particular orientations of scholars. This allowed the field to shift in tandem with shifts in political and economic orientation among those in state power.

Returning to the exchange programs beginning in the late 1970s and early 1980s, the exchange programs with Columbia and other institutions produced many prominent investment bankers and business lawyers. The Ford Foundation facilitated many of these exchanges. Edwards (2009) has noted that "many of the Chinese J.D. and LL.M. graduates from the 1980s and 90s now occupy leadership positions in American investment banks and in private Chinese and American law firms. Among them, notable graduates include Wei Christianson (J.D.), currently the managing director and CEO of Morgan Stanley in China; Charles Li (J.D.), CEO of Hong Kong Exchanges and Clearing, and formerly the chairman and CEO of JP Morgan China, and Wei Chun (LL.M.), who is now a partner in the Beijing office of Sullivan & Cromwell" (8).[4]

These examples are consistent with the fact that the elite of legal academia and the graduates produced by the leading universities were internationalized from the start, well before communism. They suffered during the Anti-Rightist Campaign and the Cultural Revolution but were able to step into leadership positions after the return of legal education and the legal profession. This, we should note, does not mean that their focus is solely on international connections and approaches, nor, as in Zhu Suli's example, does it mean they *support* foreign models. Their international orientation is not inconsistent with publishing in Chinese with the aim of getting the ear of the Chinese state, even if to oppose foreign models.

THE LEGAL FIELD TODAY: THE GROWING STRENGTH OF THE INTERNATIONALIZED LEGAL ELITE IN STATE AND SOCIETY

Legal Education: Stratification and Adaptation

Legal education and the legal profession have grown dramatically since the 1980s. The same can be said to varying degrees about the other countries examined in this book. Indeed, law in China became one of the most sought-after majors before what Minzner describes as a readjustment from overproduction (Minzner 2013). The number of law faculties reached more than 600. The profession was once dominated by state employees, whereas today, private law firms play a major role in economic and political relations. There are now at least three "grades" of law schools in China today. One group comprises the elite university law schools that have been for the most part internationalized from the start. These schools provide continuity with the past through the cosmopolitan professors who taught law prior to and after the Communist Revolution and who trained a new generation to follow in their footsteps. They include familiar names such as Peking, Renmin, and Fudan. Second are the institutes of political science and law, which can be traced to the Russian influence after the communist takeover. They are much larger in terms of student bodies and number of faculty members. We have some good information on their place today, but not as much data as we have on the elite schools. The third group includes the vast number of law schools that exist outside the major cities. We know very little about their faculties and students and, more generally, the roles that they play locally and nationally. There is some evidence that they are struggling to find places for their graduates.[5]

The Elite of Legal Education

The rapid expansion of law, and of higher education generally, "significantly increased the internal stratification in the Chinese law school community and intensified the interschool competition for government support and recognition"

(Wang, Liu, and Li 2017: 243). The period of law school expansion corresponded with the rise of "law schools affiliated with elite universities that used to specialize in natural sciences and engineering" (245). The rapidly rising law schools of Tsinghua University, Zhejiang University, and Shanghai Jiao Tong University, for example, benefited from their universities' "administrative ties with the Ministry of Education, rich alumni resources, and dedication to strengthening humanities and social studies in the state-led effort to build 'comprehensive research universities'" (245). They caught up with their "traditional elite counterparts," such as the law schools of Peking University and Renmin University (245). Global rankings have reinforced the position of the traditional elite and the newcomers in the Chinese educational hierarchies.

The elite law schools are also considered to be the most focused on theory, today as in the past: "Universities such as Peking, Tsinghua, Nankai and Wuhan were more traditionally focused on producing legal academics, researchers and public servants, so practical education was seen as less important" (Biddulph 2010: 270). They remain dominated by highly theoretical lectures. According to one recent study, "no law school is willing to define its mission as the 'training of practitioners'" (Zhao and Hu 2012: 354). Accordingly, "practice experience is not given much weight in the recruitment and promotion of law professors" (354). Scholarly publication is much more important than teaching in terms of career development. As a result, "faculty members in Chinese law schools lack incentive to invest in improving legal teaching" (354). Legal theory is at the core of these schools.

There is a movement to develop clinical legal education. More than 100 law schools now offer clinics of some kind, and an organization called the Chinese Committee of Clinical Legal Educators keeps up with developments in this system. The Ford Foundation was instrumental in launching a number of these programs (354), which are now found in the full range of law schools. Lawyers in the United States often view these clinics as central to legal education reform and as key to building the rule of law in China (e.g., Phan 2005). Those ambitions have not been realized.

The founder of the first clinic, at Wuhan University in 1980, Wan Exiang, earned an LL.M. from Yale Law School in 1987 through the Ford Foundation exchange program and has followed a remarkable path since then. He became professor of international law at the Wuhan University law school and is currently the Deputy President of the Supreme Court of the PRC, a member of the standing committee of the CPCC, and Vice-Chairman of the China Society for Human Rights Studies. His career is consistent with the fact that the clinics in China have added a more US-inspired element to legal education, but this is an add-on that has not affected China's hierarchical values and approaches more generally.

Finally, while difficult to classify according to Chinese internal hierarchies, we mention the highly innovative and internationalized Peking School of Transnational Law in Shenzhen. Founded in 2008 as a domestic initiative to provide Chinese students with an alternative to studying abroad, STL hired a prestigious founding dean from the United States and aspired to produce graduates with US JDs suitable for them to be hired by global law firms. As a result of US opposition, it failed in its goal of achieving accreditation by the American Bar Association; the school then retooled to offer both a Chinese JM and a US JD in one four-year program. With its international faculty, the school is more like one of the Hong Kong law schools than a Chinese law faculty. Despite not offering the LL.B., it has found a niche in China and has placed its 100 to 150 annual graduates in international and Chinese corporate and in-house positions. It hopes to inspire further reform in China. Its creation and survival is another indicator of China's openness to the international in legal education.

As noted earlier, the elite Chinese law faculties are highly internationalized and theory-driven. Faculty are recruited from those with advanced degrees from China or abroad, with very few from practice: "Many elite Chinese law schools have adopted the hiring policy that, except for exceptional applicants, graduates with only domestic law degrees are not considered in faculty recruitment" (Wang, Liu, and Li 2017: 260). Those who have gone abroad since around 2000 have divided their graduate studies between the civil law—mainly in Germany and France—and the common law—mainly in the United States (Int. 5–China). Accordingly, there are divisions in the law schools between those that emphasize the more practical learning and interdisciplinary approaches of US law schools and those that embrace the legal formalism identified with German approaches (Int. 4–China; Wang, Liu, and Li 2017: 253). Such differences in background may be part of the reason why some schools, such as Peking Law School and Shanghai Jiao Tong, have more of an interdisciplinary focus. An informant from Renmin noted a competition between schools that emphasize dogmatic law (i.e., the German influence) and those that lean more toward the social sciences (i.e., the US influence) (Int. 4–China). One professor at another leading school said that in the current situation, editors might criticize an article for relying on too many US sources and not enough on German ones (Int. 5–China). What unites the various groups is a focus on legal theory, even if what is seen as legal theory from a German perspective is very different from what legal theory means from a US perspective. The range of theoretical perspectives is suggested by Seppänen, who characterizes the literature on the rule of law as a "theoretical smorgasbord" (2016: 66).

The shifting debates in legal scholarship provide a sense of how the internationalized legal academy responds to shifts in the state. According to Zhang (2019), "for much of the 1980s and early 1990s, both American and German trained scholars shared a basic consensus that Chinese law should become more like foreign legal systems. They differed in which foreign legal system they preferred—for obvious and often self-interested reasons, each side preferred the legal system they were educated in—but most people seemed to agree that Chinese law needed to westernize once more and pursue a rights-based ideal of the 'rule of law'" (246).

Zhang highlights a relatively recent shift in the dominant approach of the US-educated scholars. Late in the 1990s, he suggests, a "growing number of American trained scholars, most notably Zhu Suli, dean of Peking University Law School between 2001 and 2010, began to explicitly argue *against* transplanting either American or German law, or any foreign legal system. Instead, they argued that China needed to find its own path" (247). Accordingly, "by the 2000s, the most visible opponents of westernization tended to have some sort of American academic background" (247). Most interestingly, "certain strands of American legal and political theory were especially conducive to this agenda" (247). Zhang cites law and society scholarship, various forms of critical legal studies, sociology, and economics as Western tools to "deconstruct and delegitimize the application of Western law to other societies" (247).

Academic developments thus "allowed Chinese leftists to reject the notion of universal human rights and argue for Chinese cultural and political exceptionalism" (247). These Western-based academic theories, more generally, "gave academic voice to a political mainstream that, while still very much in control of the actual levers of power, had become somewhat dormant in intellectual discourse" (248). The "state swiftly moved to support this trend, boosting the sociopolitical profile of its major advocates and enlisting their support in a number of major legislative moves" (248). The new theories fit the new politics in China. What is noteworthy is not that the legal academy shifted to accommodate a new balance of power. The chapters of this book and the theory of legal revolutions demonstrate the importance of such shifts in maintaining the position of law. What *is* remarkable in China is how internationalized the debates and the people participating in them are.

Cosmopolitan professors from the elite law schools circulate internationally and develop substantial networks abroad. They naturally play a double role similar to the role that elite Chinese law scholars and professors played in the past. They import from abroad and reshape for domestic purposes, and this links Chinese legal professors with global markets and hierarchies even while they adapt them to Chinese interests and the field of state power. They can modify their behavior for the different contexts. Chinese scholars at times encourage those abroad to see progress or at least ferment toward "the rule of law with Chinese characteristics"; at home, they are more conservative. For example, Li Buyun, one of the cosmopolitan jurists mentioned by Tiffert in regard to the drafting of the 1982 constitution, has been a leader in speaking and publishing in favor of the "autonomy of the law" (Seppänen 2016: 121), rights protection, and the rule of law within and outside China, even though his politics within China are relatively conservative (121).

An important feature of the present day is that the Communist Party now signals which scholars it sees as favorable to party orientations (Int. 12–China). Especially since the mid-1990s, scholars have been invited to lecture the top party leaders in Zhong Nan Hai, the hub and central headquarters of the Chinese ruling party's most senior leaders. It appears that those who are chosen to give these lectures—without any official statement as such—enjoy significant prominence on the basis of their political recognition by the ruling party; their careers may well blossom as a result (Int. 12–China). This treatment may also distinguish those who are loyal to the party from those who tend to disagree with it and thus gain its disapproval.

Finally, the risks that elite and cosmopolitan legal scholars face more generally are mediated by their international stature, their valued scholarly capital, and their connections to the worlds of economic and political power, whereas other legal professionals are not as protected. As shown by Liu and Halliday (2016), the lawyers who run the greatest risk of retaliation by state organs are the ones without academic credentials or ties to the state. In particular, lawyers for criminal defendants may run huge risks with few resources except the hope that media publicity will persuade the political authorities to take their side.

For aspiring students, the top law schools fit into a system of education in which "China's elite colleges are the fundamental point of entry for the scientific and political elite" (Yang and Chen 2016: 196). The number of openings is quite small, especially given that the undergraduates at the top schools—those who gain their position from national test scores—are the most favored. Peking Law School has about 2,000 students (700 undergraduates), Tsinghua has about 1,300 (300 undergraduates), and Shanghai Jiao Tong University KoGuan Law School even fewer, some 725 (220 undergraduates). Renmin Law School has some 3,000 students (800 undergraduates). These and a few other elite schools graduate a very small percentage of the more than 200,000 law graduates per year (Minzner 2013). The elite group is quite rarified.

In 1993, the Ministry of Education and Ministry of Justice began to consider creating a degree akin to the US graduate JD degree. According to Ji Weidong, writing in 2005, this was part of a plan to introduce the US way of legal education (2005: 15), with the US business lawyer as a model. The plan also drew some inspiration from the US-inspired Japanese move to replace the undergraduate LL.B. degree with the graduate JD. In 1998 the JM degree was created, and there was optimism that it would become the main vehicle for training practicing lawyers in China (15; Erie 2009: 67).

Predictably, it has not been successful. Erie writes that "so while the JM is being designed as the main degree for professionalizing PRC lawyers, in fact, the LL.M. [following the LL.B.] remains a more efficacious vehicle of professionalization. This is particularly true in terms of developing practical skills of legal reasoning, argumentation, and oral advocacy" (95). One professor noted that the JM is not a "good education" but that it "makes a profit" (Int. 6–China). The LL.B. followed by the LL.M. remains dominant.

The most respected students are those who score highest on the national exams and get into the most selective universities. A JM graduate does not get that kind of respect. Erie notes, for example, that "international law firms show a preference, in hiring first year associates, for students who obtained an LL.B. at the undergraduate level and then either went on to obtain an LL.M. in China or abroad. Domestic firms also prefer LL.M. graduates" (Erie 2009: 75). The continued importance of the first degree, where selection is based largely on the national exams, reinforces the significance of the law school hierarchy as compared to a more practical law degree modeled on the US JD.

The strategy of the Chinese elite universities, including the newer ones such as Shanghai Jiao Tong University KoGuan Law School, has therefore been to focus on the very small number of students they accept for LL.B. degree programs while also offering the JM in order to generate revenue and as a means to upgrade the less prestigious undergraduate degree. Having learned from the JD's relative failure in Japan, the dean at KoGuan, Ji Wedong, has reinforced the elitism of undergraduate education. He has created a 3 + 3 program that enables about fifty of the top undergraduates to move into an academic master's program along with the LL.B. He also sought philanthropic support to invest further in the quality of the faculty and student body, and has received some $30 million from Leo KoGuan, an American/Chinese entrepreneur. In this way he has made the elite training at his school even more selective.

According to professors at the top schools, the students of the "top ten" all come from similar family backgrounds (Int. 5—China; Int. 6–China) and forge similar careers (Wang, Liu, and Li 2017). Students come largely from the best secondary schools in the cities, and their parents have assets to invest in education. Thus, Tsinghua has fewer students from rural backgrounds than in the past (Int. 6–China). The students' backgrounds as reported by the professors and deans are consistent with more general recent sociological research on Chinese mobility. There is some mobility, to be sure, but the statistics make it clear that those with the advantaged backgrounds are strongly favored.

Xiaogang Wu, in a recent study of mobility and education in China, found that "family background directly affects access concerning the quality of college education. Other things being equal, upper-middle-class and upper-class children clearly enjoy advantages in getting into elite and other 211 universities" (roughly a top 100 based on a project of educational reform from 1995: 2017: 27). There are also advantages to coming from more urban and politically significant communities—most crucially, from "keypoint high schools," that is, those schools that especially feed the leading universities (27).

Another recent article augments this picture by showing that cadre status also plays a role: "the political status of a cadre parent is significantly correlated with the possibility of his or her child attending an elite college" (Yang and Chen 2016: 209). Again, the most important factor is access to the keypoint high schools that feed the top colleges. There is upward mobility through the relatively meritocratic system organized around the national tests, but, as these studies note, there is a family cadre advantage as well as one of resources: "approximately 30 percent of students in the elite universities came from upper- or upper-middle class families, whereas the percentages in other 211 universities and non-211 universities are 18.6 percent and 14.6 percent" (Wu 2017: 17).

The combination of local meritocratic, international, and perhaps in recent years familial capital is increasingly evident in the legal academy. One leading China expert noted that "although the intergenerational reproduction of academic legal elite in China was severely undermined by the Cultural Revolution and other political events in the Mao era, since the reform era, it has gradually re-emerged." This scholar reports seeing "an increasing number of children of distinguished Chinese legal scholars pursuing doctoral degrees in law, and some of them already hold faculty positions. It is likely that in the next 5–10 years a wave of 'second-generation law professors' will emerge in the Chinese legal academy, as happened in many other places" (email China–1).

The Institutes of Political Science and Law

The importation of Soviet models in the 1950s led to the creation of five Institutes of Political Science and Law to go with the European-inspired law departments of Peking, Renmin, Jelin, and Wuhan. The story of the relationship between the two groups is complex; that said, the relationship is more a division of labor than a competition (Wang Liu, and Li 2017; Minzner 2013). There are also overlaps and combinations and movements between the two types of law schools. A recent article on Chinese leadership, for example, notes that the justices of the Supreme People's Court of the PRC in 2013 (Li 2014) included four graduates from the Southwest University of Political Science and Law in Shanghai, three of whom had advanced degrees from Peking Law School; one from the Chinese University of Political Science and Law in Beijing; one from Jilin University and Peking Law School; and one who only graduated from Peking Law School. These judicial positions seem to link more to the schools of political science and law designed to train prosecutors and judges.

The Institutes of Political Science and Law, as noted, were modeled on Soviet schools and were meant in the first place to train loyal legal cadres for judicial and prosecutorial positions. The universities and their law departments, in contrast, were originally created to mimic the great Western (and Japanese, based on Western) universities. The division of labor in these early years is significant; however, enduring hierarchies in the legal field meant that both kinds of faculties of law sought to build the credibility of law through foreign models. Also, there was some circulation of elites when these schools were established.

After the Cultural Revolution, the basic division of labor returned as the schools reopened. According to Herman, writing in 1982, "graduates of the university law departments are educated primarily for careers in research, teaching and government. The institutes, on the other hand, are geared to train practicing lawyers to serve in the procuratorates, the Ministry of Justice and the public security organizations (police), as well as to serve in the roles of advocate and justice" (1982:

792). Sarah Biddulph's close study of the East China University of Political Science and Law, published in 2010, notes also that 30 percent of the graduates at that time "were allocated to the legal divisions of local governments, a range of government departments, and [other organizations]" (2010: 263). Furthermore, "schools within the Ministry of Justice system were traditionally more oriented toward practice as many of the graduates of these schools were employed in the state's judicial organs, as judges, prosecutors, police, justice officials and lawyers" (270). These institutes were thus closely linked to national and local government legal bureaucracies.

The institutes are much larger than the elite law schools. The Chinese University of Political Science and Law in Beijing has 14,000 students (8,000 undergraduates). The school likely graduates at least 1,000 undergraduates with LL.B.s. The East China University of Law and Political Science reportedly graduates 1,500 undergraduate LL.B.s per year (Int. 5–China). They do not have the same prestige as the more theoretical law departments, a partial exception being the Chinese University of Political Science in Law, which has close ties to the Ministry of Justice (China email 1) and has internationalized through a relationship with the European Community.

From the perspective of one who attended the East China University of Law and Political Science and has had experience with the faculty, it is a "different world" (Int. 5–China). Those who attend that university do not have near the scores on the national exam that the students at the elite law schools have. Graduates tend to go into criminal litigation or seek ("self-select") to be judges or prosecutors, rather than lawyers for state-owned enterprises (SOEs) or corporate law firms. Teaching is focused more on the bar examination. The students tend to be less eager to go abroad after graduation—"to take the TOEFL"—than those in the elite schools. The students generally are "traditional" and "stay in China" (Int. 5–China). They also tend to be from the provinces, and their future careers typically depend on family capital brought from home and connected to local networks of judges and prosecutors (a "family sector") (Int. 5–China).

The power of these schools is in general less internationally based, involves less scholarly capital, and is more tied to rank-and-file governmental and party power.

The Rank and File Law Schools and Law Students

There is reportedly a scramble to get jobs among students outside the very small elite of graduates from the top law schools and others with family or *guanxi* connections that facilitate recruitment. Those who practice criminal law, for example, have little in common with the elite law graduates (Liu and Halliday 2011–12: 838). It is suggestive that Li, Li, and Hu (2018) quote one student as stating that "our teachers told us in class that if there were no judges or government officials in our family members, we should not choose law schools. Law is the major for the people with power. The children from poor families will not have a bright future after graduation" (2018: 22).

A great number of graduates compete for a relatively small number of positions within the prosecutors' offices and the judiciary. Minzner thus writes (2013: 360) of a "spiral of degree devaluation," where "many Chinese law students are willing to spend large sums of money on advanced degrees to distinguish themselves from other graduates. Enrollment in foreign LL.M. programs (with tuition ranging up to US $50,000 a year) has surged. Chinese schools have expanded their J.M. . . . programs, charging four times as much in tuition per student as compared with the 'academic' master's degrees." Graduates of many, perhaps most, of the Chinese law schools may not enjoy the study-abroad option that Minzner suggests makes a difference. In addition, as we saw in Japan and Korea, the difficulties facing lawyers at the low end of the hierarchy have become a reason to put pressure on the low-prestige schools. One goal of recent reforms in China has been to cut down and essentially defund some of the more marginal law schools. As elsewhere, this has threatened the law schools that are more accessible to less privileged students (Minzner 2013: 374).

The Rise of Corporate Law Firms and Their Dominance by the Internationalized Elite

The Chinese corporate legal market has a short history, one that began in 1992 as a top-down initiative to mimic institutions of globalization. Corporate law firms, as elsewhere in Asia, make up a tiny percentage of the legal profession. In late 2017 there were more than 340,000 lawyers in China (Liu 2020). The small number of corporate lawyers stands out: "modelled on global law firms from Britain and the United States" in the early 1990s, "the elite club of the corporate bar is relatively easy to identify" (Wang 2018). Since it has been well-studied in several respects (especially by Sida Liu), our discussion of it will be brief.

China now has its Red Circle of law firms, comprising "a dozen elite Chinese corporate law firms such as King and Wood (today's King and Wood Mallesons), Jun He Law Offices, Haiwen and Partners, Jingtian and Gongcheng, and Zhong Lun Law Firm" (53). The largest of these has more than 4,000 lawyers. Beijing has the greatest number, but firms are also concentrated in the major cities of Shanghai, Shenzhen, Guangzhou, and Hangzho. There are also small boutique firms, and law graduates also work in the SOEs, which increasingly emphasize the need for quality in-house counsel (Liu 2020).

Drawing from the expertise of Chinese lawyers educated abroad and with work experience in global law firms, the Chinese law firms now compete from a very strong position for high-end work with the more than 100 global firms (Liu 2020) in China—most of which are in relatively small "outpost offices" (Stern and Li 2016). The Chinese firms have advantages in part because Chinese lawyers are not authorized to practice local Chinese law in international firms, which limits local recruitment. Another reason, which is only beginning to be studied in depth (Wang 2018), is the importance of connections to the Chinese government and regulatory structures. Wang writes that for a variety of reasons, there is a "growing interaction between the Chinese state and Chinese corporate lawyers" (63). We discuss this strengthening connection below.

The elite law firms hire according to the educational hierarchy, despite the fact that elite schools focus on theory and not practice. The Peking Law School, in particular, reportedly pays little attention to the bar examination, and the graduates who take it—likely to qualify for litigation—reportedly do worse than the national average. One informant from Peking Law School, perhaps exaggerating, said that the professors there, in fact, are proud to "teach the opposite of bar exam, and the students score poorly—20 percent of the 10 percent who take the bar examination pass" (Int. 7–China). According to one student at a top school, it is "easy" for the LL.B. graduates to get positions at the corporate law firms if they want them (Int. 3–China). Students from the "mediocre" law schools, however, have no chance.

Firms in Beijing, for example, reportedly recruit mainly from Peking Law School, Tsinghua, and the University of International Economics and Business (Zhu, Zhao, and Liu 2020). The Peking Law School, historically the most prestigious school, reportedly dominates in the corporate law firm sector. Very few of its graduates reportedly go into litigation (Int. 7–China). Criminal law especially is looked down upon (Int. 7–China; Liu and Halliday 2016). Other positions sought by the elite graduates are in the government and the SOEs.

The new arrivals to elite law status, including notably KoGuan and Tsinghua, are competing with their more established rivals by taking the lead in the globalization of faculty recruiting, stronger scholarly requirements, and educational programs, but the others have followed the same strategy (Wang, Liu, and Li 2017). Wang, Liu, and Li maintain that the enhanced international strategy relates to "the prestige and wealth of corporate law," which "prompt[s] law schools to develop courses, curricula, and internship opportunities tailored to the careers of international business lawyers. Accordingly, the ability to place graduates in prestigious law firms is becoming a new symbol for the success of law schools and a key attraction in law schools' recruitment of college applicants" (243). The easiest access is for those with an elite undergraduate legal education, who follow up with LL.M.s, especially from abroad (Zhu, Zhao, and Liu 2020). The internationalized law faculties thus operate in sync with the corporate law firms and SOEs in China.

The Increasing Value of Legal Capital
in Governance and the State

The value of legal capital in China has increased over the past forty years. The historically high value of elite and internationalized legal capital has returned, and it is rewarded in governmental and party careers as well as with positions in law firms and SOEs. Cheng Li's detailed recent study of the Chinese ruling elite highlights this change. He notes the shift in the educational credentials away from technocrats such as engineers, "with the so-called rule of the technocrats lasting for only about two decades" (2016: 203). The well-connected and talented children who took the path of legal and related training have been rewarded. Chinese leaders are known more today "for their educational and professional training in the social sciences, economic administration, and law" (203). These leaders invest their legal learning and capital in state governance, distinguishing themselves from those with other claims to party and governmental power. As suggested below, they quite naturally also link to the elite law graduates in corporate law firms and elsewhere.

The increased value of legal capital in governance is well explored in a recent article by Zhang and Ginsburg (2019), who point out that this change is not the same as an increased commitment to the liberal legal values, which seemed to be on the ascendency in the 1980s and '90s. Zhang and Ginsburg do not note any shift in the training and expertise of key Chinese leaders, but they make a persuasive case that there has been a shift toward law: "contrary to conventional accusations that China has 'turned against law,' Chinese politics have become substantially more law-oriented over the past 5 years, and . . . several core legal institutions, including the judiciary and the Constitution, are now more politically significant than at any point in the 69-year history of the People's Republic of China (PRC)" (2019: 309). This conclusion, they note, is not inconsistent with increasing central control by the top party leadership around President Xi Jinping. The move toward greater control at the top, they note, has been implemented "legalistically." The increasing role of law involves, among other things, "empowering courts against other state and Party entities, insisting on legal professionalism, and bringing political powers that were formerly the exclusive possession of the Party under legal authorization and regulation" (310). The changes go with more independence of the judiciary, higher pay, and the related ability to attract more talent into the judiciary.

Zhang and Ginsburg observe that prior to Xi Jinping's rise, there was a reaction to what was seen as excessive foreign-inspired legal liberalism. This led to a relatively brief and ineffective attack on law reminiscent of the dramatic attacks of the Cultural Revolution and earlier by party activists (2019). Citing Minzner's work (2013) on the "rise and fall" of legal education, they note that under President Hu Jintao, Xi Jinping's predecessor (2002–12), this reaction "included a de-emphasis on formal law and court adjudication, and the subjugation of judicial power to political imperatives" (Zhang and Ginsburg 2019: 318). In their words, "instead of formal law, the Party sought to promote mediation as the preferred means of resolving social disputes, indeed as an institutional embodiment of the 'Harmonious Society' promoted by President Hu Jintao" (318). "As part of a general program to increase the courts' responsiveness to 'the feelings of the masses,' judges were systemically evaluated on the percentage of their cases—the more the better—that were either mediated or voluntarily withdrawn" (324).

This focus on mediation, they note, was not very popular with the Chinese public, which by then had little interest in activist mediation as opposed to law. Indeed, Zhang and Ginsburg affirm the respect of the public at large toward law, courts, and the constitutions—all of which can be traced significantly to the internationalized legal elite that the Anti-Rightist Campaign and Cultural Revolution attacked. The neo-Maoist rally against them under the banner of popular mediation appears to have been defeated. The party's further distancing itself from the populism of the Cultural Revolution is one of many signs of the revival of the internationalized legal elite in the state and the economy.

Elite Legal Education, Corporate Law firms, and the State

The literature on corporate law firms and elite faculties of law notes that graduates of the elite faculties, including now especially law, occupy strong positions in the party and state. This chapter has offered several examples of graduates prominent in the state as well as in law firms. We do not, however, have a literature on personal relationships from family, school, or career between, for example, partners in corporate law firms and leaders in government. We know little, for example, about how governmental careers are converted into corporate law or whether the reverse takes place. We do have a growing literature, mentioned earlier, that emphasizes that the success of Chinese corporate law firms and their advantage over international law firms with offices in China often come from government relationships (Wang 2018).

An intriguing preliminary report by Lawrence Liu (2019) has explored some of these connections, focusing especially on the vast Belt and Road Initiative (BRI), first announced in 2013. Commenting on the growing outbound investment that characterizes the (BRI), he notes that "PRC legal professionals are increasingly relied upon to advise domestic industries, broker deals with foreign companies and states, and handle the disputes that arise in challenging foreign legal environments" (2019:1). Significantly, the Chinese state takes an active interest in this role, seeking "to implicate lawyers in the political dimensions of China's outbound efforts" (2). Liu explores efforts by the Ministry of Justice (MoJ) and the All China Lawyers Association (ACLA), beginning in 2012, to "cultivate a group of PRC cross-border legal experts" (2) and to build a government-recognized elite in the service of these transactions (see also Stern and Liu 2020).

Accordingly, "the ACLA and the MoJ jointly selected a talent pool of 300 lawyers with foreign legal expertise. . . . Over four years . . . the program aimed to produce 120 lawyers proficient in the corporate transactional work involved in outbound investment" as well as in various other transnational specialties. This effort has been expanded, again reflecting the high expectations placed on lawyers, who have been called upon in a governmental document to, among other things, "serve as good legal advisers to the government," to "promote positive economic and trade exchanges," and to "help Chinese companies go out, and defend their rights and interests abroad" (2).

What is especially interesting is that in 2017, again according to Liu, the ACLA announced a list of "BRI and Cross-Border Legal Experts" (2). Liu was able to examine the characteristics of the eighty-four PRC lawyers officially recognized as part of that group. The results are striking. First, they are mostly men. Second, there is a very strong representation from among the Red Circle firms: "A handful of lawyers have even moved to these law firms since 2017 . . . further consolidating the strength within these firms" (4). Third, "the overwhelming majority of "BRI and Cross-Border Legal Experts" hold advanced degrees (88 percent), with most of them pursuing graduate-level education abroad (60.6 percent)" (4). Fourth, they have strong ties to the party and government: "About 68 percent of these ACLA-recognized individuals hold leadership positions at some level of the bar association, and about 20 percent serve as People's Congress or People's Political Consultative Congress deputies" (5). Over 50 percent are party members, according to the lists available for Beijing and Shanghai.

These data, while preliminary, suggest three findings consistent with this chapter. First, the Chinese government today values the characteristics identified with the internationalized legal elite, high-level education (especially with study abroad), and strong foreign experience. Second, the largest law firms—staffed by such persons—have been identified as a key place to find the most elite lawyers. Finally, the government contemplates a major role for these elite lawyers along with the government in law and development, dispute resolution, contract management, and other aspects of the Belt and Road Initiative. All of this is consistent with a strong role for elite lawyers and law in the BRI as essential to the Chinese state strategy globally and at home. It also appears, as with respect to law professors, that the government today is more open about its efforts to find and identify allies with governmental strategies (which is consistent with governmental efforts to link lawyers to party ideology in bar exams and elsewhere: Stern and Liu 2019).

CONCLUSION

The internationalized elite that emerged in the late nineteenth century is thriving today after a remarkable story of challenge, adaptation, and survival—all the while making internationalized legal capital central to the process. Many were persecuted during the Anti-Rightist Campaign and Cultural Revolution, but they have returned to their previous social place. Their survival strategy was to emphasize elite, learned, and meritocratic education; to develop international expertise and contacts; and to legitimate a kind of post-Confucian elite that could occupy leading positions in the state and economy. The legal field in China is organized around a diverse group of internationalized scholars united by their commitment to legal theory and the value of international capital. The elite is also well-connected to state power. Learned law represents a kind of neutral space, and the different foreign and domestic emphases of the various contending groups have allowed the center of gravity to shift with the times and with changes in the orientation of state power. The new era of legalization has abandoned the almost pro-democracy and liberal teachings of the 1990s to emphasize anti-corruption along with higher-quality and better-paid prosecutors and judges, more judicial autonomy, less tolerance of dissent, and a greater focus on rewarding lawyers and scholars seen as best oriented to the party's agenda (Zhang and Ginsburg 2019).

Law appeared to return from out of nowhere after the Anti-Rightist Campaign and the Cultural Revolution. The law schools had all been closed, there was no legal profession, and lawyers were among those singled out as targets of the Cultural Revolution. It seemed at that point that there was no legal establishment to point to, in contrast to the situation in the other Asian countries studied in this book. But a new start developed out of the remnants of an internationalized elite, which revived its connections abroad, especially to the United States, and imprinted its approaches in the elite university law schools. This is a prime example of a revival of an elite, internationalized, and relatively meritocratic legal oligarchy akin to what we have seen in other Asian countries.

That elite has survived and adapted to changes in the state and the market as well as in global hegemonic relationships. This group helped make elite corporate careers the province of relatively privileged graduates, who typically study abroad after their initial work experiences. The faculty of the top law schools circulate globally, with impacts on both sides of the ocean. The internationalized faculty brought China into the global legal world of the WTO, international law, and international institutions (Roberts 2017), while also steering the international rules so as to be more in favor of Chinese concerns and interests. Elite graduates have now been assigned key roles in China's new Belt and Road Initiative, which will define China's relationship with much of the world.

China's situation is thus very different from India's, for example, where there is an entrenched conservative legal elite tied to the long experience of the British Empire, and from South Korea's, where the Japanese colonial legacy and the Cold War produced a deeply conservative legal establishment that resisted approaches identified with US-style globalization and the spread of large corporate law firms. The even more entrenched Japanese legal establishment is also sharply different from China's. China has various colonial legacies in law, all active prior to the communist takeover. But the genesis and history of this group has prevented it from acting as a conservative or entrenched legal establishment.

Interestingly, this internationalization has made the Chinese legal field over the past forty years seem more like Hong Kong than the other case studies in this book. The value and convertibility of international legal capital are quite high in both places. The law professors and law schools in China have much higher status than in Hong Kong. China did not inherit the British system seen in Hong Kong and India, which devalues law professors as mere teachers. In addition, Hong Kong, long a colonial entrepôt, tends to open up elite corporate law positions more to those educated abroad rather than to locals educated at Hong Kong law schools.

In China, as elsewhere, finally, a key part of the story is the growing gap between the small number of elite careers, students, and schools and the mass of schools producing many more graduates with slim prospects. Thus the relationship between Peking Law School, Tsinghua Law School, and others with the corporate law firms is very similar to what we find in South Korea or Japan. Also similar is the importance of the undergraduate school attended. The competition favors those with resources in a variety of ways, including in relation to the cherished opportunity to study abroad.

Conclusion

Combining Social Capital with Learned Capital:
Competing on Different Imperial Paths

Our long history began in medieval Bologna, where mastery of canon law and Roman civil law turned a small number of cosmopolitan elites into elite legal professionals. This was a process of empowering family capital with new knowledge. It required financial resources. Only an advantaged few had the ability to travel and to pay the costs; only they had the background to succeed in the rigorous academic work required for a doctorate from Bologna. The graduates put their social and scholarly capital to work in the in-fighting between canon law and civil law, controversies over feudal privileges, and disputes within and among the multiplicity of jurisdictions existing at that time. Growing trade and commerce made the graduates of schools of law very much in demand. As Brundage (2008) noted, they went from "strength to strength" during the medieval period.

The expertise of the small group of law graduates trained in civil and canon law, and their successful application of it, thus became central to the conversion of the old landed elite into modern-day professionals and ultimately agents and leaders of newly created states and companies. The descendants of this formative period—able to mobilize the habitus established by then of family capital, cosmopolitan scholarly learning (initially Roman civil law and Roman Catholic canon law), and proximity to power—remain keys to understanding continuity amid the constant reinvention of hierarchies, norms, and institutions of different legal fields. The continuity of the story makes that habitus of internalized behavior relevant and quite visible today.

The case studies in Part IV show the importance of relatively small cosmopolitan legal elites able to maintain their positions over time across dramatic political and social changes, including independence and global legal revolutions, most recently and notably the neoliberal revolution arising from the end of the Cold

War and the rise of US hegemony. The revolution has had varying degrees of success in the countries we have examined in this book. One clear result is that large corporate law firms have proliferated where they had not existed before, including in the countries studied here. Also, there is greater emphasis on meritocratic capital to obtain positions in such firms, even if the ability to succeed according to meritocratic criteria relates strongly to social class.

The corporate law firms started outside the cores of the local legal professions but have since found strong places within local hierarchies and co-opted their major opponents. Also, albeit to different degrees, the second phase of the legal revolution reveals the development of very close ties between the relatively small elite of corporate lawyers in magic circles, red circles, and big fours or fives, and an equally small number of elite law schools—together they build and reinforce the great distance between the mass of law graduates and an ever wealthier few. The new and reformed law schools compete for international status, and they also compete to place their graduates in corporate firms. Reforms oriented toward corporate law firms include more engaged teaching, a focus on practical problem-solving, and a new emphasis on subjects such as mergers and acquisitions. Related reforms have enhanced the visibility of interdisciplinary research and more generally the sophisticated interdisciplinary arguments that the most elite firms employ.

We now reflect on the scholarly approaches we have drawn upon and what our own approach brings. The case studies, as noted earlier, well exemplify and continue the model that Brundage and Martines portrayed of the legal profession as it emerged in medieval Italy and developed with the rise of the city-states. Lawyers served from the beginning as brokers combining arcane cosmopolitan knowledge with family capital in various ways, and they used their position to build law and states in relation to emerging economic groups, the Church, and the huge number of jurisdictions under feudalism.

The case studies also fit generally with Berman's theory of legal revolution. We interpret that theory as a theory of permanent revolutions—the rebooting of legal establishments through the challenges brought by aspiring quasi-elites as they made new investments in knowledge and linked themselves to emerging political powers. That process is quite evident in the contrast we drew between South Korea and Japan. A certain sector of South Korea's legal profession, linked to US approaches and human rights initiatives, acquired power through an alliance with its country's democracy movement (which was not necessarily pro-US) against the formerly authoritarian government and its supporters. That alliance led to very different outcome in South Korea than in Japan in terms of legal education and the power of the traditional professional hierarchies. We see various forms of political legal alliances working toward the legal revolution in India as well as China, and there are hints that aspiring legal elites were key actors within the legal profession in these battles. These case studies also bear out Bourdieu's observation that the class and family capital that undergirds the power of cosmopolitan elites is reinforced through meritocratic criteria and links to state power.

It is important to recognize, however, that legal revolutions are more complex than Berman's theory and our narratives that draw on it. These revolutions involve constantly shifting positions and blended categories such as professor/politician in the United States and prosecutor/NGO/ entrepreneur in South Korea. Nevertheless, Berman's theory provides a solid hypothesis for how legal establishments wedded to existing power change and endure in relation to new social movements. The emerging legal revolution leads to more or less significant changes while rebuilding the position of law close to power and refurbishing the established legal hierarchies that had been tied to an earlier status quo. Lauren Benton and Lisa Ford's *Rage for Order* (2016), which we also draw upon, shows how the British Empire built law out of a relationship between London and the local or expatriate imperial agents designated as representatives of a law connecting Britain to its colonies and noncolonial outposts.

The *problématiques* employed by Berman, Bourdieu, and Benton and Ford, from our perspective, miss how larger geopolitical dimensions shape the circulation of ideas and the particular mixes of social and learned capital that we find in different settings. Benton and Ford help explain the approach adopted in the British Empire, but they do not address how the larger geopolitics affects interconnected histories in different places and through changes in imperial power. In medieval times, competition and complementarity characterized not only the tensions between learned capital and social capital, but also the role of feudal justice, communal approaches, and many other approaches to dispute resolution. Interaction with these and other localized approaches helped produce a divergence relatively early in the post-medieval history of the legal profession.

The British combination of learned and social capital emerged through the transformation of local justices of the peace into learned gentlemen with different political alliances than found in medieval or Renaissance Italy. Social capital to mediate between the Crown, the aristocracy, and the gentry combined with learned law, but social capital dominated—as evidenced by the role of the Inns of Court, especially after the seventeenth century, as mainly dining clubs where apprentices were socialized into the bar. As Benton and Ford show (2016), when the British exported their approach to colonies, they exported the same focus on social capital. They sought out locals endowed with social capital, such as the Brahmins and the Parsi, and encouraged or facilitated their education—mainly through dining with members of the bar—then sent them back to India as quasi-English gentlemen. On the basis of their social capital and a little learned capital, they were able to profit tremendously. They became the "nabobs of the law."

The other model that emerged and that is important in our case studies also required social/familial capital and learned capital, but it also maintained the prominent role of selection through schools and education that characterized the Bologna model, which produced aristocrats as grand professors in the Holy Roman Empire and Continental Europe. That model's relative valuation of scholarly capital was not inconsistent with the booms and busts related to times of relative obsolescence in the value of scholarly capital, such as in the history of the French *noblesse de robe*. Similar conditions of devaluation drove the revival that took place in Prussia in the eighteenth century, which included a purge of the lawyer-courtiers serving and dependent on the aristocracy. The private bar shrank, and scholarly and educational standards improved. German legal education maintained its prestige but also became oriented toward the production of bureaucrats and statespersons. Professors were also circumscribed somewhat by the development of codification, but the mix of social and scholarly capital was still very different from that of the British. The Prussian investment in law and the state then became central to the well-known state-led industrialization spearheaded by Prussia in the nineteenth century in an effort to catch up to the British, who were a century ahead.

At the end of the nineteenth century, heightened imperial competition led to extraordinary investments in legal expertise in colonial governance and legitimacy. The revival of law during the Indian Raj is one example; the cultivation of the Javanese aristocrats sent by the Dutch to Leiden for their education is another. The earlier gradual process accelerated as a function of imperial competition. What the British exported into India, as noted, was based largely on social capital; it empowered Brahmins and Parsi, in particular, as gentlemen lawyers. Leiden-trained Javanese aristocrats in Indonesia were a similar example in a Dutch colony. This phenomenon was not evident in Hong Kong, an exception because expatriates occupied the relatively few places in the legal profession.

This second geopolitical approach we see in the case studies can be viewed as a "catch-up" strategy both in the North, exemplified by Germany and France, and in the South, exemplified in our case studies by China, Japan, and South Korea. Those from the leading samurai clans in Japan invested in the state and followed the Prussian model of a strong state legitimated by legally trained bureaucrats, with judges and lawyers coming from less powerful samurai clans and given more subordinate roles. Codes designed in part to limit the role of private lawyers and judges were mimicked as well. For China and Japan, this was clearly part of an economic catch-up strategy and a push to gain credibility in the West, and the Japanese brought that strategy to Korea. This strategy did not necessarily allow those most endowed with social capital to reap the rewards of learned legal capital akin to those enjoyed by the Indian nabobs of the law, but the investment of ambitious reformers diffused that state-oriented legal capital throughout these Asian contexts.

The third geopolitical approach central to this study is the one connected to the United States. There were British-trained barristers in the colonies, and they in turned trained others. This small cosmopolitan elite played a strong role in US independence and governance. Its ties to Britain and British legal expertise, however, led to attacks on lawyers in the Jacksonian period and a low point for lawyers' prestige. There was a boom for the elite of the legal profession later in the nineteenth century that went with an upgrading of legal education led by Harvard, which drew in part on the formalism of the Continental model. This helped the partners of the emerging corporate law firms become lawyer-statespersons and not simply hired guns for the robber barons. Those partners then international-ized, exporting an anti-imperial imperialism into the Philippines and elsewhere as the basis for a "legalist empire."

The particular blend of social and learned capital has differed in each of the settings we have examined. We find similar cycles of booms, busts, and revivals, but those cycles vary as to timing, the spaces of activity, and the direction of the circulation of people and knowledge. The colonial legal and social capital associ-ated with the Indian Brahmin lawyers, for example, grew as a result of the politi-cal capital accumulated from the independence movement, then contracted when elite lawyers resisted Nehru's social reforms.

Booms and busts can lead to new hegemonies, an example being the evolution from the Jacksonian rejection of the Toquevillian lawyer-aristocrat; to the corpo-rate lawyer statesperson armed with an upgraded legal discourse, close relation-ships with a few elite law schools, and ties to powerful corporate and individual clients and the philanthropic foundations they founded with their clients' money. They became the basis of the foreign policy establishment (FPE) that, with rela-tively minor ups and downs, thrived at least into the 1970s.

The FPE's approach led to the law and development movement as a new form of export of moral imperialism and scholarly selectivity. That movement sought to develop lawyer-statespersons to open up economies and invest in moderate social reform. The key goals were legal education reform and the development of the tools wielded by US "first-rate metropolitan lawyers." It failed in part because of the weakness of the liberal establishment in the United States, which found itself divided over the Vietnam War. The main reason, however, was resistance from the South. The investment that was imported by or poured into India and Japan (then to South Korea), in particular, in the late nineteenth century resulted in legal pro-fessions with bunker mentalities that resisted reform as threats to the status and rewards enjoyed by those at the top.

The shape of the resistance related to the geopolitics of the nineteenth century. India's elite bench and bar mobilized the social and family capital central to their status and practice. Japan and South Korea mobilized the quasi-family capital that grew out of their respective "cradles of the legal mafia" in the Judicial Research and Training Institute in South Korea and the Legal Research and Training Institute in Japan, which trained those few who succeeded in passing the bar examination. Ties to conservative economic and political power also helped maintain the legal status quo. Bar passage into the select group entering the training institutes came from mastery of the codes, which meant "excelling in memorization, requiring one to in effect 'memorize all the textbooks and theories'" about the codes.

In China, by contrast, investors in foreign legal expertise began their work during an era in which classical Chinese knowledge and political expertise were devalued. Their learned investment was a survival strategy, not a defensive one, and the flexibility of the cosmopolitan legal elite today reflects the same approach.

The most recent phase of legal revolution is connected to but different from the moral imperialism of the law and development movement that was launched in India, Japan, and South Korea roughly a generation earlier. There has been a counter-offensive against the various embodiments of legal oligarchies, with different alliances in India, Japan, and South Korea. They have had some degree of success in each country. The major changes are the emphasis on corporate law firms, financial markets, and neoliberal policies. Also, there have been recent changes in legal education, including new law schools and new law degrees, more engaged and practical teaching, and more investment in interdisciplinary scholarship and discourse and in "modern" legal arguments suitable for corporate law firms. The embrace of US-style legal theory has drawn scholars around the globe into the debates and approaches that succeed in global centers, especially in the "highest ranking" law schools such as Harvard.

The revolution has enhanced meritocracy, but we see no evidence that it has opened the profession to the relatively disadvantaged, who cannot as a rule muster the resources to succeed under the meritocratic criteria. They may enter the legal profession through the schools at the bottom of the hierarchy, which are quite numerous in China and India, or through the relatively few schools at the bottom, as in Japan and South Korea. But their inability to get into the most select schools, and perhaps to gain access to a foreign LL.M. or other degree, eliminates any chance for them to join the magic circles of elite law firms and top in-house positions. The mass of lawyers is strongly separated from the small fraction at the top.

The reforms have created some meritocratic openness, however. Outsiders to legal families, for example, who come from business and professional families, may gain access to the resources to get into and succeed in a select law school. We see this especially in India. These outsiders represent some of the leaders in the legal revolution, in part because they have observed that without family capital they face a glass ceiling.

The dramatic divide in the legal profession between the few and the very many who may have law degrees but practice a very different kind of law is reminiscent of the medieval period, when only a very few could practice formalized and rarified dispute resolution under the civil law and the canon law. Looking backward, while we may exalt the rise of professionalized Roman and canon law in dispute resolution in the medieval period, we need to remember that that story coexists with a huge variation in approaches, formalities, and authorities at the same time in different areas. Since legal history tends to be by and for lawyers, there has been neglect of the many gradations in the boundary between what gets before the law, what is above or below the gaze of the law, and how the boundaries change. In short, there are ebbs and flows in the role of professionalized law in relation to other forms of authority, and ideally these should be subject to historical and sociological inquiry. We do not have detailed information, but there are suggestions that in China, for example, the growing importance of law in global business transactions and as a tool of regulation from the top may be very different from local dispute resolution, where social capital may be more important than legal argument. The general point is that part of the tension in legal fields—and hence instability, conflict, and reform—comes from the challenge and contestation it has to confront from the second tier of "petty" disputes and second tier of legal professionals.

There are also tensions arising from counter-developments away from the narrative of professionalization and legalization stemming from notables who seek to displace the role of law as local authority or in relation to empire and hegemony. A strong instrumentalism in the Cold War and in the War against Terror, for example, provided international leeway for local leaders to diminish the role of law. Notables in particular circumstances may ground their decisions in law, in indigenous norms, in clientelistic relationships, in religious texts, or in various mixes of these. Law identified with a hegemon who becomes an enemy might be purged. If the Maoist and peasant-led Cultural Revolution had succeeded, for example, what kind of party governance and clientelism might have replaced the role, however weak, of law in China? We cannot be sure. The legal revolutions we refer to in our analyses of the case studies have succeeded in keeping law close to power, but that result is not inevitable.

Finally, these potential challenges to the authority of professional justice raise a related complexity that we could not take up in this work. Bourdieu appropriately emphasizes the complementarity and competition between social capital and meritocratic capital in legal fields (2021). This mode of analysis also suggests a pull of social capital because those able to mobilize it can use it maintain their positions in legal fields with limited investment in scholarship and meritocracy— leading to potential devaluations of scholarly capital. Bourdieu's focus on the role of social capital and legal capital did not, however, lead him to address the ways that professional justice and what we can call a kind of feudal justice continue to coexist in different ways. We have referred to dual justice, but the two sides are not separate. The concept of dual justice in the sense of a "lower" justice dominated by social capital versus a more "professionalized" justice of formal law masks this coexistence.

As E.P. Thompson in *Whigs and Hunters* (1975) showed, the professional justice system in the eighteenth century in Britain doled out draconian punishments for those who committed minor crimes, but he noted also that some of those convicted could mobilize mentors, notables, neighbors, or others, to gain some kind of recourse, ultimately perhaps to the Crown, suggesting that the ultimate resolution could stem from both formal professional justice and a kind of feudal justice drawing much more on social capital. Thompson's narrative, therefore, is not just about his famous assertion that the formal law has some autonomy despite its service to power. This additional power of social elites on the perimeter of professional justice is different. That power can modify or avoid professional justice or even mobilize professional justice on behalf of particular interests. The Trump administration provided many examples of what can be seen as the personalistic mobilization of professional law to punish enemies and reward friends. Similarly, it may be that the *chaebols* in South Korea still have the power, as suggested in a Korean interview, to mobilize prosecutors to target perceived critics. The connections between social capital and professional justice change in relation to evolving power relationships. An exploration of these connections would add a further dimension to studies of the relations between law, social change, and stability that could be developed in the future.

CONCLUDING WORDS

This book is ambitious, covering long interconnected histories and countries, each of which has a cadre of legal and other scholars much more knowledgeable than we can be about any single country or historical period. The terrain we seek to examine here is too large for us to master, even with the help of area legal and other experts. We have tried to use the tools of historical sociology and the best sources available to provide a novel but convincing account of a story that extends from medieval Bologna to cosmopolitan elites in imperial settings to a new legal revolution. The narratives show at a minimum that the global rise of corporate law firms is not just about the demand for such services or global isomorphism. It is about a legal revolution related to global hegemonic power, hierarchies in national legal fields created out of the older European empires, the role of challengers drawing on learned law emanating initially from the United States to build their positions and the role of scholarly law, and the resistance, embrace, or co-optation of the new by those who occupy the leading positions in legal fields. These are hard-fought battles that have shaped the national credibility of law and lawyers in the competing global context.

The stories leading to the financial and neoliberal legal revolution emanating from the United States, in addition, provide an opportunity to reexamine the relationship between law and social change. We found tools for that examination by going back to the origins of the legal profession, as examined by Martines (1968) and Brundage (2008), and those tools exposed for us how the cosmopolitan broker model developed in Bologna both stayed the same and diverged in different settings, especially vis-à-vis Britain and Germany and, later, the United States. Berman's theory of legal revolution (1983; 2002) provided a framework for examining law and social change in particular settings. Bourdieu's insistence on the competing and complementary relationship between social capital and learned capital and between lawyers and the state fits well with Berman. So do Bourdieu's conceptual tools such as the field and the concept of habitus. Successful legal revolutions bring change, but the change comes with continuity, often through the refurbishment of a legal establishment and the interests embedded in it.

What we especially bring in this book, we think, is a missing geopolitical dimension. What emerged within legal fields depended on imperial competition, specific developments in competing empires, and interactions with local settings. Changes, including legal revolutions, depended in large part on learned law, whose credibility stemmed from geopolitical developments, including, for example, the rise of US hegemony in the aftermath of the Cold War. Our approach makes clear that today's universe of "best practices" in legal education and legal practice must be understood in relation to the geopolitics that have *made* them "best."

NOTES

CHAPTER 3. LEARNED LAW, LEGAL EDUCATION, SOCIAL CAPITAL,
AND STATES: EUROPEAN GENESES OF THESE RELATIONSHIPS
AND THE ENDURING ROLE OF FAMILY CAPITAL

1. "Poised between centers of power, able to play one against the other, the university managed to develop its own institutional structure and traditions with remarkably little interference. Thus allowed to get a good running start, the university had become largely unstoppable and indispensable by the time of the emergence of the modern nation-state" (Labaree 2017: 17).

2. The story of continuity was pointed out by Max Rheinstein: "In the fourteenth century, a young man who aspired to a career in the service of his prince, or who intended to practice before the prince's boards and tribunals as an advocate, or as a notary, went to the Italian seats of learning. In later times, the princes provided their young men with universities in their own territories, but in all universities the same Corpus Juris was taught by the professors. The Corpus Juris, the work of the sixth century, was to be adapted to the needs of new times. This task was fulfilled by the professors, who were creative men of great learning and authority" (1938: 6).

3. These opinions are both lucrative and prestigious. According to Rheinstein, "It brought the law professors into continuous contact with the facts of life and the actual problems of legal practice; it was a consequence as well as a cause of their enormous influence on the development of the law" (1938: 7).

4. "The most striking feature of the history of the inns during the later seventeenth century was the decline of legal education" (Lemmings 1990: 25).

CHAPTER 4. LEGAL HYBRIDS, CORPORATE LAW FIRMS, THE LANGDEL-
LIAN REVOLUTION IN LEGAL EDUCATION, AND THE CONSTRUCTION
OF A US-ORIENTED INTERNATIONAL JUSTICE THROUGH AN ALLIANCE
OF US CORPORATE LAWYERS AND EUROPEAN PROFESSORS

1. Even a C average would get a job on Wall Street, but according to a student at the time, "we all wanted to get into the best office" (Coquillette and Kimball 2015: 587).

CHAPTER 6. INDIA: COLONIAL PATH DEPENDENCIES REVISITED:
AN EMBATTLED SENIOR BAR, THE MARGINALIZATION OF LEGAL
KNOWLEDGE, AND INTERNATIONALIZED CHALLENGES

1. NLS training has slowly become more corporate-focused. With new changes to NLS coursework requirements, one could go through law school and not take a single class that prepares one for litigation (Int. 23-India).

2. According to a recent editorial by two academics who went through the system, "NLUs tend to prioritize the number of hours spent in the classroom over the quality of teaching; the timelines of evaluation over the quality of evaluation; and the number of courses taught per year over development of good courses" (Surendranath and Arun 2012).

3. We focus our interviews and analysis on those at the top of the national hierarchies, but the national hierarchies are mimicked in regional and local settings throughout India. We would find the same processes and familial relationships among the "elites" not known at the national level. Email from Jayash Krishnan.

4. For example, Nick Robinson shows that "in about half of Indian states, including Bihar and Madhya Pradesh, there are public ombudsmen called lokayuktas, i.e., 'People's Commissioners' in Hindi. These ombudsmen are usually retired High Court or Supreme Court judges" (Robinson 2015: 353).

5. There is some progress. One US academic observed, "I wouldn't go too far on this. I know many young, talented Indians who are making a career of being a legal academic and they are published in the newspapers, appear on TV" (Int. 25-India). Still, the interviews within India suggest that, outside of the Jindal Global Law School, the career is still not established.

6. Jayish Krishnan notes a group from the big seven law firms that break off and go specifically into litigation in part to challenge the entrenched group (email communication).

CHAPTER 8. SOUTH KOREA AND JAPAN: CONTRASTING ATTACKS
THROUGH LEGAL EDUCATION REFORM ON THE TRADITIONAL
CONSERVATIVE AND INSULAR BAR

1. An exception was the Handong International Law School—part of a Christian university—which early embraced the notion of a JD and a common law education.

2. "First, the Council's ambition to create a more diverse bar composed of lawyers with expertise in fields outside the law—to ensure lawyers would be better able to understand their clients' legal problems—fell short almost immediately. Of the first class of admitted students, 5% were graduates of law faculties, 22.0% were graduates of humanities or social science departments, and only 8.4% were graduates of science departments. Since then, the

numbers of non-law graduates admitted to graduate law programs has steadily declined, and the class admitted in 2007 included about half as many graduates of engineering and science programs . . . as the class admitted in 2004" (Riles and Uchida 2009: 13).

3. Foote noted that the expensive bar dues—as much as $10,000 per annum—meant that the one or two people working in the public interest in the labor union sector let their memberships lapse.

CHAPTER 9. LEGAL EDUCATION, INTERNATIONAL STRATEGIES,
AND REBUILDING THE VALUE OF LEGAL CAPITAL IN CHINA

1. "Chinese students went to Moscow for advanced legal training, and both countries exchanged fact-finding delegations to learn first-hand about the professionalized legislative organs, courts, prosecutors, legal aid offices and public defenders contemplated under the new Constitution. . . . In these and other outlets, lawyers and academics, influenced by Soviet jurisprudence, translated the notions of rule of law and constitutionalism that had entered China during the early Republican period, and that have proved vital to its numerous constitutional movements ever since, into a discourse of 'socialist legality' that promised many of the same deliverables" (Tiffert 2009: 22).

2. "Advising the drafters as the text moved forward were a pair of philologists (Ye Shengtao and Lü Shuxiang) and two principal teams of lawyers (Zhou Gengsheng, Qian Duansheng, Fei Qing, Lou Bangyan and Wang Tieya). None of these advisors were members of the CCP. The legal advisors in particular had had extremely distinguished academic careers, and were well-traveled, multi-lingual and conversant in the dominant trends in international legal scholarship at the time" (Tiffert 2009: 16).

3. Tiffert notes further: "The structural and normative connections between the 1954 and 1982 Constitutions are too numerous to list here, but one Chinese scholar sums up the relationship this way: "[t]he 1982 Constitution takes the 1954 Constitution as the basis of its formulation" (25).

4. Some information on Wei Christianson is suggestive. According to a Wikipedia entry, "Wei Sun Christianson, born on August 21, 1956, to an army officer father and doctor mother . . . grew up in Beijing as the youngest of four daughters. . . . Her parents believed strongly in a Western education, going as far as to spend a month's salary buying her a tape recorder so she could play English tapes. . . . During college, she met visiting Columbia University professor Randle Edwards and was urged to set her goals higher, aiming to become a lawyer as it would be a more respected profession and highly atypical of women at the time. . . . Edwards advised that she first attain a degree from a top liberal arts college in the U.S. in order to better her chances of acceptance . . . .

In 1983 she transferred to Amherst College and became its first student from mainland China following China's opening to the Western world in the early 1980s. She graduated *cum laude* with a B.A. in political science in 1985. She immediately continued on to Columbia Law School, where she met her future husband Jon Christianson and received her J.D. degree in international law in 1989" (Christianson 2020).

5. One observer said that fewer than 100 provide any quality legal education and that they have low bar passage rates (Int. 5–China). Minzner (2013: 350) reports that there are many of low quality and with poor employment statistics.

Abel, Richard, and Philip Lewis, eds. 1988–89. *Lawyers in Society*. Berkeley: University of California Press.

Abel-Smith, Brian, and Robert Stevens. 1968. In *Search of Justice: Law, Society, and the Legal System*. Penguin Books.

Academy of Humanities and Social Sciences. 2020. Han Depei. http://ahss.whu.edu.cn /info/1018/1084.htm.

Alford, William P., Johannes M.M. Chan, Mayo Moran, Mariana Mota Prado, Anthony Sebok, and Zhenmin Wang. 2010. "In Memoriam: Professor Betty May Foon Ho." *Tsinghua China Law Review* 3, no. 2.

Arrighi, Giovanni. 2010. *The Long Twentieth Century: Money, Power, and the Origins of Our Times*. New York: Verso.

Auerbach, Jerome. 1976. *Unequal Justice: Lawyers and Social Change in Modern America*. Oxford.

Baade, Hans. 2001. "The Education and Qualification of Civil Lawyers in Historical Perspective: From Jurists and Orators to Advocates, Procurators, and Notaries." In *Critical Studies in Ancient Law, Comparative Law, and Legal History*, edited by John Cairns and Olivia Robinson, 213–34. Oxford: Oxford University Press.

Ballakrishnen, Swethaa. 2009. "Where Did We Come From? Where Do We Go? An Enquiry into the Students and Systems of Legal Education in India." *Journal of Commonwealth Law and Legal Education* 7(2): 133–54.

———. 2012. "Homeward Bound: What Does a Global Legal Education Offer the Indian Returnees?" *Fordham Law Review* 80: 2441–80.

———. 2013. "'Why I am not a lawyer': An Institutional Analysis of the Indian National Law School Model and Its Implications for Global Legal Education." In *The State of Legal Education in India: Essays in Honour of Professor Ranbir Singh*, edited by Lokendra Malik, 131–52. Lexis Nexis.

_____. 2019. "Just Like Global Firms: Unintended Parity and Speculative Isomorphism in India's Elite Professions." *Law and Society Review* 53(1): 108–140.

Barnet, Richard. 1971. *Roots of War*. New York: Atheneum.

Basheer, Shamnad, K.V. Krishnaprasad, Sree Mitra, and Prajna Mohapatra. 2017. "The Making of Legal Elites and the IDIA of Justice." In *The Indian Legal Profession in the Age of Globalization: The Rise of the Corporate Legal Sector and Its Impact on Lawyers and Society*, edited by David Wilkins, Vikramaditya Khanna, and David Trubek, 578–605. Cambridge: Cambridge University Press.

Baxi, Upendra. 1976. "Notes towards a Socially Relevant Legal Education." *Journal of the Bar Council of India* 5: 23.

Bell, David A. 1994. *Lawyers and Citizens: The Making of a Political Elite in Old Regime France*. Oxford: Oxford University Press.

Benton, Lauren, and Lisa Ford. 2016. *Rage for Order: The British Empire and the Origins of International Law, 1800–1850*. Cambridge, MA: Harvard University Press.

Berman, Harold J. 1983. *Law and Revolution: The Formation of the Western Legal Tradition*. Cambridge, MA: Harvard University Press.

_____. 2003. *Law and Revolution II: The Impact of the Protestant Reformations on the Western Legal Tradition*. Cambridge, MA: Belknap Press of Harvard University Press.

Biddulph, Sarah. 2012. "Legal Education in the People's Republic of China: The Ongoing Story of Politics and Law." In *Legal Education in Asia: Globalization, Change, and Contexts*, edited by Stacey Steele and Kathryn Taylor, 260–75. New York and London: Routledge.

Bird, Kai. 1992. *The Chairman: John J. McCloy and the Making of the American Establishment*. New York: Simon and Schuster.

_____. 1998. *The Color of Truth: McGeorge Bundy and William Bundy: Brothers in Arms*. New York: Simon and Schuster.

Biskupic, Joan, Janet Roberts, and John Shiffman. 2014. "Special Report: At U.S. Court of Last Resort, Handful of Lawyers Dominate Docket." *Reuters*, 8 December. https://www.reuters.com/investigates/special-report/scotus.

Bohmer, Martin. 2013. *Imagining the State: The Politics of Legal Education in Argentina, USA, and Chile*. JSD diss., Yale Law School.

Bourdieu, Pierre. 1986. "The Force of Law: Toward a Sociology of the Juridical Field." *Hastings Law Journal* 38(5): 814–85.

_____. 1989. *La Noblesse d'État. Grandes écoles et esprit de corps*. Paris: Minuit.

_____. 1991. "Les Juristes, gardiens de l'hypocrisie collective." In *Normes juridiques et régulation sociale*, edited by F. Chazel and J. Commaille, 95–99. Paris: LGDJ.

_____. 1993. "Esprits d'Etat. Genèse et structure du champ bureaucratique." *Actes de la recherche en sciences sociales* 96–97: 49–62.

_____. 2002. "Les conditions sociales de la circulation des idees." *Actes de la recherches en sciences sociales* 145: 3–8.

_____. 2012. *Sur l'état: Cours au Collège de France (1989–1992)*. Paris: Seuil.

_____. 2015. *On the State: Lectures at the College de France, 1989–1992*. Stanford: Stanford University Press.

Bourgon, Jerome. 2000. "Sauver la Vie." *Actes de la recherches en sciences sociales* 133: 32–39.

Boussebaa, Mehdi, and James Faulconbridge. 2019. "Professional Service Firms as Agents of Economic Globalization: A Political Perspective." *Journal of Professions and Organization* 6(1): 72–90.

Boyd, Susan. 1993. *The ABA's First Section: Assuring a Qualified Bar*. Section of Legal Education and Admissions to the Bar. Chicago: American Bar Association.

Brennan, Tom. 2013. "Foreign Firms Stumble Going Local in Japan." *The Asian Lawyer*, 15 July.

Brundage, James. 2008. *The Medieval Origins of the Legal Profession*. Chicago: University of Chicago Press.

Burbank, Jane, and Frederick Cooper. 2010. *Empires in World History: Power and the Politics of Difference*. Princeton: Princeton University Press.

Burgis-Kasthala, Michelle. 2018. "Teaching on the Periphery: The Politics of Studying International Criminal Law in Postcolonial Africa." (unpublished manuscript).

Carbonneau, Thomas E. 1980. "The French Legal Studies Curriculum: Its History and Relevance as a Model for Reform." *McGill Law Review* 25: 455–77.

Chan, Johannes M.M. 2010. "In Memoriam: Professor Betty May Foon Ho." *Tsinghua China Law Review* 3: 4.

Chan, Kay-Wah. 2011. "The Reform of the Profession of Lawyers in Japan." In *Lawyers and the Rule of Law in an Era of Globalization*, edited by Yves Dezalay and Bryant Garth, 185–217. New York and London: Routledge.

Chandrachud, Justice D.Y. 2016. "Address by Hon'ble Justice D.Y. Chandrachud at the Sesquicentenary event of the Bombay Bar Association on 19th November 2016." https:// www.youtube.com/watch?v=mIyo2WrbtoE.

Cheng, Kris. 2015. "Johannes Chan Appointment to HKU Key Position Rejected, 12 votes to 8." *Hong Kong Free Press*. September. https://www.hongkongfp.com/2015/09/29/johannes -chan-appointment-to-hku-key-position-rejected.

Christianson, Wei. 2020. Wikipedia [4 February 2020]. https://en.wikipedia.org/wiki/Wei _Christianson.

Coates, Benjamin. 2015. "Securing Hegemony through Law: Venezuela, the U.S. Asphalt Trust, and the Uses of International Law, 1904–1909." *Journal of American History* 102(2): 380–405.

———. 2016. *Legalist Empire: The United States, Civilization, and International Law in the Early Twentieth Century*. Oxford: Oxford University Press.

Coe, Aebra. 2016. "Plans to Open Up Legal Sector in India Hit a Snag." *Law 360*, 4 October. https://www.law360.com/articles/848269/plans-to-open-up-legal-sector-in-india-hit -a-snag.

Cohen, Jerome. 2010. "Introduction to Part V." In *Legal Reforms in China and Vietnam: A Comparison of Asian Communist Regimes*, edited by J. Gillespie and A.H.Y. Chen, 271–76. New York and London: Routledge.

Comaroff, Jean, and John Comaroff. 2011. *Theory from the South*. New York and London: Routledge.

Connor, Alison W. 1994. "Training China's Early Modern Lawyers: Soochow University Law School." *Journal of Chinese Law* 8: 1–46.

Coquillette, Daniel R., and Bruce A. Kimball. 2015. *On the Battlefield of Merit: Harvard Law School, the First Century*. Cambridge, MA: Harvard University Press.

Dasgupta, Lovely. 2010. "Reforming Indian Legal Education: Linking Research and Teaching." *Journal of Legal Education* 59: 432.

Dezalay, Sara. 2017. "Lawyers' Empire in the (African) Colonial Margins." *International Journal of the Legal Profession* 24(1): 25–32.

Dezalay, Sara, and Yves Dezalay. 2017. "Professionals of International Justice: From the Shadow of State Diplomacy to the Pull of the Market of Arbitration." In *International Law as a Profession*, edited by A. Nollkaemper, J. d'Aspremont, W. Werner, and T. Gazzini, 311–37. Cambridge: Cambridge University Press.

Dezalay, Yves. 1992. *Marchands de Droit*. Paris: Fayard.

Dezalay, Yves, and Bryant G. Garth. 1996. *Dealing in Virtue: International Commercial Arbitration and the Construction of a Transnational Legal Order*. Chicago: University of Chicago Press.

————. 2002. *The Internationalization of Palace Wars: Lawyers, Economists, and the Contest to Transform Latin American States*. Chicago: University of Chicago Press.

————. 2010. *Asian Legal Revivals: Lawyers in the Shadow of Empire*. Chicago: University of Chicago Press.

————. 2016. "Constructing a Transatlantic Marketplace of Disputes on the Symbolic Foundations of International Justice." In *Contractual Knowledge: One Hundred Years of Legal Experimentation in Global Markets*, edited by Gregoire Mallard and Jerome Sgard, 185–214. Cambridge: Cambridge University Press.

Dinnerstein, Leonard. 1983. "Jews and the New Deal." *American Jewish History* 72(4): 461–76.

Dinovitzer, Ronit, and Bryant G. Garth. 2020. "The New Place of Corporate Law Firms in the Structuring of Elite Legal Careers." *Law and Social Inquiry* 45(2): 339–71.

Duxbury, Neil. 1995. *Patterns of American Jurisprudence*. Oxford: Oxford University Press.

The Economist. 2017. "Elevator Malfunction: Britain Ignores Social Mobility at Its Peril." 9 December. https://www.economist.com/britain/2017/12/09/britain-ignores-social -mobility-at-its-peril.

Edwards, R. Randle. 2009. "Thirty Years of Legal Exchange with China: The Columbia Law School Role." *Columbia Journal of Asian Law* 23: 3–16.

Elman, B.A. 2013. *Civil Examinations and Meritocracy in Late Imperial China*. Cambridge: Cambridge University Press.

Erie, Mathew. 2009. "Legal Education Reform in China through U.S.-Inspired Transplants." *Journal of Legal Education* 59(1): 60–96.

Feeley, Malcolm M., and Setsuo Miyazawa. 2007. "The State, Civil Society, and the Legal Complex in Modern Japan: Continuity and Change." In *Fighting for Political Freedom: Comparative Studies of the Legal Complex and Political Liberalism*, edited by Terence C. Halliday, Lucien Karpik, and Malcolm M. Feeley, 151–92. Oxford and Portland: Hart.

Feldman, Eric. 1993. "Mirroring Minds: Recruitment and Promotion in Japan's Law Faculties." *American Journal of Comparative Law* 41(3): 465–79.

Ferguson, Niall. 2012. *Empire: How Britain Made the Modern World*. London: Penguin Books.

Flaherty, Darryl. 2013. *Public Law, Private Practice: Politics, Profit, and the Legal Profession in Nineteenth-Century Japan*. Cambridge, MA: Harvard University Press.

Foote, Daniel H., ed. 2008. *Law in Japan: A Turning Point*. Seattle: University of Washington Press.

————. 2013. "The Trials and Tribulations of Japan's Legal Education Reforms." *Hastings International and Comparative Law Review* 36: 369–442.

_____. 2018. "The Advent of Lawyers in Japanese Government." https://ssrn.com/abstract
=3121476.

Friedman, Lawrence. 2005. *A History of American Law*. 3rd ed. New York: Touchstone
Books.

Galanter, Marc and Thomas Palay. 1991. *Tournament of Lawyers: The Transformation of the
Big Law Firm*. Chicago: University of Chicago Press.

Galanter, Marc, and Nick Robinson. 2017. "Grand Advocates: The Traditional Elite Lawyers." In *The Indian Legal Profession in the Age of Globalization: The Rise of the Corporate
Legal Sector and Its Impact on Lawyers and Society*, edited by David Wilkins, Vikramaditya Khanna, and David Trubek, 455–85. Cambridge: Cambridge University Press.

Gane, Christopher, and Robin Hui Huang, eds. 2016. *Legal Education in the Global Context:
Opportunities and Challenges*. Farnham: Ashgate.

Ganz, Kian. 2016. "A Ranking of India's 25 Largest Law Firms," *Legally India*, 5 December.
https://www.legallyindia.com/law-firms/india-25-largest-law-firms-by-headcount
-00011130-8166.

Gardner, James. 1980. *Legal Imperialism*. Madison: University of Wisconsin Press.

Gelatt, Timothy A., and Frederick E. Snyder. 1980–81. "Legal Education in China: Training
for a New Era." *China Law Reporter* 1: 41–60.

Gingerich, Jonathan, and Nick Robinson. 2017. "Responding to the Market: The Impact of
the Rise of Corporate Law Firms on Elite Legal Education in India." In *The Indian Legal
Profession in the Age of Globalization: The Rise of the Corporate Legal Sector and Its Impact on Lawyers and Society*, edited by David Wilkins, Vikramaditya Khanna, and David
Trubek, 519–47. Cambridge: Cambridge University Press.

Ginsburg, Tom. 2004. "Transforming Legal Education in Japan and Korea." *Penn State
International Law Review* 22: 433–40.

Gobe, Éric. 2013. *Les avocats en Tunisie de la colonisation à la révolution (1883–2011):
sociohistoire d'une profession politique*. Paris: Karthala.

Gomez, Manuel, and Rogelio Pérez-Perdomo, eds. 2018. *Big Law in Latin America and Spain:
Globalization and Adjustments in the Provision of High-End Legal Services*. Houndmills:
Palgrave Macmillan.

Gordon, Robert W. 1984. "The Ideal and the Actual in the Law: Fantasies and Practices of
New York City Lawyers, 1870–1910." In *The New High Priests: Lawyers in Post-Civil War
America*, edited by Gerald W. Gawalt, 51–74. Westport: Greenwood Press.

_____. 2008. "The American Legal Profession, 1870–2000." In *The Cambridge History of
Law in America*, vol. 1: *Early America (1580–1815)*, edited by Michael Grossberg and
Christopher Tomlins, 73–126. Cambridge, MA: Cambridge University Press.

Grey, Thomas C. 1983. "Langdell's Orthodoxy." *University of Pittsburgh Law Review* 45: 1–53.

Gross Cunha, Luciano, Jose Garcez Ghirardi, David M. Trubek, and David B. Wilkins. 2018.
"Globalization, Lawyers, and Emerging Economies: The Case of Brazil." In *The Brazilian
Legal Profession in the Age of Globalization: The Rise of the Corporate Legal Sector and Its
Impact on Lawyers and Society*, edited by Luciana Gross Cunha, Daniela Monteiro Gab-
bay, Jose Garcez Ghirardi, David M. Trubek, and David B. Wilkins, 1–32. Cambridge:
Cambridge University Press.

Hackney, James. 2012. *Legal Intellectuals in Conversation: Reflections on the Construction of
Contemporary American Legal Theory*. New York: NYU Press.

Halpern, Charles. 2008. *Making Waves and Riding Currents*. Oakland: Berrett-Koehler.

_____. 2017. "Cultivating Wisdom for Justice and Social Transformation." *Awakin.org*, 28 January. http://www.awakin.org/calls/297/charles-halpern/transcript.

Han, Depei and Stephen Kanter. 1984. "Legal Education in China." *American Journal of Comparative Law* 32: 543–82.

Harding, Andrew, Jiaxiang Hu, and Maartje de Visser, eds. 2017. *Legal Education in Asia: From Imitation to Innovation*. Leiden: Brill.

Hattori, Tataaki. 1963. "The Legal Profession in Japan: Its Historical Development and Present State." In *Law in Japan: The Legal Order in a Changing Society*, edited by Arthur Taylor von Mehren, 109–187. Cambridge, MA: Harvard University Press.

Henretta, James A. 2008. "Magistrates, Common Law Lawyers, Legislators: The Three Legal Systems in British America." In *The Cambridge History of Law in America*, vol. 1: *Early America (1580–1815)*, edited by Michael Grossberg and Christopher Tomlins, 555–92. Cambridge, MA: Cambridge University Press.

Herman, Richard A. 1981–82. "The Education of Chinese Lawyers." *Albany Law Review* 46: 789–804.

Hilbink, Thomas Miguel. 2006. *Constructing Cause Lawyering: Professionalism, Politics, and Social Change in 1960s America*. Ph.D. diss., NYU. https://papers.ssrn.com/sol3/papers.cfm?abstract_id=2417253.

Hollis-Brusky, Amanda. 2011. "Support Structures and Constitutional Change." *Law and Social Inquiry* 36: 516–36.

_____. 2015. *Ideas with Consequences: The Federalist Society and the Conservative Counterrevolution*. *Oxford*: Oxford University Press.

Hsu, Ching-fang. 2020. "Taiwan and Hong Kong: Localisation and Politicisation." In *Lawyers in 21st Century Society*, edited by Richard Abel, Ole Hammerslev, Hilary Sommerlad, and Ulrike Schultz, 801–30. Oxford and Portland: Hart.

Huang, Jingjing. 2017. "Hong Kong's Foreign Judges Target of Criticism amid Political Tension." *Global Times*, 28 February. https://www.globaltimes.cn/content/1035291.shtml.

Isenberg, Nancy. 2016. *White Trash: The 400-Year Untold History of Class in America*. New York: Penguin Books.

Jain, Chirayu, Spadika Jayaraj, Sanjana Muraleedharan, and Harjas Singh. 2016. *The Elusive Island of Excellence: A Study on Student Demographics, Accessibility, and Inclusivity at National Law School 2015–16*.

Jamin, Christophe. 2013. *La cuisine de droit*. Paris: LGDJ.

Jamin, Christophe, and William van Caenegem, eds. 2016. *The Internationalisation of Legal Education*. Berlin: Springer.

Ji, Weidong. 2005. "Legal Education in China: A Great Leap Forward of Professionalism." *Kobe University Law Review* (international edition) 39: 1–21.

Jodhka, Surinder S., Boike Rehbein, and Jesse Souza. 2018. *Inequality in Capitalist Societies*. New York and London: Routledge.

Johnson, Earl, Jr., 2013. *To Establish Justice for All: The Past and Future of Civil Legal Aid in the United States*. Westport: Praeger.

Jones, Carol. 2009. "Producing the Producers: Legal Education in Hong Kong." In *Legal Education in Asia*, edited by Stacey Steele and Kathryn Taylor, 107–36. New York and London: Routledge.

Kabaservice, Geoffrey. 2012. *The Guardians: Kingman Brewster, His Circle, and the Rise of the Liberal Establishment*. New York: Henry Holt.

Kalman, Laura. 2005. *Yale Law School in the Sixties: Revolt and Reverberations*. Chapel Hill: University of North Carolina Press.

Kang, David. C. 2010. *East Asia before the West: Five Centuries of Trade and Tribute*. New York: Columbia University Press.

Kantorowicz, Ernst. 1997. *The King's Two Bodies: A Study in Medieval Political Theology*. Princeton: Princeton University Press.

Karnow, Stanley. 1989. *In Our Image: America's Empire in the Philippines*. New York: Random House.

Katcher, Susan. 2006. "Legal Training in the United States: A Brief History." *Wisconsin International Law Journal* 24: 335–75.

Kawar, Leila. 2015. *Contesting Immigration Policy in Court: Legal Activism and Its Radiating Effects in the United States and France*. Cambridge: Cambridge University Press.

Kim JaeWon. 2001. "The Ideal and the Reality of the Korean Legal Profession." *Asian-Pacific Law and Policy Journal* 2: 45–68.

———. 2020. "South Korea: Reshaping the Legal Profession." In *Lawyers in 21st Century Society*, edited by Richard Abel, Ole Hammerslev, Hilary Sommerlad, and Ulrike Schultz, 789–800. Oxford and Portland: Hart.

Kim, Sarah. 2014. "Concerns rise over new law school system. High tuition bars students otherwise qualified, experts say," 28 Aug, *Korea JoongAng Daily*, http://mengnews.joins .com/view.aspx?aId=2994143.

Kimball, Bruce and Blake Brown. 2004. "'The Highest Legal Ability in the Nation': Langdell on Wall Street 1855–1870." *Law and Social Inquiry* 29: 39–104.

Kolko, Gabriel. 1965. *Railroads and Regulation: 1877–1916*. Princeton: Princeton University Press.

Konefsky, Alfred S. 2008. "The Legal Profession: From the Revolution to the Civil War." In *The Cambridge History of Law in America*, vol. 2: *The Long Nineteenth Century (1789–1920)*, edited by Michael Grossberg and Christopher Tomlins, 68–105. Cambridge: Cambridge University Press.

Koskenniemi, Martti. 2001. *The Gentle Civilizer of Nations: The Rise and Fall of International Law 1870–1960*. Cambridge: Cambridge University Press.

Kostal, Randa. 1994. *Law and English Railway Capitalism 1825–1875*. Oxford: Clarendon Press.

Krishnan, Jayath. 2004. "Professor Kingsfield Goes to Delhi: American Academics, the Ford Foundation, and the Development of Legal Education in India," *American Journal of Legal History* 46: 447–99.

———. 2005. "From the ALI to the ILI: The Efforts to Export an American Legal Institution." *Vanderbilt Journal of Transnational Law* 38: 1255–94.

———. 2013. "Peel-Off Lawyers: Legal Professionals in India's Corporate Law Firm Sector." *Socio-Legal Review* 9: 1–59.

Kronche, Jedidiah. 2016. *The Futility of Law and Development: China and the Dangers of Exporting American Law*. Oxford: Oxford University Press.

Kumar, C. Raj. 2017. "Experiments in Legal Education in India: Jindal Global Law School and Private Nonprofit Legal Education." In *The Indian Legal Profession in the Age of Globalization: The Rise of the Corporate Legal Sector and Its Impact on Lawyers and Society*, edited by David Wilkins, Vikramaditya Khanna, and David Trubek, 606–30. Cambridge: Cambridge University Press.

Labaree, David. 2017. *A Perfect Mess: The Unlikely Ascendancy of American Higher Education.* Chicago: University of Chicago Press.

Lacey, Nicola. 2006. *A Life of HLA Hart: The Nightmare and the Noble Dream.* Oxford: Oxford University Press.

Lee, Chulwoo. 2014. "Hegemony, Contestation, and Empowerment: The Politics of Law and Society Studies in South Korea." *Asian Journal of Law and Society* 1(2): 275–304.

Lee, Eddy. 2017. "Beijing Throws the Book at Hong Kong's Foreign Judges," *South China Morning Post*, 9 March. https://www.scmp.com/news/hong-kong/law-crime/article /2077521/experts-line-throw-book-hong-kongs-foreign-judges.

Lee, Jae-Hyup. 2009. "Legal Education in Korea: Some Thoughts on Linking the Past and the Future." *Kyung Hee Law Review* 44: 605–23.

———. 2017. "Six Law Firm Hires of Lawyers Who Graduated at the Law Schools—by Law School Name" (unpublished manuscript).

———. 2018. "The Introduction of the Law School System and the Structure of the Legal Profession in Korea: Status and Prospects." *Journal of Legal Education* 68(2): 460–490.

———. 2019. "After the JD: The Introduction of the Law School System and the Structure of the Legal Profession in Korea: Status and Prospects" (unpublished manuscript).

Lee, Jootaek. 2017. "The Crisis and Future of Korean Legal Education: Compared with the American Legal Education System." *Korean University Law Review* 2017: 41–56.

Lee, Man Yee Karen. 2017. "Lawyers and Hong Kong's Democracy Movement: from Electoral Politics to Civil Disobedience." *Asian Journal of Political Science* 25(1): 89–108.

Legally India. 2019. "Indian Rhodes Scholars." https://www.legallyindia.com/tag/rhodes -scholarship-india.

Legemann, Ellen Condliffe. 1989. *The Politics of Knowledge: The Carnegie Corporation, Philanthropy, and Public Policy.* Chicago: University of Chicago Press.

Lemmings, David. 1990. *Gentlemen and Barristers: The Inns of Court and the English Bar 1680–1730.* Oxford: Oxford University Press.

Leung, Christy, and Tony Cheung. 2017. "Hong Kong Lawmaker Brands British Judge a 'Yellow Heart' after Seven Policemen are jailed." *South China Morning Post*, 17 February. https://www.scmp.com/news/hong-kong/law-crime/article/2071853/hong-kong-law maker-brands-british-judge-yellow-heart-after.

Levi, Ron, Ronit Dinovitzer, and Wendy Wong. 2017. "Strategic Philanthropy and International Strategies: The Ford Foundation and Investments in Law Schools and Legal Education (1951–2003)." (unpublished manuscript).

Li, Cheng. 2014. "The Rise of the Legal Profession in the Chinese Leadership." *China Leadership Monitor* 42: 1–25.

———. 2016. *Chinese Politics in the Xi Jinping Era: Reassessing Collective Leadership.* Washington, D.C.: Brookings Institution.

Li, Victor H. 1980. "Reflections on the Current Drive toward Greater Legalization in China." *Georgia Journal of International and Comparative Law* 10: 221–32.

Li, Xueyao, Li Yiran, and Hu Jiaxiang. 2018. "Globalisation and Innovative Study: Legal Education in China." In *Legal Education in Asia: From Imitation to Innovation*, edited by Andrew Harding, Jiaxiang Hu, and Maartje de Visser, 251–75. Leiden: Brill Nijhoff.

Liu, Lawrence. 2019. "The Role of PRC Lawyers and Law Firms in Chinese Outbound Initiatives." *China, Law, and Development*, Research Brief no. 7. Oxford University. https:// cld.web.ox.ac.uk/file/430561.

Liu, Sida. 2020. "China: A Tale of Four Decades." In *Lawyers in 21st Century Society*, edited by Richard Abel, Ole Hammerslev, Hilary Sommerlad, and Ulrike Schultz, 697–712. Oxford and Portland: Hart.

Liu, Sida, and Anson Au. 2020. "The Gateway to Global China: Hong Kong and the Future of Chinese Law Firms." *Wisconsin International Law Journal* 37: 308–49.

Liu, Sida, and Terence Halliday. 2011–12. "Political Liberalism and Political Embeddedness: Understanding Politics in the Work of Chinese Criminal Defense Lawyers." *Law and Society Review* 45(4): 831–39.

––––––. 2016. *Criminal Defense in China: The Politics of Lawyers at Work*. Cambridge: Cambridge University Press.

Macdonald, Ronald S.J. 1980–81. "Legal Education in China Today." *Dalhousie Law Journal* 6: 313–38.

Mandhani, Apoorva. 2014. "NLU Delhi Faculty Dr Anup Surendranath Appointed as Dy Registrar (Research) in the Supreme Court." http://www.livelaw.in/nlu-delhi-faculty-dr -anup-surendranath-appointed-dy-registrar-research-supreme-court.

Markovits, Daniel. 2015. "A New Aristocracy." Yale Law School Commencement Address, May. https://law.yale.edu/sites/default/files/area/department/studentaffairs/document /markovitscommencementrev.pdf.

Martin, Albro. 1992. *Railroads Triumphant: The Growth, Rejection, and Rebirth of a Vital American Force*. Oxford: Oxford University Press.

Martines, Lauro. 1968. *Lawyers and Statecraft in Renaissance Florence*. Princeton: Princeton University Press.

Mathur, Justice N.N. 2017. "National Law Universities, Original Intent, and Real Founders," 24 July. http://www.livelaw.in/national-law-universities-original-intent-real-founders.

Mazower, Mark. 2012. *Governing the World: The History of an Idea, 1815 to the Present*. New York: Penguin Books.

Mazzacane, Aldo. 1995. "A Jurist for United Italy: The Training and Culture of Neopolitan Lawyers in the Nineteenth Century." In *Society and the Professions in Italy, 1860–1914*, edited by Maria Malatesta, 80–111. Cambridge: Cambridge University Press.

McSweeney, Thomas J. 2019. *Priests of the Law: Roman Law and the Making of the Common Law's First Professionals*. Oxford: Oxford University Press.

Menon, N.R. Madhava. 2009. *Turning Point: The Story of a Law Teacher*. Delhi: Universal Law Publishing.

Minzner, Carl. 2013. "The Rise and Fall of Chinese Legal Education." *Fordham International Law Journal* 36(2): 334–95.

Mitchell, A. 2000. *The Great Train Race: Railways and the Franco-German Rivalry, 1815–1914*. New York: Berghahn.

Miyazawa, Setsuo. 2002. "Education and Training of Lawyers in Japan: A Critical Analysis." *South Texas Law Review* 43: 491–98.

Miyazawa, Setsuo, Kay-Wah Chan, and Ilhyung Lee. 2008. "The Reform of Legal Education in East Asia." *Annual Review of Law and Social Science* 4: 333–60.

Murayama, Masayuki. 2020. "Japan: Toward Stratification, Diversification and Speciali-sation," in *Lawyers in 21st Century Society*, edited by Richard Abel, Ole Hammerslev, Hilary Sommerlad, and Ulrike Schultz, 753–74. Oxford and Portland: Hart.

Murphy, Jay. 1967. *Legal Education in a Developing Nation: The Korea Experience*. Korea Law Study Series no. 1. Korea Law Research Institute, Seoul National University.

Murphy, John. 1982. "Legal Education in China: Some Impressions." *China Law Reporter* 2: 50–53.

Musella, Luigi. 1995. "Professionalism in Politics. Clientelism and Networks." In *Society and the Professions in Italy, 1860–1914*, edited by Maria Malatesta, 313–36. Cambridge: Cambridge University Press.

Mustafa, Faizan, Jagteshwar Singh Sohi, Sidharth Chauhan, Sudhanshu Kumar, and Vaibhaav Ganjiwale. 2018. *Suggestions for Reforms at the National Law Universities Set Up through State Legislations*. National Academy of Legal Studies and Research. https://ssrn.com/abstract=3171842.

Nakamura, Mayumi. 2014. "Legal Reform, Law Firms, and Lawyer Stratification in Japan." *Asian Journal of Law and Society* 1(1): 99–123.

Nanda, Ashish, David B. Wilkins, and Bryon Fong. 2017. "Mapping India's Corporate Law Firm Sector." In *The Indian Legal Profession in the Age of Globalization: The Rise of the Corporate Legal Sector and Its Impact on Lawyers and Society*, edited by David Wilkins, Vikramaditya Khanna, and David Trubek, 69–114. Cambridge: Cambridge University Press.

National Law School of India. 2020. Linked-In Alumni [4 February]. https://www.linkedin.com/school/national-law-school-of-india-university/people.

Nie, Kevin. 2010. "Guo Shoukang: A 'National Treasure' Master." China IP, [Comprehensive Reports]. http://www.chinaipmagazine.com/en/journal-show.asp?id=636.

Nikkei Asian Review. 2017. "Fewer Prospective Lawyers Clearing the Bar in Japan. Test Losing Appeal as Law Schools Struggle to Recruit." 13 September. https://asia.nikkei.com/Politics-Economy/Policy-Politics/Fewer-prospective-lawyers-clearing-the-bar-in-Japan.

Oguamanam, Chidi, and Wesley Pue. 2007. "Lawyers' Professionalism, Colonialism, State Formation, and National Life in Nigeria, 1900–1960: 'The Fighting Brigade of the People.'" *Social Identities* 13(6): 769–785.

Ohnesorge, John. 2003. "The Rule of Law, Economic Development, and the Developmental States of Northeast Asia." In *Law and Development in East and Southeast Asia*, edited by Christopher Antons, 70–94. New York and London: Routledge.

Park, Yong Chui. 2018. "Legal Education in South Korea: Does Continuance of the Old Judicial Examination Style Ruin the Dream of Ideal Legal Education?" In *Legal Education in Asia: From Imitation to Innovation*, edited by Andrew Harding, Jiaxiang Hu, and Maartje de Visser, 176–96. Leiden: Brill Nijhoff.

Peking University. 2011. Professor Rui Mu: Forever Young. 2 June. http://newsen.pku.edu.cn/News_Events/News/Focus/8342.htm.

Peking University School of Law. 2020. Professor Zhu Suli. http://en.law.pku.edu.cn/faculty/faculty1/21797.htm.

Pérez-Perdomo, Rogelio. 2006. *Latin American Lawyers: A Historical Introduction*. Stanford: Stanford University Press.

Phan, Pamela N. 2005. "Clinical Legal Education in China: In Pursuit of a Culture of Law and a Mission of Social Justice." *Yale Human Rights and Development Law Journal* 8: 117–52.

Pitts, Jennifer. 2006. *A Turn to Empire: The Rise of Imperial Liberalism in Britain and France*. Princeton: Princeton University Press.

Powell, Michael J. 1988. *From Patrician to Professional Elite: The Transformation of the New York City Bar Association*. New York: Russell Sage.

Prest, Wilfred. 1986. *The Rise of the Barristers: A Social History of the English Bar 1590–1640*. Oxford: Clarendon Press.

Priestland, David. 2012. *Merchant, Soldier, Sage: A New History of Power*. New York: Penguin.

Reddy, B. Varun. 2017. "NALSAR Class of 2017: Conclusion of Recruitment Process." *SCC Online Blog*, 2 May. http://blog.scconline.com/post/2017/05/02/nalsar-class-of-2017 -conclusion-of-recruitment-process.

Rheinstein, Max. 1938. "Law Faculties and Law Schools—A Comparison of Legal Education in the United States and Germany." *Wisconsin Law Review* 1938: 5–42.

Riles, Annelise, and Takashi Uchida. 2009. "Reforming Knowledge? A Socio-Legal Critique of the Legal Education Reforms in Japan." *Drexel Law Review* 1: 3–51.

Roberts, Anthea. 2017. *Is International Law International?* Oxford: Oxford University Press.

Robinson, Nick. 2015. "Closing the Implementation Gap: Grievance Redress and India's Social Welfare Programs." *Columbia Journal of Transnational Law* 53: 321–62.

Rosen, Dan. 2017. "Japan's Law School System: The Sorrow and the Pity." *Journal of Legal Education* 66: 267–88.

Rosenberg, Emily. 2003. *Financial Missionaries to the World: The Politics and Culture of Dollar Diplomacy 1900–1930*. Durham: Duke University Press.

Rueschemeyer, Dietrich. 1997. "State, Capitalism, and the Organization of Legal Counsel: Examining an Extreme Case—the Prussian Bar, 1700–1914." In *Lawyers and the Rise of Western Political Liberalism: Europe and North America from the Eighteenth to Twentieth Centuries*, edited by Terence C. Halliday and Lucien Karpik, 207–28. Oxford: Oxford University Press.

Sacriste, Guillaume. 2011. *La République des constitutionnalistes. Professeurs de droit et légitimation de l'État en France (1870–1914)*. Paris: Sciences-Po.

Sacriste, Guillaume, and Antoine Vauchez. 2007. "The Force of International Law: Lawyers' Diplomacy on the International Scene in the 1920s." *Law and Social Inquiry* 32: 83–107.

Saegusa, Mayumi. 2009. "Why the Japanese Law School System Was Established: Co-optation as a Defensive Tactic in the Face of Global Pressures." *Law and Social Inquiry* 34: 365–98.

Sathe, S.P. 2002. *Judicial Activism in India: Transgressing Borders and Enforcing Limits*. Oxford: Oxford University Press.

Scarfi, Juan Pablo. 2017. *The Hidden History of International Law in the Americas: Empire and Networks*. Oxford: Oxford University Press.

Schlegel, John Henry. 1995. *American Legal Realism and Empirical Social Science*. Chapel Hill: University of North Carolina Press.

Schmidhauser, John R. 1997. "The European Origins of Legal Imperialism and Its Legacy in Legal Education in Former Colonial Regions." *International Political Science Review* 18(3): 337–51.

Schmitt, Mark. 2005. "The Legend of the Powell Memo." *The American Prospect*. http://prospect.org/article/legend-powell-memo.

Seppänen, Samuli. 2014. "Ideological Renewal and Nostalgia in China's Avant-Garde Legal Scholarship." *Washington University Global Studies Law Review* 13: 83–125.

_____. 2016. *Ideological Conflict and the Rule of Law in Contemporary China: Useful Paradoxes*. Cambridge: Cambridge University Press.

Shamir, Ronen. 1995. *Managing Legal Uncertainty*. Durham: Duke University Press.

Sharafi, Mitra. 2014. *Law and Identity in Colonial South Asia: Parsi Legal Culture, 1772–1947*. Cambridge: Cambridge University Press.

_____. 2015. "South Asian Legal History." *Annual Review of Law and Social Science* 11(1): 309–36.

Shrivastava, Prachi. 2017. "'Largest employer of NLU graduates': Jindal Law School Hires 25 New Teachers, 32% NLU Alums." *Legally India*, 9 August. http://www.legallyindia.com /home/jindal-law-we-are-the-largest-non-corporate-employer-of-nlu-graduates-32-of -25-newest-teachers-are-nlu-alums-20170809-8708.

Silver, Carole, and Swethaa Ballakrishnen. 2018. "Sticky Floors, Springboards, Stairways, and Slow Escalators: Mobility Pathways and Preferences of International Students in U.S. Law Schools." *University of California Irvine Journal of International, Transnational, and Comparative Law* 3: 39–70.

Skinner, Quentin. 1978. *The Foundations of Modern Political Thought*. 2 vols. Cambridge: Cambridge University Press.

Smigel, Erwin. 1964. *The Wall Street Lawyer: Professional Organizational Man*. New York: Free Press.

Sood, Mansai. 2017. "Legal Education and Its Outcomes: Digging Deeper into the Successes and Failures of India's National Law Schools." 9 August. https://ssrn.com/abstract =3062519 or http://dx.doi.org/10.2139/ssrn.3062519.

Southworth. Ann. 2008. *Lawyers on the Right: Professionalizing the Conservative Coalition*. Chicago: University of Chicago Press.

Standing Committee On Legal Education and Training. 2018. *Comprehensive Review of Legal Education and Training in Hong Kong Final Report of the Consultants*. April.

Steele, Stacey, and Kathryn Taylor, eds. 2010. *Legal Education in Asia: Globalization, Change, and Context*. New York and London: Routledge.

Steering Committee. 2002. *Review of Legal Education and Training in Hong Kong Second Progress Report*. LC Paper no. CB (2)2351/01–02(02). https://www.legco.gov.hk/yr01-02 /english/panels/ajls/papers/ajo624cb2-2351-2e.pdf.

Steinmetz, George. 2007. *The Devil's Handwriting: Precoloniality and the German Colonial State in Qingdao, Samoa, and Southwest Africa*. Chicago: University of Chicago Press.

Stern, Rachel E., and Su Li. 2016. "The Outpost Office: How International Law Firms Approach the China Market." *Law and Social Inquiry* 41(1): 184–211.

Stern, Rachel E., and Lawrence J. Liu. 2020. "The Good Lawyer: State-Led Professional Socialization in Contemporary China." *Law and Social Inquiry*. 45(1): 226–48.

Stevens, Robert. 1983. *Law School: Legal Education in America from the 1850s to the 1980s*. Chapel Hill: University of North Carolina Press.

Stone, Diane. 1996. *Capturing the Political Imagination: Think Tanks and the Policy Process*. London: Frank Cass.

Subramanian, Ajantha. 2015. "Making Merit: The Indian Institutes of Technology and the Social Life of Caste." *Comparative Studies in Society and History* 57(2): 291–322.

Sugarman, David. 2009. "Beyond Ignorance and Complacency: Robert Stevens' Journey through Lawyers and the Courts," *International Journal of the Legal Profession* 16(1): 7–31.

Surendranath, Anup, and Chinmayi Arun Friday. 2012. "Opinion: Crisis of Teaching at In-dia's Law Schools," http://www.legallyindia.com/newsletters/opinion-crisis-of-teaching -at-indias-law-schools-20120427-2775.

Teles, Steven. 2008. *The Rise of the Conservative Legal Movement: The Battle for Control over the Law*. Princeton: Princeton University Press.

_____. 2009. "Transformative Bureaucracy: Reagan's Lawyers and the Dynamics of Political Investment." *Studies in American Political Development* 23: 61–83.

Thompson, E.P. 1975. *Whigs and Hunters*. London: Allen Lane.

Thwink.org. 2006. "The Powell Memo with Commentary." http://www.thwink.org/sustain /articles/017_PowellMemo/index.htm.

Tiffert, Glen. 2009. "Epistrophy: Chinese Constitutionalism and the 1950s." In *Building Constitutionalism in China*, edited by Stephanie Balme and Michael W. Dowdle, 59–76. Houndmillls: Palgrave Macmillan.

_____. 2015. *Judging Revolution: Beijing and the Birth of the PRC Judicial System (1906–1958)*. UC Berkeley Electronic Theses and Dissertations.

Tomlins, Christopher. 2000. "Framing the Field of Law's Disciplinary Encounters: A Historical Narrative." *Law and Society Review* 34(4): 911–72.

Trubek, David. 2009. "Interview with David Trubek." *História Oral do CEPED*. Escola de Direito do Rio de Janeiro da Fundação Getulio Vargas. https://direitorio.fgv.br/sites /direitorio.fgv.br/files/DavidTrubek.pdf

Tsinghua University School of Law. 2020. The Master of Law Program (LL.M. Program) in International Arbitration and Dispute Settlement (IADS) [4 February]. https://www .tsinghua.edu.cn/publish/lawen/8090/index.html.

Tushnet, Mark. 1979. "Truth, Justice, and the American Way: An Interpretation of Public Law Scholarship in the Seventies." *Texas Law Review* 57: 1307–59.

Twining, William. 1994. *Blackstone's Tower: The English Law School*. London: Sweet and Maxwell.

Upham, Frank K. 2005. "Who Will Find the Defendant If He Stays with His Sheep?: Justice in Rural China," *Yale Law Journal* 114: 1675–718.

van Caenegem, R.C. 1987. *Judges, Legislators, and Professors*. Cambridge: Cambridge University Press.

Vauchez, Antoine. 2014. "The International Way of Expertise: The First World Court and the Genesis of Transnational Expert Fields." EUI Working Paper Series 2014/80.

Vauchez, Antoine, and Pierre France. 2017. *Sphère publique, intérêts privé, Enquête sur un grand brouillage*. Paris: Presses de Sciences Po.

Vidhi Centre for Legal Policy. 2020. https://vidhilegalpolicy.in/about [10 February].

von Mehren, Arthur Taylor, ed. 1963. *Law in Japan: The Legal Order in a Changing Society*. Oxford: Oceana.

Wallerstein, Immanuel. 2004. *World-Systems Analysis: An Introduction*. Durham: Duke University Press.

Wang, Tieya. 2020. https://en.wikipedia.org/wiki/Wang_Tieya. [4 February].

Wang, Zhenmin. 2010. "In Memoriam: Professor Betty May Foon Ho." *Tsinghua China Law Review* 3: 14.

Wang, Zhizhou (Leo). 2018. "Global–Local Dynamics and the Rise of Chinese Corporate Lawyers." *China Law and Society Review* 3: 49–78.

Wang, Zhizhou, Sida Liu, and Xueyao Li. 2017. "Internationalizing Chinese Legal Education in the Early Twenty-First Century." *Journal of Legal Education* 66: 238–66.

Warsh, David. 1993. *Economic Principals: Masters and Mavericks of Modern Economics*. New York: The Free Press.

Whaley, Joachim. 2012. *Germany and the Holy Roman Empire (1493–1806)*. 2 vols. Oxford: Oxford University Press.

Wilkins, David B., and Maria J. Esteban Ferrer. 2018. "The Integration of Law into Global Business Solutions: The Rise, Transformation, and Potential Future of the Big Four Accountancy Networks in the Global Legal Services Market." *Law and Social Inquiry* 43(3): 981–1026.

Wilkins, David B., and Vikramaditya S. Khanna. 2017. "Globalization and the Rise of the In-house Counsel Movement in India." In *The Indian Legal Profession in the Age of Globalization: The Rise of the Corporate Legal Sector and Its Impact on Lawyers and Society*, edited by David Wilkins, Vikramaditya Khanna, and David Trubek, 114–69. Cambridge: Cambridge University Press.

Wilkins, David, Vikramaditya Khanna, and David M.Trubek, eds. 2017. *The Indian Legal Profession in the Age of Globalization: The Rise of the Corporate Legal Sector and Its Impact on Lawyers and Society*. Cambridge: Cambridge University Press.

Wilkins, David B., David M. Trubek, and Bryon Fong. 2020. "Globalization, Lawyers, and Emerging Economies: The Rise, Transformation, and Significance of the New Corporate Legal Ecosystem in India, Brazil, and China." *Harvard International Law Journal* 61(2): 281–355.

Williams, Alexander. 2020. "Imagining the Post-Colonial Lawyer: Legal Elites and the Indian Nation-State." *Asian Journal of Comparative Law*. 15(1):1–31.

Wong, Alan. 2017. "7 Hong Kong Police Officers Convicted of Assaulting Protester in 2014." *New York Times*, 14 February. https://www.nytimes.com/2017/02/14/world/asia/hong-kong-police-ken-tsang-conviction.html?_r=0.

Wu, Xiaogang. 2017. "Higher Education, Elite Formation, and Social Stratification in Contemporary China: Preliminary Findings from the Beijing College Students Panel Survey." *Chinese Journal of Sociology* 3(1) 3–31.

Yang, Wenhui, and Ling Chen. 2016. "Political Capital and Intergenerational Mobility: Evidence from Elite College Admissions in China." *Chinese Journal of Sociology* 2(2): 194–213.

Yeo, Jun-suk. 2015. "Debate Grows over Fate of South Korea's Traditional Bar Exam." *South Korea Herald*, 8 September. http://www.SouthKoreaherald.com/view.php?ud=20150908001142.

Yukihiko, Motoyama. 1997. *Proliferating Talent: Essays on Politics, Thought and Education in the Meiji Era*. Honolulu: University of Hawai'i Press.

Zhang, Anna. 2019. "Will Hong Kong Remain a Critical Financial Center for Law Firms?" *The Asian Lawyer*, 1 August. https://www.law.com/2019/08/01/will-hong-kong-remain-a-critical-financial-center-for-law-firms.

Zhang, Taisu. 2019. "The Development of Comparative Law in China." In *The Oxford Handbook of Comparative Law*, 2nd ed., edited by Matthias Reimann and Reinhardt Zimmerman, 229–57. Oxford: Oxford University Press.

Zhang, Taisu, and Tom Ginsburg. 2019. "China's Turn Toward Law." *Virginia Journal of International Law* 59: 306–89.

Zhao, Jun, and Ming Hu. 2012. "A Comparative Study of the Legal Education System in the United States and China and the Reform of Legal Education in China." *Suffolk Transnational Law Review* 35: 329–62.

Zhu, Jingqi, Yang Zhao, and Sida Liu. 2020. "Inside the 'Red Circle': The Production of China's Corporate Legal Elite." *Journal of Professions and Organization* 7(1): 87–100.

INDEX

ABA (American Bar Association), 81, 85
Abel, Richard, 3
Adams, John Quincy, 60
All China Lawyers Association (ACLA), 189
alliances: as central to legal revolutions, 17, 19, 23;
    China, 194; feudalism and, 31; India, 194;
    Japan, 194; marital, 23; South Korea, 194
Americanization: modernization as, 7, 98;
    in South Korea, 156
American Society of International Law, 69, 70
Anglican revolution, 27, 45–47
anti-corruption reforms, 58, 59, 191
anti-imperial imperialism (US), 9, 58, 60, 197
Anti-Rightist Campaign (China), 11, 165, 172–73,
    178, 189, 190–91
apprenticeships, 9, 22, 61
aristocratic capital, 21, 195, 196
Arnold and Porter (law firm), 78, 83–84, 93
Arrighi, Giovanni, 8
Arun, Chinmayi, 204n2(ch6)
Asian Journal of Law and Society (periodical), 161
Asian Law and Society Association, 161
Asian Legal Revivals (Dezalay and Garth), 12
Association of Korean Law Professors, 145
Auerbach, Jerome, 66, 78
authority: challenges to, 199; classic bases
    of political, 72; decline of church's, 62;
    hierarchies of, 71; international law and,
    70; of judicial institutions, 37–38; learned

authority of law, 46; legal authority, 42, 62;
    Lutheran revolution's challenge to, 37;
    mobilization of legal authority, 24, 26; papal
    authority, 25; of *Professorenrecht*, 73; of
    professors, 203n2. *See also* religious authority

Baade, Hans. *See specific countries*
Bar Council of India (BCI), 103–6, 111
bar memberships: in Britain, 47, 195; in China,
    167–68, 205n5; in France, 39–40; in India, 23,
    101–20; in Japan, 162; in Prussia, 196
bar memberships (South Korea): bar dues,
    205n3(ch8); diversity of, 204–5n2(ch8); elite
    law schools and, 152–53; in Japan, 138–39,
    142, 158–59; Korean Bar Association, 144–45,
    148, 149; lapsed, 205n3(ch8); legal education
    and, 155
Barnet, Richard, 79
barriers to entry: in Britain, 48; in France, 21;
    in India, 129; in Korea, 145; in medieval
    Bologna, 4; in United States, 58
barristers (Britain): in colonies, 196–97; as
    double agents, 46; Queen's Counsel, 6,
    47–48; rise of, 44–49, 72; triumph of, 22
Baxi, Upendra, 104, 105, 112, 119, 208
BCI (Bar Council of India), 103–6, 111
Belt and Road Initiative (BRI) (China), 189,
    190, 191
bengoshi, 162

Benton, Lauren, 5–6, 8, 28, 51, 195
Berman, Harold: on Anglican revolution, 27,
    45, 46–47; beyond theories of, 17, 19–30, 195;
    on British law, 45, 46–47; consistency with,
    97; on Gregorian revolution, 17, 27, 46–47;
    historical model of law, 19, 25; on holders
    of political power, 26; *Law and Revolution*,
    24; legal revolution theory, 4, 11, 17, 24–27,
    194, 200; on Lutheran revolution, 24, 27, 37;
    on meritocratic criteria, 30; on Protestant
    revolution, 17, 27, 46–47; on Roman civil law,
    33; theoretical perspectives and, 8, 17
Biddulph, Sarah, 185
Big Four (Japanese law firms), 157, 160, 194
Big Seven (Indian law firms), 109–11
Big Six (Seoul law firms), 153, 155
Bologna, University of: about, 4, 8–9; Bologna
    model, 195–96, 200; canon law at, 25;
    cosmopolitan legal elites, 12, 193, 200;
    degrees offered by, 32, 193; influence on
    Britain, 45, 196; influence on Germany, 36,
    37, 195–96; influence on legal field, 193; jurists
    from, 34; Martines on, 23; religious sponsors
    of study, 24; student payments, 33
boom and bust periods: Bourdieu's neglect of,
    22–23; civil rights era as, 58, 75; deregulation,
    75; German model of law, 196; imbalances
    in legal field and, 22; in Japan and China, 18;
    neoliberalism, 75; neoliberalism as, 58; New
    Deal as, 58, 75; processes central to, 23; in US,
    59, 197; variety and similarities in, 197
Bourdieu, Pierre: Berman and, 200; on boom
    and bust periods, 22–23; on change and
    continuity, 19, 23–24, 200–201; concept of
    field (term), 12; on cosmopolitan elites,
    194–95; "Esprits d'etat," 20, 24; on family
    capital, 194–95; field concept of, 200;
    "The Force of Law," 20, 22; going beyond,
    17, 19–30, 195; habitus concept, 200; on
    internal conflicts, 24; "Les juristes, gardiens
    de l'hypocrisie collective," 20; on legal
    capital, 20, 26–27; on legal challengers, 5;
    on legal education, 21; on legal fields, 21;
    on meritocratic criteria, 30, 194–95; "Les
    robins et l'invention de l'Etat," 20; on role of
    lawyers, 19; *On the State (Sur l'Etat)*, 20; on
    state power, 18, 19, 20–24, 194–95; structural
    contradictions, 17; theoretical perspectives, 8
Bracton's Treatise, 45
Brahmins, 101, 107, 113, 195, 196, 197
Braudel, Fernand, 8
Brazil: corporate law boom in, 6; jurists in, 3, 5;
    legal elites in, 52, 97–98

British colonialism: about, 5; in America, 52,
    53, 57, 59, 60; Benton and Ford on, 8, 51,
    195; Hong Kong and, 9, 52; India and, 9, 52;
    legacy of, 52, 59. *See also* Hong Kong; India
British Empire: analyses of, 21; barristers in
    colonies, 196–97; British model of courts, 20;
    British model of law, 195; industrialization,
    196; international law and, 51; Jacksonian
    democracy and ties to, 197; learned/social
    capital combination, 195; social capital
    and, 196; universities, 46, 49, 110. *See also*
    barristers (Britain); Inns of Court
British law: Benton and Ford on, 8; Bracton's
    Treatise, 45; British model of law, 9, 44–45;
    canon law and, 45, 46; Roman civil law and,
    45, 46
brokers: cosmopolitan broker model, 200;
    lawyers as, 18, 19, 32, 53, 194
Brundage, James, 24, 32–33, 36, 193, 194, 200
Buchanan, James, 87–88
Bundy, McGeorge, 76–78, 78–79, 85
Bushimata, Atsushi, 162

Caenegem, R. C. van, 19
Califano, Joe, 91
California Rural Legal Assistance, 105
canon law: British law and, 45, 46; civil law and,
    193; in European Continent, 9; French law
    and, 39, 41, 42; Gregorian revolution and,
    25; in medieval Bologna, 25, 193, 198; US law
    and, 61. *See also* Catholic Church
Carbonneau, Thomas E., 39, 41
careers: career trajectories of interviewees,
    12; elite corporate careers (China), 191;
    employment statistics (China), 205n5;
    legal academic career (India), 204n5; legal
    academic careers (India), 204n5; local
    options for in Hong Kong, 132–35
Carnegie, Andrew, 65, 66, 70, 71, 73
case method (US), 9, 64, 66
catch-up strategies, 37–39, 196
catch-up strategy, 196
categories of legal field: Berman's, 19; Bourdieu's,
    20–21, 24, 29–30; destabilizing of, 19; double
    agent, 24; elite/non-elite categories, 12–13;
    emergence of fixed, 29; limitations of, 20–21;
    manipulation by medieval jurists, 32
Catholic Church: Gregorian reforms, 24–25, 32–33;
    Holy Roman Empire and, 36; jurists and, 24,
    33, 35, 194; papal authority, 25; Papal Courts,
    34; universities and, 36. *See also* canon law
CCEJ (Citizens' Coalition for Economic Justice)
    (South Korea), 143, 144

CCP (Chinese Communist Party). *See* Chinese Communist Party (CCP)

chaebols, 144, 146, 147, 148, 151, 154, 161, 200

Chan, Kay-Wah, 155

Chandrachud, Shri Y. V., 114–15

change in legal fields: Bourdieu on, 23–24, 200–201; learned law and, 201. *See also* legal revolutions

Chen Shouyi, 174

China: All China Lawyers Association (ACLA), 189; alliances in, 194; Belt and Road Initiative (BRI), 189, 190, 191; catch-up strategy, 196; colonial legacies in law, 191; Confucianism, 164, 165; cosmopolitan legal elites in, 5; German model of law adoption in, 9; Hong Kong and, 121–36, 123–27; internationalization and, 11, 191–92; Kuomintang (KMT) government, 11, 165, 168, 169; law professors in, 167, 170, 174–76; law students in, 167, 185–86; Mao Zedong, 165, 168, 171, 184; Ministry of Education, 167, 179, 182; Ministry of Justice, 169, 182, 184–85, 189; national governance model of, 164; Open Policy, 174–75; Republican Period, 165, 166, 205n1; Sino-Japanese War, 166; social capital in, 168, 193–201; Soviet Union model of law, 168–69, 171, 184, 205n1; state restrictions on litigation, 166; think tanks, 177; Tiananmen Square movement, 177; tribute system, 164. *See also* Cultural Revolution (China); international strategies (China); lawyers (China); learned capital (China); legal capital (China); legal education (China); People's Republic of China (PRC); universities (China)

Chinese Communist Party (CCP), 125, 169–70, 171, 181–82, 205n2. *See also* Cultural Revolution (China); Maoists

Christianson, Wei (Sun), 177, 205n4

Christopher, Warren, 84

church/state relationship: Bourdieu on, 24; jurists and, 33, 35; in United States, 62; universities and, 36, 62

Citizens' Coalition for Economic Justice (CCEJ) (South Korea), 143, 144

city-states (Italy): familial capital and, 35, 67, 194; rise of, 33–34, 50, 194

civil law: in Britain, 45; canon law and, 193, 198; in China, 169, 177, 180; common law and, 61, 72; in European Continent, 9; in France, 41, 180; in Germany, 180; in Hong Kong, 124; in medieval Bologna, 29, 32, 34; in South America, 52; in South Korea, 145, 156; in United States, 53, 61. *See also* Code of

Justinian (Corpus Juris Civilis); codification; Roman civil law

civil rights: activism in India, 105; activism in United States, 80–86, 87; LCCRUL, 81–82, 83, 85

clergy: Bourdieu on lower legal clergy, 20; Gregorian revolution and, 24–25

clinics: in China, 179; emphasis on, 7; in South Korea, 151, 154, 155

Coates, Benjamin, 69–70, 71

Code of Justinian (Corpus Juris Civilis), 4, 25, 32–33, 61

codification, 52–53; in China, 124, 196; domination by, 49; export of national codes, 39; in France, 39, 40–41, 52, 53; in Germany, 38, 39, 52, 196; in Japan, 196, 198; legal education and, 52–53, 147, 150; in Naples, 43–44; in South Korea, 147, 150, 196, 198. *See also* civil law; Code of Justinian (Corpus Juris Civilis); Roman civil law

Cohen, Jerome, 171, 174–75

Cold War: globalization after, 9, 99, 143; instrumentalism in, 199; legal education after, 53, 99, 155; legal education during, 77; US hegemony after, 191, 193–94

colonialism: Asian merchants and, 51; brokers of capital in, 18, 52; centrality to interconnected histories, 8, 30; colonial legal profession, 58; French colonialism, 51–52; German colonialism, 51, 52; imperial competition and, 30, 196; law in support of, 27–29; lawyers as brokers and converters of capital and, 53; lawyers as brokers of capital and, 18; Spanish colonialism, 52

colonialism (British). *See* British colonialism

colonialism (Japanese), 10–11, 52, 137, 140, 142. *See also* South Korea

Columbia Law School, 64, 69, 76, 106, 144, 175, 177, 205n4

commercial law (Britain), 47–48

Committee of Clinical Legal Educators, 179

common law: in Britain, 27, 45–47, 49; in Hong Kong, 126, 132–33; in India, 107; in South Korea, 145, 204n1(ch8); in United States, 60, 61, 72, 180

concept of field (term), usefulness of, 12

Confucianism, 142, 146, 164–65, 166, 190–91

conservativism, 10, 89

continuity in legal fields: Berman and Bourdieu on, 30; Bourdieu on, 23–24; change and, 200–201; in China, 169; medieval Bologna and, 193; Rheinstein on, 203n2. *See also* interconnected histories co-optation process (British colonies), 5, 22, 200

Coquillette, Daniel R., 63, 64, 204n1(ch4)

corporate law firms: competition for graduate placement, 194; conservatism and, 10; diffusion of, 10, 11; in Europe, 6; existing literature on, 8; exportation of, 7; globalization of, 200; growth and expansion of, 7; institutionalization of, 10; in Japan and South Korea, 11, 137, 160–61, 163; in Latin America, 6; legitimating of, 9; legitimating of at top of hierarchy, 9; meritocracy and, 62–64; meritocratic capital and, 9, 194; neoliberalism and, 10; open market for in Hong Kong, 121–36; partners as lawyer-statespersons, 197; proliferation of, 194; resources of, 72; social capital and, 9; welfare state and, 10

corporate law firms (China): elite legal education and, 189–90; Red Circle of, 186, 190; rise of, 186–87; Xi Jinping administration, 165

corporate law firms (India): Big Seven (Indian law firms), 109–11; following economic liberalization, 5; NLS training's focus on, 204n1(ch6)

corporate law firms (US): boom in, 6; growth and expansion of, 7, 19; New Deal and, 10, 76; political change and, 58; rise of, 7

Corpus Juris Civilis (Roman Body of Civil Law), 4, 25, 32–33, 61, 203n2

cosmopolitan legal elites: overview, 3–13, 200; in Britain, 9; in China, 165, 169; in colonial America, 59, 196–97; importance of, 193; law/social change relationship involving, 12; in medieval Bologna, 193, 194

credibility in law: autonomy as basis of, 35; in China and Japan, 196; geopolitical developments and, 201; resistance resulting in decline of, 22–23; shaping national credibility of law in competing global context, 200

Critical Legal Studies, 88–89, 94, 181

Cultural Revolution (China): effects of, 165, 199; legal elites purge during, 11, 170; legal elites' revival after, 173–78; legal elites' survival during, 168–73, 184, 190–91; Xi Jinping administration and, 188–89. See also Maoists

customary law, 6

Cutler, Lloyd, 83, 91

democracy movement (South Korea), alliance with, 194

deregulation: adaptability in relation to, 75; corporate legal services market growth from, 6; US corporate law firms and, 6

Dinovitzer, Ronit, 139

diplomats between fields of power, role of lawyers as, 18

Djavan, Rajeev, 105

Doctor of Jurisprudence degree. See Juris Doctorate (JD)

domestic political power, strategies linking, 10

Dongcheon Foundation, 154

double agency concept, 24, 32, 33, 34–35, 46, 51, 132

Douglas, William O., 98

Drinan, Robert, 81–82

Dutch colonization, 28, 51, 196

East China University of Law and Political Science, 185

The Economist (periodical), 99

Edwards, R. Randle, 175, 205n4

elite bench and bar (India): challenges to, 116–20; corporate law firms and, 109–11; NLSs and, 111–13; structure of, 113–16

elites (term), 12

entrepreneurs, 7, 10, 11, 195

Erie, Mathew, 182–83

"Esprits d'etat" (Bourdieu) (1993), 20, 24

Ewha Women's University, 153

familial capital: about, 8; assimilation and, 27; Bourdieu and, 19, 21, 23, 24; in Britain, 9, 49–50; change and continuity processes, 24; city-states (Italy) and, 35, 67, 194; as criteria for advancement, 8; family alliances, 23; in France, 23; in India, 23, 109; legal capital from, 23; legal education reform and, 11; Martines on, 23; in medieval Bologna, 193, 194; meritocratic capital and, 19; Mexican camarillas, 23; role of, 31–53; scholarly capital and, 19; strategies and, 10, 18; symbolic capital and, 22; US hybrid model of legal education and, 61, 62; US model's challenges to, 8

Federalist Society, 91–92

Feeley, Malcolm M., 138

Feldman, Eric, 23

feudalism: alliances and, 31; in Britain, 45; feudal privileges, 193; jurisdictions under, 194; in medieval Bologna, 193

field (term), as differentiated space, 20

Flaherty, Darryl, 137

fluidity: of legal field, 18; of roles lawyers play, 21; terminology and, 12

Fong, Byron, 110

Foote, Daniel H., 139–40, 162, 205n3(ch8)

"The Force of Law" (Bourdieu), 20, 22

Ford, Lisa, 5–6, 8, 28, 51, 195
Ford Foundation: Bundy and, 78–79; China
    and, 177, 179; India and, 102, 103–5, 106, 112,
    139; Japan and, 139; LCCRUL and, 82; liberal
    establishment and, 84–86, 87; Vance and, 79
foreign policy establishment, 9, 78–81, 94, 197
formal law: challengers to, 6; local elites
    competition with, 6; role of, 20
France: French Revolution, 21, 39, 40, 53;
    geopolitical approach of, 196; legal education
    in, 39–42; legal scholarly capital blending
    with family capital in, 23, 50; Napoleonic
    reforms, 40–41, 42; Parlement of Paris, 20.
    See also French law; noblesse de robe
Frankfurter, Felix, 65, 66, 76, 77
French law: analyses of field of, 21; French Civil
    Code, 40–41, 43; Roman civil law and, 39,
    41, 42
Friedman, Milton, 87

Galanter, Marc, 10, 106, 113
Gandhi, Indira, 102
Gandhi, Mahatma, 102
Garth, Bryant, 12
Gelatt, Timothy A., 171
gentry: in Britain, 195; political recognition of, 27
geopolitical approaches: about, 201; first, 195;
    idea circulation shaped by, 195; second,
    195–96; third, 196–97. See also British model
    of law; German model of law; Prussian
    model of law; Soviet model of law; US model
    of law
German model of law, 20, 21, 34–39, 52; influence
    on China, 166, 167, 174, 180, 181; influence on
    Japan and South Korea of, 9, 52, 137, 138, 139,
    150, 166
Germany: geopolitical approach of, 196; German
    model of state, 9; Japanese Meiji period and,
    164; law professors in, 147; legal education,
    42, 196; model of law, 147; Professorenrecht,
    20, 38, 50, 72, 73; Prussia, 37–39, 50, 52, 196;
    Roman civil law and, 36, 38. See also German
    model of law; Holy Roman Empire; lawyers
    (Germany)
Ginsburg, Tom, 188–89
globalization: of corporate low firms, 200;
    cosmopolitan legal elites and, 193; of legal
    education, 11; US corporate law firms and, 6;
    US-style, 7, 136. See also liberalization
Gonggam (public interest organization), 154
Gong Xiangrui, 173, 177
Gossett, William, 85
Government Law College (GLC) (India), 115

Graduate School of Law, Seoul National
    University (GSL) (South Korea), 140–41, 144,
    145, 153–54
grassroots groups, 89–90
Gregorian revolution: Berman on, 4, 17, 27;
    Brundage on, 32; defined, 24–25
Gregory I, Pope, 24–25
Grey, Thomas, 65
GSL (Graduate School of Law, Seoul National
    University) (South Korea), 140–41, 144, 145,
    153–54
Gunasekhere, Savitri, 106
Guo Shoukang, 175–76

Hall, Carlyle, Jr., 84
Halliday, 182
Halpern, Charles, 83–85, 90
Han Depei, 171, 172, 173
Harrison, Gordon, 85
Hart, H. L. A., 49
Harvard Law School: case method, 9, 64, 66;
    Continental model and, 197; founding of,
    61–62; graduates of, 110, 114; Japanese
    professors and, 139; legal education reform,
    62–67; legal education reform at, 58, 59;
    meritocratic reforms at, 9; Wall Street
    lawyers produced by, 9
Harvard Law Schools, Socratic method, 7
Hattori, Tataaki, 138
hegemonic relationships: boom/bust periods and,
    197; China's dominance in, 164; credibility in
    law and, 201; strategies linking, 10
Henretta, James A., 60
Henry II, King of England, 45
Heritage Foundation, 87, 88, 92
Herman, Richard A., 184
Hidayatullah, Mohammad, 104
hierarchical relationships: in Japan, 194;
    reinventions of, 193; in South Korea, 151–55,
    194; terminology and, 12
hierarchies, national (India): focus on, 204n3;
    grand advocates in, 10
hierarchies, national (Japan): alliances, 194;
    judges in, 10; prosecutors in, 10
hierarchies, national (Latin America), 10
hierarchies, national (South Korea): alliances,
    194; judges in, 10; prosecutors in, 10
hierarchies, national (US), historical uniqueness
    of, 10
Hilbink, Thomas, 80–84, 85
Hollis-Brusky, Amanda, 92
Holy Roman Empire, 36–38, 196
Hong Jin-Ki, 142

Hong Kong, 121–36; adaptation to global balance of power, 10; British colonialism and, 9; China comparison, 191–92; elite careers in, 132–35, 136; expatriates in legal profession in, 98, 196; growing power of, 10; India comparison, 136; internationalized scholarly production in, 135–36; international strategies in, 132–35; interviews in, 12; lawyers in, 130–32, 136; legal education in, 127–30, 136; legal education reform in; neoliberal revolution and, 10; post-1997 period, 124–27; pre-1997 period, 122–25; University of, 119; US-style globalization in, 136

Hong Seok-hyun, 142

Horowitz, Michael, 90–91

hôsô sansha, 140

Hu Jiaxiang, 166, 168, 169, 185

Hu Jintao, 189

human rights initiatives (US), 194

hybrid model of legal education. See US hybrid model of legal education

imperial competition: changes in imperial power, 195; in China and Japan, 9, 165; colonial governance and, 30, 196; different paths of, 193–201; in early 20th century, 72–74; imperial relationship links and, 10; importance of, 17, 19; legal and social capital from, 31; legal fields and, 201; local capital and, 57; rise of US power in, 9; role of, 12; symbolic capital and, 22; US exceptionalism as, 58, 60

imperial exams (China), 166, 170

independence movements, 193, 197

India: alliances in, 194; Big Seven (Indian law firms), 109–11; British colonialism and, 9, 191; British legal education and, 164; colonial legal capital in, 197; colonial path dependencies in, 101–20; Common Law Admission Test, 107; Congress Party, 29, 98, 102, 103; corporate law boom in, 6; corporate law firms, 109–11; corporate law firms proliferation in, 10; coursework in, 204n2(ch6); cram schools, 159; family capital in, 23; Government Law College (GLC), 115; grand advocates (leading senior barristers), 10; high court advocates (India), 3, 10; Hong Kong comparison, 136; Indian Raj, 29, 101, 107, 196; Institutes of Technology, 107, 108; interviews in, 12; Jawaharlal Nehru University (JNU), 119; legal education reform in, 139; legal elites in, 191; legal oligarchies

of grand advocates and high judiciary, resistance by, 10; legal revolution and, 10; litigation in, 114, 204n1(ch6), 204n6; NLS training, 204n1(ch6); NLUs, 204n2(ch6); requirement changes, 204n1(ch6); traditional bar in, 165; US-oriented law schools and, 10; Vidhi Centre for Legal Policy, 117–18, 120. See also elite bench and bar (India); National Law Schools (NLSs) (India)

Indonesia, 28, 51, 196

industrialization, in Prussia, 196

Inns of Court: evolution of, 22, 49; history of, 203n4; legal education and, 203n4; role of, 195; training at, 45, 46, 51, 101

Institutes of Political Science and Law, 173, 184–85

interconnected histories: overview, 3–13, 200; differences and similarities of, 12; geopolitics affects on, 195; imperial competition and, 30

interdisciplinary approaches (US): as global standard, 7; in reformed law schools, 194; in US law schools, 180

internationalization: anti-imperial imperialism and, 197; China and, 191–92; in Hong Kong, 135–36

internationalized legal elites (China): corporate law firms and, 186–87; during Cultural Revolution, 168–73; domestic power growth of, 11; emergence of, 190; international capital and, 191; legal education and, 178; purging of, 11; during Republican Period, 11; survival of, 166, 168, 191

international justice, US-oriented: construction of, 59–74; The Hague and, 73, 74; Permanent Court of International Justice, 73, 74

international law: American Society of International Law, 69, 70; British Empire and, 51; China and, 191; Peking School of Transnational Law and, 180; South Korea and, 155; United States and, 58

international strategies (China): after Cultural Revolution, 173–78; legal elites and, 165

Iron Triangle, 156, 161, 162

Isenberg, Nancy, 60

Italy: Bologna model of law, 195–96, 200; cosmopolitan legal elites in, 6; medieval seats of learning in, 4, 203n2; Neapolitan legal system, 43–44; political alliances in Renaissance, 195; state building in, 42–44. See also Bologna, University of; Naples

Ivy League universities, 78, 79, 80, 87

Iyer, Krishna, 105

Jacksonian democracy, 59–61, 197
Jaffe, Sanford, 85
Jamin, Christophe, 40–41
Japan, 137–63; Asian financial crisis of, 161;
    Big Four (law firms), 157, 160, 194; Boxer
    Rebellion, 166; China and, 164, 166, 167, 174;
    co-optation of reforms, 155–59; corporate law
    firms in, 137; economic catch-up strategy,
    196; geopolitical approach of, 196; German
    influence on, 164; German model of law
    adoption in, 9, 52, 137, 138, 139; hybrid law
    school system, 157–59; interviews in, 12;
    Iron Triangle, 156, 161, 162; judges in legal
    hierarchy, 10, 138; keiretsu, 147, 155, 161,
    162; law professors in, 23, 147, 161; lawyers
    as brokers of capital and, 18; lawyers in,
    137–38; legal education reform in, 11, 155–57;
    legal market in, 159–61; Liberal Democratic
    Party (LDP), 161, 162; Meiji Revolution, 11,
    52, 98, 137, 137–38, 164; Ministry of Justice,
    157–58, 159; political interventions in, 139;
    prosecutors in legal hierarchy, 10; Provisional
    Justice System Investigation Committee
    (PJSIC), 139–40; Prussian model in, 196;
    samurai clans, 98, 138, 196; Sino-Japanese
    War, 166; South Korea in contrast with, 137,
    194; South Korea's colonial relationship to,
    10–11, 52, 137, 140, 142, 164, 191; stratification,
    159–61; Taiwan's colonial relationship to, 52;
    universities of, 139, 142, 158; US influence
    in, 139
Javanese elites, 28, 51, 196
JD (Juris Doctorate). See Juris Doctorate (JD)
Jiang Ping, 174, 177
Jindal Global Law School (India), 112, 118–20,
    204n5
Ji Weidong, 176
Johnson, Earl, Jr., 82
JRTI (Judicial Research and Training Institute
    (South Korea), 137, 141, 142, 145–49, 151
judges: in India, 204n4; in Japan, 196; in
    Japanese hierarchy, 10; in South Korea,
    142; in South Korean hierarchy, 10. See also
    specific Supreme Courts
judicialization, 70, 111
Judicial Research and Training Institute (JRTI)
    (South Korea), 11, 137
Juris Doctorate (JD), 7, 11, 204n1(ch8)
jurists: alliances with, 37; Bourdieu on, 24; in
    Brazil, 3, 5; in China, 174; as double agents,
    34–35; in Latin America, 10
Justinian's Digest, 25, 32

Kabaservice, Geoffrey, 78–79
Kalman, Laura, 85
Kang, David, 164
Kanter, Stephen, 171, 173
Kantorowicz, Ernst, 26, 35
keiretsu, 147, 155, 161, 162
Kennedy administration: civil rights and, 82;
    foreign policy establishment during, 78–81;
    Gossett during, 85; Keynesian advisors to, 87;
    Trubek to, 97
Keynesians, 87, 94
Khanna, Vikramaditya, 114
Kimball, Bruce A., 63, 64, 204n1(ch4)
Kim Young Sam, 144
King's Bench, 45
KoGuan, Leo, 183
Korean Bar Association, 144–45, 148, 149
Korean Law Schools Association, 153
Kostal, Randa, 47–48
Krishnan, Jayash, 103, 106, 107, 109, 117, 204n3,
    204n6
Kronche, Jedidiah, 168
Kumar, Raj, 119
Kuomintang (KMT) government, 11, 165, 168,
    169

Labaree, David, 62, 203n1
Langdell, Christopher Columbus, 9, 62–67, 73
Latin America: corporate law boom in, 6;
    hierarchies in, 10; legal education in, 52;
    Venezuela, 69–72. See also Brazil
Law and Economics, 88, 89, 92, 93
Law and Revolution (Berman), 24
Law and Society scholarship, 86, 88, 89, 144,
    161–62, 176, 181
law faculties (China): imperial pressures on, 164;
    internationalization of, 180, 191; as theory-
    driven, 180
law faculties (European Continent), 9
law faculties (Japan), 11
law faculties (South Korea), 11
law firms (India): bar privileges and, 23; Big
    Seven, 109–11; entrenched, 204n6
law firms (Japan), 160–61
law firms (South Korea), 153–54, 155
law firms (US): Arnold and Porter, 78, 83–84, 93;
    New Deal liberalism and, 76–78; Simpson
    Thatcher, 79, 85. See also Wall Street law firms
law graduates (China): in Belt and Road
    Initiative, 191; career paths of, 185, 186;
    faculty recruitment of, 180; going abroad, 11;
    in-house law sector and, 11; internationalism

of, 165; Soviet Union model of law and, 171; study abroad, 191

law graduates (Japan), 158, 162

law graduates (South Korea), 204–5n2(ch8)

Law in Japan (von Mehren, ed.), 139

law professors: alliance with US corporate lawyers, 59–74; Bourdieu and Berman on relationships with, 19; and changes in economic and political power, 19; in China, 167, 170, 174–75, 175–76; in Germany, 37, 147, 196; internationalization of, 191; invention of, 17; in Japan, 23, 147, 158, 161; from Japan in US, 139; in Latin America, 10; opposition to, 23; professor/politician (US), 195; recruiting of, 7; Rheinstein on opinions of, 203n3; in South Korea, 140–41, 145, 147, 149–50, 158, 195

law schools: in France, 21; invention of, 17

law schools (China): Chaoyang Law School, 167; Comparative Law School of China, 167–68; Cultural Revolution and, 11, 191; elite of, 178–84; expansion of, 179; hiring policies of, 180; KoGuan Law School, 176, 179, 180, 182, 183, 187; Peking Law School, 173–74, 180, 182, 184, 187; Peking School of Transnational Law, 180; Tsinghua Law School, 132, 132–33, 176, 179, 182, 183, 187, 192

law schools (India), 204n1(ch6)

law schools (Japan): alternatives to, 158–59; applications to, 159; graduates of, 158; Kobe University, 176; resources of, 163

law schools (South Korea): focus of, 155; German influence on, 150; Handong International Law School (South Korea), 204n1(ch8); impacts of reform on, 149–50; US-oriented faculty, 150

law schools (US): Columbia Law School, 64, 76, 79, 205n4; elite schools, 10, 194, 197; NYU Law School, 141, 168; rank and file of, 185–86; reforms at, 62–64; selection process of, 9; in South Korea, 147; Yale Law School, 64, 76, 79. *See also* Harvard Law School

law students (China): in Japan, 167; rank and file of, 185–86; in United States, 167

law students (India), grades (India), 204n1(ch4)

lawyers: barristers (Britain). *See* barristers (Britain)as brokers, 18, 19, 32, 53, 194; credibility of, 22; differentiated by social origins, education and royal power proximity, 20; as double agents, 24, 32, 33, 46; in France, 40; in Hong Kong, 130–32; in India, 108–9, 197; in Japan, 137–38, 196; in Prussia, 196; role as courtiers and diplomats,

18; role of, 19, 21, 24; in South Korea, 140, 141–42

lawyers (China): "barefoot" lawyers, 6; foreign expertise of, 168, 186–87; as legal advisors to drafters, 205n2; party's agenda and, 191; translated rule of law and constitutionalism from early Republican period, 205n1

lawyers (Germany), serving the state, 20

lawyers (term), use of, 12

lawyers (US): during colonial period, 59, 60, 196–97; effects of boom and bust periods on, 197; during Jacksonian period, 60–61, 197; role of, 72

Lawyers Committee for Civil Rights Under Law (LCCRUL), 81–82, 83, 85

Lawyers Constitutional Defense Committee (LCDC), 81–82

Lawyers for a Democratic Society (Minbyun) (South Korea), 144, 154

LCCRUL (Lawyers Committee for Civil Rights Under Law), 81–82

LCDC (Lawyers Constitutional Defense Committee), 81–82

LDP (Liberal Democratic Party) (Japan), 155–56, 159, 161, 162

learned capital: British combination of social and, 195; decline of, 22; medieval law (Italy) and, 195; model requiring, 195; social capital and, 195, 197

learned capital (China): devaluing of, 22; social capital and, 193–201

learned law: change in legal fields and, 201; and changes in economic and political power, 19; credibility of, 22; European geneses of, 31–53; invention of, 17; role in family capital, 31–53; role in social change and stability, 17; role of, 17–18, 19

learned law (China), 191

Lee, Chulwoo, 144, 148

Lee, Jae-Hyup, 140, 141, 148, 152, 153–54

Lee Byung-chul, 142

Lee Kun-hee, 142

LEET (legal education eligibility test), 148

legal capital: Bourdieu on, 17; holders of, 17, 20, 21; state-oriented, 196; symbolic capital and, 22

legal capital (China): foreign legal capital, 168; in governance and state, 187–89; increased value of internationalized, 165

legal education: alliances and, 194; best practices of, 201; codification and, 52–53; decline during 17th century, 203n4; European geneses of, 31–53; globalization of, 11;

globalization of by entrepreneurs, 7; in Hong Kong, 127–30; investment of cosmopolitan legal elites in, 5; in Japan, 139, 163; process of legal revolutions and, 7–8; role in family capital, 31–53; role of, 19; in South Korea, 140, 155; US hybrid model of, 61–62. *See also* hybrid model of legal education, US

legal education (Britain), 48, 49

legal education (China): adaptation in, 178; after Cultural Revolution, 11; clinics, 179; during Cultural Revolution, 172–73; elite of, 178–79, 189–90; internationalization of, 167; Japanese influence on, 167; quality of, 205n5; stratification in, 178; Xi Jinping administration, 165

legal education (France), 39–42

legal education (Germany), prestige of, 196

legal education (India): quality of, 204n2(ch6); reluctance reform of, 105–9

legal education (US): export of model of, 9; Litchfield School, 61. *See also* Harvard Law School

legal education, US: about. *See* Harvard Law School

legal educational reform, about, 8

legal education eligibility test (LEET), 148

Legal Education in a Developing Nation (Murphy), 140

legal education reform: efforts by groups allied with corporate law firms to, 11; familial capital and, 11; in India, 139; in Japan, 11, 137–63, 176; scholarly capital and, 11; in South Korea, 11, 137–63, 139, 141, 143, 146; technologies of in Hong Kong, 121–36; in United States, 62–64; US influence on, 97

legal elites: alliances and, 194; in Brazil, 97–98; corporate law firms ostracization by, 7; elite law schools and reproduction of, 10; in Japan, 163; long history of, 8; in medieval Italy, 4, 6. *See also* internationalized legal elites (China)

legal elites (China): adaptability of, 166, 171; after Cultural Revolution, 173–78; continuity of, 170; internationalization of, 165; persecution of, 172

legal elites (South Korea), *chaebols*, 144, 146, 147, 148, 151, 154

legal elites, cosmopolitan (China): in China, 5; law/social change relationship involving, 12; long-established internationalized, 11; during Republican Period, 11

legal field: Bourdieu's field of state power and, 20–24; in contemporary China, 178–90; fluidity and shifting of, 18, 21; usefulness of term, 12

legalization, 70, 162, 191, 199

legal profession: comparative studies, 6; controlled access to, 10; divergence in post-medieval, 195; genesis of, 12; origins of, 200

legal profession (China): Depei and Kanter on, 171; imperial pressures on, 164; near eradication during Anti-Rightist Campaign, 11; near eradication during Cultural Revolution, 11

legal profession (Japan): after Meiji Revolution, 11; history of, 137–38

legal profession (South Korea): as Japanese-led replica, 11; US ambitions for, 141

legal realism, 76–78

Legal Research and Training Institute (LRTI) (Japan), 142, 158

legal revolution(s): overview, 3–13; about, 8; alliances as central to, 17; Berman on, 4, 11, 17, 24–27, 200; global hegemonic power and, 200; legal education and process of, 7–8; legal oligarchies challenged by, 7; long history of, 8; modernist challenges associated with, 10; resistance of those shaping impacts of, 13; second phase of, 194; seeking to shake up law/social change relationship involving cosmopolitan legal elites, 12; structural contradictions of, 17; United States and promotion of, 57–58, 57–94; US inspired, 137; US power in imperial competition and, 9. *See also* Anglican revolution; Gregorian revolution; Lutheran revolution; Meiji Revolution; neoliberal revolutions; Protestant revolution; social revolutions in United States

Legal Services Corporation, 89

Lemmings, David, 47, 203n4

"Les juristes, gardiens de l'hypocrisie collective" (Bourdieu) (1991), 20

"Les robins et l'invention de l'Etat" (Bourdieu) (1989), 20

Levi, Ron, 139

Li, Charles, 177

Li, Cheng, 177, 187–88

Li, Xueyao, 187

Liberal Democratic Party (LDP) (Japan), 155–56, 159, 161, 162

liberalism (China), 11

liberalism (US): legal realism and, 76–78; liberal establishment, 78–88, 89, 91, 94, 197
liberalization (India): corporate law firms and, 5, 109–10, 111; economic liberalization, 5, 6
liberalization (US): corporate law firms and, 6; US corporate law firms and, 6
Li Buyun, 174, 181
Li Keqiang, 176–77
Li Mu'an, 170–71
Lindsay, John, 79
Liu, Lawrence, 189–90
Liu, Sida, 6, 182, 187
Li Xueyao, 166, 168, 169, 185
Li Yiran, 166, 168, 169, 185
LL.B. (Legum Baccalaureus) (Bachelor of Laws) degree: China and, 174, 180, 182–83, 185, 187; Hong Kong and, 127, 128, 129, 130, 134; India and, 114, 119; Japan and, 11; legal education reform and, 11; South Korea and, 11, 142
LL.M. (Legum Magister) (Master of Laws) degree: access to, 198; China and, 176, 177, 179, 182–83, 186, 187; Hong Kong and, 129, 130, 133; India and, 110, 114, 119; South Korea and, 154
The Long Twentieth Century (Arrighi), 8
LRTI (Legal Research and Training Institute) (Japan), 142, 158
Lutheran revolution, 24, 27, 37

Macaulay, Thomas Babington, 101
Macdonald, Ronald S. J., 167
Madhya Pradesh (India), public ombudsmen (lokayuktas) in, 204n4
Magic Circles, 11, 99, 116, 137, 160–61, 194, 198
Mangaldas, Cyril Amarchand, 108, 109
Maoists, 165, 170, 189, 199. *See also* Chinese Communist Party (CCP)
Mao Zedong, 165, 168, 171, 184
Marden, Orison, 85
Markovits, Daniel, 4
Marshall, Burke, 80–81
Martines, Lauro, 23, 32, 34, 36, 132, 194, 200
Mazower, Mark, 71
McDougal, Myres S., 141
McSweeney, Thomas J., 45
mediation practices, 170–71
medieval law (Italy): about, 8–9; canon law and, 193, 198; competition and complementarity in, 195; European structures evolving out of, 17–18; familial processes, 24; learned capital and, 195; legal profession in, 194; Roman civil law and, 193, 198; social capital and, 195. *See also* Bologna, University of

Meese, Edwin, 91–92
Meiji Revolution, 11, 52, 98, 137, 137–38, 164
Menon, N. R. Madhava, 105–6
mentor-professor relationships, 23, 147, 161
meritocratic capital, 11; about, 8; corporate law firms and, 9; criteria for, 4; families/quasi-families and, 23; hiring and, 7; in India, 109; over inheritance or familial capital, 21; social class and, 194; tensions between family capital and, 19; tensions between scholarly capital and, 19
meritocratic criteria, in France, 21
Mexico, camarillas as scholarly/familial capital, 23
Minbyun (Lawyers for a Democratic Society) (South Korea), 144, 154
Minzner, Carl, 178, 186, 188, 205n5
mirror images, 9, 28, 29, 30
Miyazaya, Setsuo, 138
modernization: Americanization as, 7, 97, 98; challenges of, 10; in China, 165, 168–69, 170, 173; of growth in demand, 7; Jamin on, 40; in Japan, 140; moral imperialism and, 98–99, 197, 198; in Naples, 44; opposition to, 29
Mody, Zia, 110
Moon Jae-in, 144, 161
Moore, John Bassett, 69, 71
moral imperialism, modernization and, 98–99, 197, 198
Murayama, Masayuki, 159
Murphy, Jay, 140, 141
Musella, Luigi, 44

nabobs of the law (India), 29, 51, 101, 195, 196
Nader, Ralph, 83
Nakamura, Mayumi, 159–61
Nanda, Ashish, 110
Naples, 43–44
Nariman, Rohinton, 114
National Law School of Bangalore (India), 5
National Law Schools (NLSs) (India), 204n1; access to, 107–8; curriculum of, 106; development of, 102, 104; elite bench and bar and, 109, 111–13; graduates of, 108–9, 115, 116–17, 118; influence of, 107; research and, 117, 118; rise of, 107
Natural Law Jurisprudence, 41, 92
Neapolitan legal system, 43–44
Nehru, Jawaharlal, 5, 102, 119, 197
Nehru, Motilal, 102
neoliberalism: adaptability in relation to, 75; in Asian countries, 6; as boom and bust periods, 58; corporate law firms adaptations

to, 10; corporate law firms and, 10; diffusion of abroad, 10; economists and, 93; use of term, 12; US models and, 10

neoliberal revolutions: about, 97–99, 97–201; in Asian countries, 8; cosmopolitan legal elites and, 193; in United States, 75–94, 200

New Deal: academic legal theory during, 86; adaptability in relation to, 75; Berman's model applied to, 25; as boom and bust periods, 58; corporate law firms adaptations to, 10; corporate law firms and, 10; corporate law firms opposition to, 76; leaders of corporate bar as opposed to, 67; legal realism and, 77–78; liberalism of, 78, 83

New York & Bermudez (NY&B) Company, 69
Ngai-man, Simon Young, 126
NGOs (nongovernment organizations), 5, 195
Nilekani, Rohini, 118
Niles, Russell, 141
Nixon, Richard, 80, 82, 84
noblesse de robe, 3, 20, 21, 38, 196
nongovernment organizations (NGOs), 5, 195

Olson, Ted, 93
On the State (Sur l'Etat) (Bourdieu), 20
Originalism, 92, 94
Ottoman Empire, 31
Oxford University, 46, 49, 61, 118

Park, Yong Chui, 146, 147
Park Chung-hee, 141–42
Park Geun-hye, 149
Park Se-Il, 144
Park Won-soon, 144, 154
Parlement of Paris, 20
Parsis, 101, 110, 113, 114, 195, 196
Peking School of Transnational Law, 180
People's Commissioners (lokayuntas) (India), 204n4
People's Republic of China (PRC), 165, 169–70, 179, 184, 188, 190
People's Solidarity for Participatory Democracy (PSPD) (South Korea), 143–44, 154
Philippines, 197
Piketty, Thomas, 93
PIL (public interest litigation), 104–6, 110
PILSARC (Public Interest Legal Support and Research Center), 105
Posner, Richard, 88, 176
Pound, Roscoe, 169–70
Powell, Lewis, 90
pro bono litigation, 154, 162

Professorenrecht, 20, 38, 50, 72, 73. See also Weberian model (Professorenrecht)
prosecutors: from China and Moscow, 205n1; in Japan, 10; in South Korea, 10, 195
Protestant revolution, 4, 17, 27
Provisional Justice System Investigation Committee (PJSIC) (Japan), 139–40
Prussia, 37–39, 50, 52, 196
Prussian Code of 1794, 38
Prussian model of law, 196
PSPD (People's Solidarity for Participatory Democracy) (South Korea), 143–44, 154
Public Interest Advisory Committee, 85
Public Interest Legal Support and Research Center (PILSARC), 105
public interest litigation (PIL), 104–6, 110, 154–55, 162, 205n3(ch8)
public ombudsmen (lokayuktas) (India), 204n4
pure law (term), 12, 20

Qian Duansheng, 170, 174, 205n2
Qing dynasty, 164, 165–66, 167, 170
quasi-familial capital: Bourdieu on, 21; in India, 195; meritocratic legal capital leading to production of, 23; US model's challenges to, 8
Queen's Counsel (Britain), 6, 47–48

Rage for Order (Benton and Ford), 195
railroad industry, 47, 48, 61
Rao Geping, 126
Reagan administration, 88–92
Red Circle law firms, 186, 190, 194
Reginald Heber Smith program, 82
religious groups: alliances with, 19; authority of, 24, 37; in construction of state, 24; discrimination against, 64–65; place of, 6; as sponsors of study, 24
Renaissance Italy, 32–36, 39, 195
Renmin University, 169, 177, 179, 180, 182, 184
Republican Period (China), 11, 165, 166, 167–68, 170
La république des constitutionalistes (Sacriste), 41
research methodology, 3–4, 4, 8
resistance, 11, 200; decline of learned capital from, 22
Rhee, Syngman, 142
Rheinstein, Max, 203nn2–3
Riles, Annelise, 204–5n2(ch8)
robber barons, 48, 58, 59, 65, 68, 197
Robinson, Nick, 10, 113, 204n4
Rockefeller, John D., 65, 71
Roh Moo-hyun, 144, 148, 161

Roman Catholicism. *See* canon law; Catholic Church

Roman civil law: British law and, 45, 46; Corpus Juris Civilis (Roman Body of Civil Law), 4, 25, 32–33, 61; European legal systems and, 31; French law and, 39, 41, 42; Germanic law and, 36, 38; in medieval Bologna, 193, 198; universities and, 36, 43, 203n2; US law and, 61

Roman model of governance, 31, 34

Roosevelt, Franklin D., 77, 94

Roosevelt, Theodore, 69

Root, Elihu, 65, 66, 67, 69–71, 71, 78

Roots of War (Barnet), 79

Rosen, Dan, 156, 160–61

royal power, 20, 24

Rueschmeyer, Dietrich, 38

Rui Mu, 175, 177

rule of law (China), 11

Sacriste, Guillaume, 23, 41

Saegusa, Mayumi, 156, 157–58

Samsung Group, 142

samurai clans, 98, 138, 196

Sathe, S. P., 105

Savigny, Friedrich Carl von, 43

Scalia, Antonin, 92

Schmitt, Mark, 90

scholarly capital: about, 8, 9; family capital and, 19, 23; family capital blending with, 23; legal education reform and, 11; in medieval Bologna, 193; Mexican camarillas, 23; in Prussia, 196; relative decline in value of, 18, 49–50; role of, 17, 200; tensions between meritocratic capital and, 19

scholarly production, 17, 22

Scott, James Brown, 69, 70

Segal, Bernard, 81, 85

Sengupta, Arghya, 118

Seoul National University (SNU), 145, 149, 152–55

Seppänen, Samuli, 180

Seymour, Whitney North, 85

Shamir, Ronen, 76–77

Shen Junru, 170

Shen Zonglin, 174

Shroff, Pallavi, 110

Simpson Thatcher (law firm), 79, 85

Singapore, 117

Sino-Japanese War, 166

Skinner, Quentin, 24

SKY schools, 149, 152–54

SNU (Seoul National University), 145, 149, 152–55

Snyder, Frederick, 171

social capital: about, 8; British combination of learned and, 195; in China, 168, 193–201; corporate law firms and, 9; European geneses of, 31–53; imbalances in legal field and, 22; learned capital and, 195, 197; in medieval Bologna, 193; medieval law (Italy) and, 195; model requiring, 195; in Prussia, 196; role in family capital, 31–53; strategies linking, 10

social change: Bourdieu on, 19, 23; in India, 197; law and, 12, 17–18, 19; social stability and, 17

social continuity: Bourdieu and Berman on role of learned law and legal education in, 19; Bourdieu on centrality of process of, 23

social origins of lawyers: differentiation by, 20; recruitment in conformance with, 22

social revolutions in United States, 75–94

sociological perspectives: about, 19; Bourdieu's field of state power, 20–24; evolution of Bourdieu's, 17; on role of learned law and social change, 19–30; on social change and role of learned law, 19–30

Socratic method, 7

Sorabjee, Soli, 110

South Korea: China and, 164; corporate law firms in, 137, 191; corporations in, 142; economic catch-up strategy, 196; geopolitical approach of, 196; German model of law adoption in, 9, 52, 147; graduate level reforms, 147–49; Graduate School of Law, Seoul National University (GSL), 140–41, 144, 145; Handong International Law School, 204n1(ch8); interviews in, 12; Japan in contrast with, 137, 194; Japan's colonial relationship with, 10–11, 52, 137, 140, 142, 164, 191; judges in legal hierarchy, 10; Judicial Research and Training Institute (JRTI) in, 11, 137, 141, 142, 145–49, 151; Juris Doctorate (JD) in legal education reform, 11; law colleges of, 140; law firms in, 153; law professors of, 140–41; legal education reform in, 11, 137; legal profession in, 140; legal sector allied with democracy movement, 194; legal system/legal profession in, 10–11, 137; prosecutor/NGO/entrepreneur, 195; prosecutors in legal hierarchy, 10; reform impacts, 149–51; resistance to legal establishment in, 143–47; Supreme Court, 141, 145. *See also* Asian countries

Southworth, Ann, 89–90, 92

Soviet model of law, 168–69, 171, 174, 184, 205n1

Spanish colonialism, 52

Starr, Kenneth, 93

State Department, US, 69, 70, 78

state power, field of: adaptation to changes in, 11; Bourdieu on, 20–24; marginalization of law and, 50; pure law relationship to, 20; usefulness of term, 12
Stiglitz, Joseph, 93
stratification: in China, 178; in Japan, 159–61, 163; in South Korea, 151–55
Sugarman, David, 49
Sullivan and Cromwell (law firm), 64, 85, 177
Supreme Court (China), 170, 179, 184
Supreme Court (India): as employer, 108; hierarchical relationships and, 111; Indira Gandhi and, 102; justices of, 104–5, 110, 114, 204n4; reform challenges, 115, 116, 120; retirement from, 113, 114
Supreme Court (Japan), 139, 157, 158
Supreme Court (South Korea), 141, 145
Supreme Court (US), 86, 90, 92, 93
Surendranath, Anup, 117, 204n2(ch6)
symbolic capital, 22

Taiwan, 52, 137, 162, 165, 168, 169
Tammany Hall politics, 63
Teles, Steven, 89, 91
think tanks, 87, 88, 116, 117–18, 120, 177
Tiffert, Glen, 165, 166–67, 169–70, 171, 181, 205nn1–3
Tilly, Charles, 8
Tomlins, Christopher, 65–66
Tong Rou, 177
Toqueville, Alexis de, 60, 61, 197
Tripathi, P. K., 106
Trubek, David, 6, 97–98
Tushnet, Mark, 86
Twining, William, 49, 106

Uchida, Takashi, 204–5n2(ch8)
United States: American Revolution, 60, 61; challengers to entrenched legal oligarchies in, 200; Chinese graduates in, 11; civil rights era, 58, 75; colonial legacy of Britain, 52, 53, 57, 59, 60; common law in, 60, 61, 72, 180; conservativism and, 10; corporate law firms in, 6, 59; global neoliberalism, 58; golden age of legal theory, 88–89; Great Depression, 67, 76; hybrid model of legal education, 61–62; impact on China, 167; influence on China, 167–68; international legal field in, 68, 69–72; Jacksonian democracy, 59–61, 197; Japan and, 139, 140; legal revolution and, 52, 53; neoliberalism and, 10, 58; neoliberal revolutions in, 75–94; New Deal, 10, 25, 58, 67, 75, 76; Peking School

of Transnational Law and, 180; professor/politician, 195; Progressive Era, 65, 67; rise of US power in imperial competition, 9; social revolutions in, 75–94; South Korea and, 140–41, 194; Vietnam War, 79, 80, 84, 197; welfare state, 10, 25. See also corporate law firms (US); Ford Foundation; Harvard Law School; lawyers (US); legal education, US; universities (US)
universities: church/state relationship and, 36, 62; of Japan, 139, 142, 158; Roman civil law and, 43; US borrowing from German, 58
universities (Britain): Cambridge University, 46, 49, 110; law faculties of, 46, 49
universities (China): Beijing University, 126, 169, 170, 176; Hubei University, 172; Institutes of Political Science and Law, 169, 184–85; law departments at, 5, 169, 173, 179, 184; Nanjing University, 172; Peking University, 167, 173, 175, 176, 177, 179, 184; Renmin University, 169, 177, 179, 180, 182, 184; Shanghai Jiao Tong University, 176, 179, 180, 182, 183; Soochow University, 167; Wuhan University, 169, 172, 173, 176, 179, 184
universities (South Korea), 140; Handong International Law School, 204n1(ch8); hierarchy of, 152–53; Seoul National University (SNU), 145, 149; SKY schools, 149, 152, 153–54
universities (US): Columbia Law School, 175; Ivy League universities, 78, 79, 80, 87; Japanese professors and, 139; New York University, 141, 168; Stanford University, 139; University of Michigan, 139, 168. See also Harvard Law School
US hegemony: boom and bust periods and, 197; cosmopolitan legal elites and, 193–94; rise of, 72, 201; universals consistent with, 97. See also hierarchies, national (US)
US hybrid model of legal education, 59–74; about, 196–97; challenges to familial and quasi-familial establishments, 8; convergence with, 7; development of, 58, 61–62, 72; family capital and, 61, 62; influence on China, 180, 181, 182; influence on Japan and South Korea of, 150, 156; local, distorted variation of, 10; neoliberal legal revolution and, 10; as revolutionary break, 9

Vance, Cyrus, 79, 91
Venezuela, 69–72
Vietnam War, 79, 80, 84, 197
von Mehren, Arthur Taylor, 103, 139

Wallerstein, Immanuel, 8
Wall Street law firms: emergence of, 59; Ivy
    League colleges and, 80; LCCRUL and, 81;
    New Deal and, 76–78; resistance to, 65
Wall Street lawyers: control over law production
    by, 73; criticism of, 78; elevation of legal
    argument by, 69; Harvard's production of, 9;
    Langdell as, 63–64; as lawyers-statespersons,
    68; public service activities of, 65; Yale
    idealists and, 85
Wan Exiang, 179
Wang, Zhizhou, 164–92
Wang, Zhizhou (Leo), 12, 164–92, 187
Wang Jiafu, 177
Wang Tieya, 170, 174–76, 175–76, 205n2
Weber, Max, 20
Weberian model (*Professorenrecht*), 20, 38,
    72, 73
Wei Christianson, 177
Wei Chun, 177
welfare state, 10, 25

Wilkins, David, 6, 110, 114, 117
women lawyers (China), 205n4
Wong, Wendy, 139
writ system, 45
Wu, Xiaogang, 166
Wuhan University, 169, 172, 173, 176, 179, 184

Xiaogang Wu, 183
Xi Jinping administration, 165, 188

Yale Law School, 64, 76, 79, 85–86, 90, 92,
    141, 179
Yang Zhaolong, 169–70
Yonsei Law School, 153, 154
Yu Shengtao, 205n2

Zhang, Taisu, 164, 166, 180–81, 188–89
Zhang Sizhi, 174
Zhong Nan Hai, 181
Zhou Gengsheng, 205n2
Zhu Suli, 176, 178, 180, 181

Founded in 1893,
UNIVERSITY OF CALIFORNIA PRESS
publishes bold, progressive books and journals
on topics in the arts, humanities, social sciences,
and natural sciences—with a focus on social
justice issues—that inspire thought and action
among readers worldwide.

The UC PRESS FOUNDATION
raises funds to uphold the press's vital role
as an independent, nonprofit publisher, and
receives philanthropic support from a wide
range of individuals and institutions—and from
committed readers like you. To learn more, visit
ucpress.edu/supportus.